Financial Analysis

A Managerial Introduction

Richard M.S. Wilson

School of Management and Economic Studies, University of Sheffield

Gerard McHugh

School of Business and Administrative Studies, University of Dublin

Cassell

Cassell Educational Limited
Artillery House
Artillery Row
London SW1P 1RT

British Library Cataloguing in Publication Data

Wilson, Richard M.S.
    Financial analysis: a managerial introduction.
    1. Business enterprises—Finance
    I. Title   II. McHugh, Gerard
    658.1'51   HG4026

    ISBN 0-304-31395-5

Typeset by Scribe Design, Gillingham, Kent

Printed and bound in Great Britain by Mackays of Chatham Ltd

Last digit is print no. 987654321

To
Derek and Mary Wilson
and
Thomas and Marie McHugh
for their
parental support
and
encouragement

Other books by R.M.S. Wilson

Technological Forecasting (with Gordon Wills, Neil Manning and Roger Hildebrandt)
Management Controls in Marketing
Financial Control
Cost Control Handbook
Management Controls and Marketing Planning
The Marketing of Financial Services
Financial Dimensions of Marketing (2 volumes)
The Application of Management Accounting
 Techniques to the Planning and Control of Marketing of Consumer Non-Durables (with
 Anne Bancroft)
Personal Investment and Financing Decisions (with Colin Dodds)
Managerial Accounting: Method and Meaning (with Wai Fong Chua)
Marketing Management: Planning and Control (with Colin Gilligan)

Contents

Foreword

It gives me great pleasure to introduce this book, both because of its content and because one of the co-authors, Dick Wilson, has for some years been a professional associate of mine. Any book that enables those in non-financial roles to understand financial information, and to insist on management accounting systems which suit their needs, has considerable potential to help improve overall organizational performance. This book, clearly written and with understandable examples, should make a real and positive impact on the businesses of those who study it.

Why is there such a gap of understanding between accountants and managers? Why is it that, in too many situations, intelligent people are separated by a gulf of mystique, with many accountants having very little knowledge of the other management functions, and many managers willing to be blinded by what they see as the 'black art' of accountancy?

In my professional work I see three facets of this problem. Firstly, in strategy consulting, we frequently have to help managers to understand the economic reality of their businesses by re-analysing and re-presenting the management accounts. It is not that these are 'wrong', it is just that management has never had the knowledge to suggest more suitable information, and the accountants have been too far away from the sharp end of the business to produce better information by themselves. This book will certainly help those who may want to open a dialogue with their accountants so that they obtain the information they really need.

The second facet is in the provision of management training to teach finance and accounting to people of other disciplines. It is in this activity that I have frequently worked with Dick Wilson. Even if the management accounting system is ideal for the business, managers have to understand it in order to make appropriate decisions. A manager who cannot see, for example, the connection between his or her marketing policies and the firm's cash flow position runs the risk of making the wrong decision for the firm. This book does a superb job of showing the financial implications of management actions.

My third facet lies outside the direct scope of the book, and is included to show that the problem is not one-sided. We also provide courses in management to many levels in one of the top accounting firms. While this book is not designed to teach management to accountants, it can indirectly do much to improve this side of the problem. Managers who understand finance and accounting are likely to improve the management knowledge of accountants, simply because they expose them to more demands, and more specific requests. Most accountants of my acquaintance would welcome this.

There is little doubt that those who read this book will add to both their financial and management skills, and will be able to improve their ability to make good decisions.

It is a book which I heartily recommend.

David E. Hussey
Managing Director
Harbridge Consulting Group Limited
London W1

Preface

Our aims in writing this book are twofold: to help its readers see how better decisions can be made by encouraging them to obtain better financial information (and to insist on accounting systems being designed to suit their *managerial* needs); and to explain, in a decision-oriented context, much of the jargon associated with financial matters.

The book is very specifically targeted on two groups of potential readers. Its primary target consists of students pursuing courses that require them to become 'financially literate' (e.g. courses in marketing, catering or engineering management, as well as in general management) rather than for those who are intending accountants. As a secondary market the book is directed towards managers who have had little or no financial training. It is applicable to manufacturing and service companies, and especially to those of medium size.

In terms of its approach the book's main characteristics are that:

- It adopts a *managerial orientation* (i.e. how can financial analysis help the manager make better decisions to solve his company's problems?).
- It focuses on the *meaning* of financial analyses in a managerial context (rather than on the detailed mechanics of accounting techniques or double-entry book-keeping).
- It emphasizes *action* following on from diagnosis (which requires identification of alternative courses of action) and their evaluation prior to choice and implementation, followed by further evaluation and modification.

We pursue this approach by reference to a detailed set of data relating to a fictitious enterprise. This is introduced and discussed in Chapters 2 and 3, following an opening chapter that sets financial analysis in a broad business context. These three chapters make up the first of the book's five parts. Part 2 seeks to analyse an enterprise's overall financial performance, with specific reference to liquidity, profitability, capital structure, and the impacts of inflation.

Within Part 3 we focus on the sources of profit, which involves an examination of different segments of a business with a view to identifying opportunities for improving profit performance. The key managerial tasks of planning, decision-making and control are covered, along with the analysis of different costs for these different purposes.

Part 4 takes a longer-term perspective than Part 3, and in it we look at investment decision-making, as well as offering an overview of the book's coverage.

Finally, we have included a note on the institutional framework of accounting, and a glossary.

We hope that this book offers a concise yet comprehensive guide to help students and practising managers harness financial analysis to their decision-making endeavours in order to enhance corporate performance.

RMSW (Sheffield)
GMcH (Dublin)
June 1987

Acknowledgements

We would like to offer our thanks to:

Simon Lake, the Business and Reference Editor at Cassell, for his patient support, and Miranda Walker for her editorial guidance.

Gillian Wilson, Marie Boam, and Sue Clewes for their magnificent application to purpose in producing the typescript.

Moira Greenhalgh for compiling the Index.

Vannessa Thornsby for her characteristically unassuming yet invaluable secretarial support throughout the preparation of the book.

Gower Publishing for permission to reproduce certain extracts from *Cost Control Handbook* by R.M.S. Wilson (2nd edition, 1983).

Accountancy Age and *British Business* for permission to reprint Figures 1.1 and 1.2 (published in this form in the former, but based on data from the latter).

Part 1

Introduction

Chapter 1
——A Perspective——

1.1 Introduction

Whether one is concerned with business success or business failure, it is apparent that financial issues figure prominently. A report from the Confederation of British Industry in 1985 concluded that the key element in the success of the UK's most outstanding companies over the past 15 years was the progress made in improving

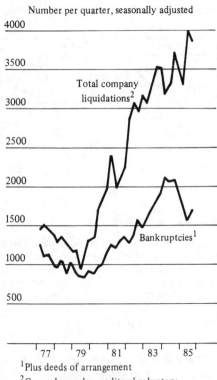

Number per quarter, seasonally adjusted

[1] Plus deeds of arrangement
[2] Compulsory plus creditors' voluntary

Figure 1.1 *Business failures, 1977–1985*
Source: *Accountancy Age* (1985).

The graph shows the quarterly figures for insolvencies in England and Wales from 1977 up until the third quarter of 1985, divided into total company liquidations and bankruptcies.

The third quarter of 1985 shows bankruptcies rising to 1,720, compared to 1,570 in the second quarter. But they are still below the levels of the fourth quarter of 1984. Liquidations fell from around 4,000 in the second quarter to 3,860 in the third, but are still 16 per cent higher than in the first quarter.

The figures are taken from *British Business*.

financial control and management. Survival in the face of inflationary pressures and high interest rates has demanded rigorous financial management.

However, not all businesses have managed to survive the hazards of commercial life over the past few years. As Fig. 1.1 shows, the trend in both liquidations and bankruptcies has been strongly upwards since 1979. (Only individuals become bankrupt; it is companies that go into liquidation.)

More detailed data relating to 1985 (on a month-by-month basis) is given in Fig. 1.2. While the failure of any commercial enterprise is usually represented at the end of the day by an inability to meet financial obligations, it should not be assumed that the fundamental causes of failure are of a financial nature. It is more likely that an inability to meet financial obligations has arisen as a *consequence* of, say, products that do not match those of competitors; poor customer service; or any number of other causes. On the other hand, if products are selling well but amounts due from customers are not being collected in a controlled way, or if the costs associated with offering an unnecessarily high level of customer service are allowed to escalate, then financial issues are more clearly identifiable as being potential causes of failure.

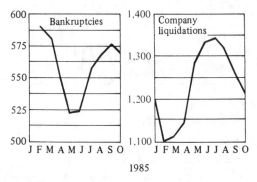

Figure 1.2 *Business failures, 1985*
Source: *Accountancy Age* (5 December 1985).

The graphs show the changes in bankruptcies and liquidations from January to October 1985. Each monthly figure is a three-month seasonally adjusted average.

The figures have remained roughly stable over the course of the year. Bankruptcies dipped in the spring and have since been rising, although October shows a marginal fall.

Liquidations have fallen and risen over the year. But the level for October was slightly above the January level.

The figures are taken from *British Business*.

Taking a company-wide view it is the responsibility of management to ensure that each business is well-run and in order to achieve this, the manager must be financially literate and financially aware—even if (or, perhaps, especially if) his or her background is in sales, design, or production—since financial matters underlie all business activities.

As the Preface has indicated, this book is concerned with the non-financial manager's need for improved financial awareness in order to perform more effectively. It is not the authors' aim to indoctrinate the reader with unnecessary jargon, nor to seek to make an accounting technician out of her or him. The aim is to adopt a managerial orientation (i.e. that of the user of financial data as opposed to that of the compiler) that relates to action based, at least in part, on financial reports.

1.2 An Organizational Perspective

Within every commercial enterprise, of whatever size, there are inevitably many different interests to be served. Fig. 1.3 identifies some of these interest groups and it is possible to suggest what their various expectations might be.

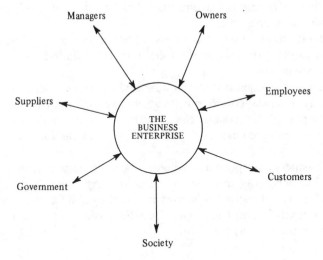

Figure 1.3 *Interest groups*

Customers will typically expect value for money and continuity of supply.

Suppliers will also be interested in continuity of supply and payment in accordance with agreed terms.

Employees will seek adequate reward for their labour and security of employment.

Owners will usually be concerned with the financial return on their investment (whether in the form of income or capital growth) relative to the risks involved.

Managers will look for satisfaction from their work in addition to material inducements.

Government will expect legal compliance—including the generation of revenue via income/corporation tax and VAT.

Society will have expectations regarding the social responsibility of business (which will be reflected in the activities of pressure groups such as Friends of the Earth).

Some of the legitimate expectations of these groups are clearly non-financial, so in developing any argument about the role of financial analysis it is vital to recognize at the outset the *partiality of financial considerations*. This can be highlighted in the following ways:
• Financial analysis is partial in that it only encompasses issues that can be expressed

in financial terms. This excludes such critical elements as managerial competence, employee morale, and an enterprise's reputation in the marketplace.

- Much of the information on which decisions might be based is non-financial (such as that relating to market share, productive capacity expressed in terms of machine hours, and the speed with which customers' orders can be fulfilled). It follows from this that the financial system of an enterprise has no monopoly over the information that is available to management.
- Many considerations in running a business are not predominantly financial, and few issues are exclusively financial, so the role of financial analysis needs to be viewed in its proper perspective.

The points listed above suggest that any advocate of financial analysis must have a degree of humility: financial considerations are not everything. But a lack of financial awareness on the part of the manager can easily lead to undesirable consequences that might threaten the continued existence of the business, so one cannot ignore financial considerations.

If we view a business enterprise as a whole, it becomes apparent that it needs to be managed in a balanced way in order to meet the expectations of all the groups represented in Fig. 1.3. This can be shown in a slightly different manner (as in Fig. 1.4) that emphasizes the *inputs* and *outputs* from the business—in other words, we can portray the typical business as a *system*.

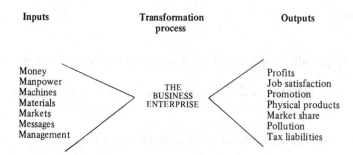

Inputs	Transformation process	Outputs
Money Manpower Machines Materials Markets Messages Management	THE BUSINESS ENTERPRISE	Profits Job satisfaction Promotion Physical products Market share Pollution Tax liabilities

Figure 1.4 *The business as a system*

A little poetic licence has been used in Fig. 1.4 to express all the inputs in words beginning with the letter 'M': thus information has been termed 'Messages', but the main point is to identify the range of inputs. A simple but useful analogy is to compare the mix of inputs to the list of ingredients in a recipe for a cake. Once assembled the ingredients need to be baked (i.e. processed or transformed) in order to be converted into output—the finished cake. This is equivalent to the way in which a finished unit of manufactured output is produced, but a business enterprise converts a wider variety of inputs into a wider range of outputs than is contained within its saleable products. Some of these outputs are much less tangible (e.g. job satisfaction), while others are not desirable (e.g. pollution).

The range of inputs portrayed in Fig. 1.4 are *resources* of one kind and another. Managers need to focus on three phases in relation to the management of resources:

1. In the first instance resources must be *acquired*—whether to facilitate the initial setting up of a business, or to allow for its continued existence. This is not purely a

financial matter, although 'money' is one vital resource and we will need to analyse the extent to which trading activities generate sufficient funds for continued existence. If additional financial resources are needed in order to acquire other resources (such as new equipment), then consideration should be given to the alternative sources and terms. Resource acquisition needs to be planned.

2. Once acquired, resources must be *allocated* to purposes that managers have determined. This requires that choices be made among alternative purposes, since resources will invariably be insufficient to allow managers to undertake every available alternative. But how, and by whom, are alternatives to be identified and evaluated? Financial criteria will have a role to play in this decision-making process, even though issues of a non-financial nature will also need to be taken into account.

3. Having been allocated to particular purposes the *utilization* of resources needs to be monitored to ensure that some satisfactory balance is maintained between the actual inputs and the achieved versus the desired outputs. Thus the *efficiency* and *effectiveness* of resource utilization need to be considered in the following ways:

Efficiency (or productivity) relates to the ratio of outputs to inputs (i.e. %), so an enterprise that produces £1,000,000 sales revenue from a marketing outlay of £250,000 is more efficient than an enterprise producing the same sales results from marketing expenditure of £300,000. Their respective efficiency measures are $£1,000,000/£250,000 = 4$ and $£1,000,000/£300,000 = 3.33$.

Effectiveness relates to the achievement of that which one set out to achieve. In other words, did the actual results (or outputs) for a given period of time correspond with the desired results? Using the above example, the desired sales revenue may have been £900,000 for the time period in question, in which event the performance is apparently effective. However, if the costs of achieving this result were £300,000 rather than, say, a budgeted expenditure of £250,000, the performance is inefficient. Moreover, if the market is growing and the target sales figure of £900,000 represented an estimated 10 per cent market share (i.e. the total market was estimated to be £9,000,000) but the actual sales revenue of £1,000,000 only amounted to 8 per cent (because the rate of market growth was inaccurately predicted), this would represent an ineffective level of performance.

As shown in Fig. 1.5 there are four logical outcomes that take into account rather polarized levels of efficiency and effectiveness. Each 'cell' contains a combination of either positive or negative levels of efficiency and effectiveness. In cell 1 both are positive, which is a happy situation since resources are being used efficiently in producing a desired (i.e. effective) outcome. In sharp contrast, cell 4 contains an extremely unhappy situation which has connotations of failure. Between these extremes are the greyer pictures of cells 2 and 3: in cell 3 the level of efficiency is good but the degree of effectiveness is poor, and vice versa in cell 2. Interpretation of these logical possibilities depends upon the relative importance attached to efficiency and effectiveness.

Put simply, effectiveness refers to doing the right thing, whereas efficiency refers to doing the thing right. There should be no doubt that effectiveness is much more important than efficiency, even though both qualities are desirable. If this is accepted, it can be seen that cell 2 (effective but inefficient) in Fig. 1.5 is a better place to be than is cell 3 (efficient but ineffective).

Referring back to Fig. 1.3, an enterprise needs to meet the expectations of its

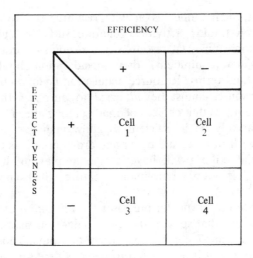

Figure 1.5 *Efficiency versus effectiveness*

constituent interest groups if it is to be effective. Survival depends upon this. The more efficiently the enterprise can use its available resources in striving to be effective, the more profitable it is likely to be.

1.3 The Time Perspective

In considering profitability, or any other indicator of performance, to which time period should one seek to relate it?

Clearly time is a continuum, but we habitually divide it into broad bands (past, present, future) and into specific intervals (years, months, weeks). Every manager is accustomed to the annual accounts that the law requires limited companies to produce, and which the Inland Revenue requires other types of enterprise to submit. These accounts reflect, in a partial and stylized manner, the results of a year's activity in the recent past. As we will see in subsequent chapters, it is possible to analyse these historical documents in considerable detail in order to help tell a story about business performance. But the details relate to water that has passed under the bridge: one cannot change these past events, and actions that were taken to produce the results of earlier time periods cannot retrospectively be changed. So what are the benefits of historical accounts? The basic answer to this question is simple: we can seek to learn from the past. If we are able to associate a given action in an earlier period with a particular result, we should be able to use this knowledge—however approximate it may be—to guide our future decision-making.

In order that we might learn effectively from the past we need to keep a reasonably open mind about cause-and-effect relationships, avoiding too many preconceived views. This can be illustrated by the opening paragraphs of this chapter: to assume that businesses fail because of financial problems is usually to miss the point of what it was that actually caused those financial problems. An analysis of annual accounts might help in raising further questions—such as why costs may have increased significantly over the last year with no change in the volume of business, or how trading income failed to cover the financing requirement of re-equipping a factory—but it will not supply all the necessary answers.

The smaller a business is, the more likely it is to have little in the way of financial reports other than its annual accounts. This highlights the need for a sound level of financial awareness on the part of managers of small businesses, since decisions made today affect the future, and the future is not a straightforward extension of the past. We cannot learn everything from the past since the world around us is changing so rapidly; nevertheless, we can learn something about the future avoidance of past errors, and the approximate linkages between actions and results.

In planning and controlling business activities the critical time perspective must be the future: specifying what one wishes to achieve—and how; acquiring and allocating resources; monitoring performance (and the utilization of resources) in a way that constantly seeks to modify plans in the light of changing circumstances.

1.4 Scope of Financial Analysis

There are three elements constituting the scope of financial analysis: its origins, aims, and limitations.

Origins

The main sources are to be found within the branches of accounting and financial management. As Fig. 1.6 suggests, investors need to be persuaded to provide finance to enable an enterprise to get underway, or to grow or diversify once it has become established. Investors put their funds into enterprises in exchange for either a share of

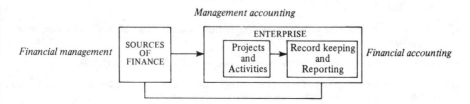

Figure 1.6 *Scope of financial analysis*

ownership or a commitment from the owners/managers to repay the investors on specified terms. It is among the tasks of financial management to balance the sources of finance, and to ensure that the enterprise is able to 'service' its sources of finance (whether via the payment of dividends to shareholders, or of interest to those who have lent funds to the enterprise), and to repay loans on their due date. Appropriate financial analysis will clearly be necessary for these tasks.

However, the above observations relate primarily to the *supply* of funds rather than to the *demand* for funds. Enterprises demand funds to facilitate their on-going activities (e.g. paying suppliers, ensuring wages and salaries can be paid) and to facilitate new (or expanding) projects of one kind and another. Determining these needs is another task for financial management—in association with management accounting. Once projects are underway, the routine handling of financial transactions and the production of annual financial reports is within the province of financial accounting.

These three activities (financial management, management accounting, financial accounting) constitute the main contributors to financial analysis.

Aims

In broad terms, financial analysis aims to help managers in controlling the efficiency and effectiveness of their enterprises. Each of the underlying source activities has specific aims.

- Financial management aims to raise funds in the most suitable and economic manner, to guide investment where opportunity is greatest, and to maintain liquidity.
- Management accounting aims to assist managers in planning, decision-making, and controlling the enterprise's activities, as well as helping to improve internal co-ordination and communication within the enterprise.
- Financial accounting aims to record and report on the financial transactions of an enterprise to help in the decision-making of those groups having a legitimate interest, and to fulfil a stewardship function (involving the maintenance of records on behalf of the enterprise's owners).

It is often argued that accounting is the 'language of business', and financial analysis (which is based on accounting *and* financial management) seeks to apply this language

---

(a) to aid in selecting business objectives that are capable of being measured;

(b) to assist in establishing, co-ordinating, and administering, as an integral part of management, an adequate plan covering all aspects of business activities (with particular reference to liquidity and profitability);

(c) to compare performance with plans and standards, and report to all levels of management accordingly;

(d) to develop suitable information and control systems, in line with company policy;

(e) to consult with all segments of management responsible for policy or action in connection with objectives, adequacy of policies, organization structure, and procedures;

(f) to administer tax policies and procedures;

(g) to analyse and interpret the implications of the economic situation, government policies, and social pressures;

(h) to negotiate acquisitions and mergers;

(i) to maintain credit lines with banks;

(j) to ensure that the business's assets are protected by adequate insurance and systems of internal control;

(k) to establish and maintain good relations with investment analysts, financial journalists, and the investing public;

(l) to formulate accounting and financial policy.

Figure 1.7 *Role of financial analysts*

to any business situation within any industrial/commercial setting on which it might help throw some light. While financial accounting is necessarily carried out in accordance with strict statutory and professional requirements, with an historical slant, financial analysis needs to be undertaken in a future-oriented manner that emphasizes those aspects of business life (in so far as they can be expressed in financial terms) that are critical to survival and success.

In summary, the role of financial analysts is outlined in Fig. 1.7. There are no legal imperatives stating that financial analysis must be undertaken by a business enterprise, nor is there any single way in which financial analysis may be carried out. Approximate figures, provided they are relevant to the task in hand, are acceptable outputs from financial analysis whereas the reports, etc., that emerge from financial accounting/reporting are typically very precise. It inevitably takes time to produce more precise reports, and there can be no guarantee of their relevance, so prompt approximations are likely to be more useful for managerial purposes.

Limitations

As we have seen, the role of financial analysis is partial, which suggests some limits to its value. If one accepts that decisions emerge from the interaction of a purpose to be served, the available information, and managerial judgement, then financial analysis can be seen to contribute to only one or two of these (depending on whether the purpose in question is specifically financial):

$$\text{DECISION} = \text{PURPOSE} + \text{INFORMATION} + \text{JUDGEMENT}$$

The higher one's status in an enterprise, the more significant is the input of judgment into decision-making; and the greater the scope one has for specifying the purpose to be served by any given decision. In a similar way, the less routine and more future-oriented is the situation requiring a decision to be made, the more limited will be the role of financial analysis. This is indicated in Fig. 1.8.

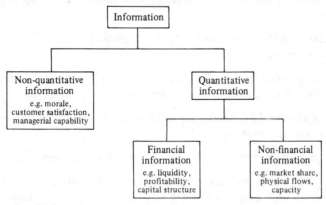

Figure 1.8 *Categories of information*

1.5 Summary

In this introductory chapter we have sought to define the role of financial analysis as a service to managers.

Financial analysis aims to help managers in controlling the performance of their enterprises. At the least this will mean helping in the avoidance of bankruptcy/liquidation, but the potential of financial analysis is much greater than this and should be seen in the context of improving an organization's effectiveness and efficiency.

In improving their financial awareness, managers are unlikely to lose sight of the partiality of financial information. However, while finance as a specific input to any business system is but one factor, the value of other factors is usually expressed in financial terms (in so far as this is feasible). It follows that questions associated with the acquisition, allocation, and utilization of resources are typically discussed in financial terms, and the manager—whatever his or her functional role—must be financially aware.

The origins of financial analysis are seen in the fields of financial management, management accounting, and financial accounting. Its aims focus on maintaining adequate liquidity, improving profitability, and securing an appropriate capital structure to facilitate the enterprise's activities.

1.6 Exercises

Review questions

1. What are the main questions that financial analysis seeks to address?

2. Identify the major constituents of financial analysis (as outlined in Chapter 1) and explain their distinctive roles.

3. Can an enterprise be effectively managed purely on the basis of financial information? Justify your answer.

4. Explain your understanding of 'system' and illustrate this with reference to an organization with which you are familiar.

5. Distinguish between 'efficiency' and 'effectiveness'. Indicate which you consider to be the more important, and illustrate this in the context of an organization of your choice.

6. Why is it desirable for every manager to be 'financially literate'? Give examples to illustrate your answer.

7. Discuss the significance of the time dimension in financial analysis. How important do you consider the past to be relative to the future?

8. To what extent should financial systems be designed to suit the needs of managers rather than, say, accountants?

9. What is meant by the notion of action-oriented financial reports?

10. Do you think there are any major differences between commercial (i.e. profit-oriented) and non-commercial (e.g. educational) organizations in their needs for financial analysis?

1.7 Further Reading

There are many introductory books on aspects of financial analysis, but most tend to be rather preoccupied with accounting mechanics, principles, and associated jargon.

Readers may find the following useful:

Bird, P. (1979), *Understanding Company Accounts*, London: Pitman.

Fanning, D., & M. Pendlebury (1984), *Company Accounts: A Guide*, London: Allen & Unwin.

Hitching, C., & D. Stone (1984), *Understand Accounting!*, London: Pitman.

Mott, G. (1984), *Accounting for Non-Accountants*, London: Pan.

Reid, W., & D.R. Myddelton (1982), *The Meaning of Company Accounts*, Aldershot: Gower. (3rd edition)

Sizer, J. (1979), *An Insight into Management Accounting*, Harmondsworth: Penguin. (2nd edition)

Chapter 2

——Introduction to Data: CKD Ltd ——

2.1 Introduction

In order to render the ideas about financial analysis as useful as possible it seems most appropriate to develop them in the context of a case study. The case study is built around a fictitious family-run business, CKD Ltd. Details are given in the remainder of this chapter, and a commentary follows in Chapter 3.

Once the background to CKD Ltd has been assimilated, the chapters that follow will discuss a variety of approaches to developing and using tools of financial analysis in relation to performance measurement, the evaluation of liquidity and profitability, and the assessment of capital expenditure. Specific applications of these approaches will be illustrated in the setting of CKD Ltd, so that the interplay of different decisions and alternative approaches can be better understood.

The time is the beginning of 19x6.

2.2 Background to CKD Ltd

Contemporary Kitchen Designs Limited (hereafter CKD Ltd) is a small but expanding company engaged in manufacturing and marketing an intentionally limited range of kitchen fittings. It has not yet engaged in exporting any of its output.

In addition to the main activity of manufacture/marketing of kitchen fittings, the company has developed a kitchen design service through which it advises clients on suitable layouts, etc., for their kitchens. This activity generated 2 per cent of turnover in 19x1, growing to 17 per cent in 19x5.

The company's offices, factory and warehouse are located in the Midlands. All the company's products are manufactured by CKD, but use is made of outside carriers for all deliveries to customers since CKD has not yet thought it appropriate to invest in its own transportation facilities.

CKD Ltd sells its products to department stores, builders' merchants and major DIY outlets, offering a high level of service in what is a strongly competitive market. No stocks are held other than at CKD's central warehouse.

The design services are sold to clients via advertisements in such up-market periodicals as *Homes & Gardens*, *Ideal Home* and *The Lady*. This activity is conducted entirely by correspondence/telephone rather than by visits to clients' premises.

Organization

CKD Ltd. is managed by five directors (see Fig. 2.1):

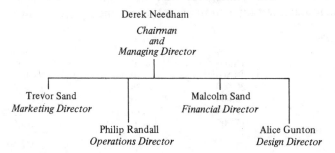

Contemporary Kitchen Designs Ltd.

Figure 2.1 *Contemporary Kitchen Design's management structure as at 1 January 19x6*

Chairman and Managing Director Derek Needham (aged 64), who founded the company almost 20 years ago.

Marketing Director Trevor Sand (aged 42), a nephew of Derek Needham, has been with CKD for 15 years.

Operations Director Philip Randall (aged 38), in charge of production and distribution, is newly-recruited having spent his career to date with a major furniture manufacturer in northern England.

Financial Director Malcolm Sand (aged 40), brother of Trevor, joined CKD 10 years ago after several years spent in private practice as an accountant.

Design Director Alice Gunton (aged 35), Derek Needham's daughter, introduced the kitchen design service when she joined the company in 19x0.

The majority of shares in CKD are held by the directors and other members of the Needham family, giving closely-held control. However, in recent years, additional capital funding has been raised via further issues of shares and long term loans. Various financial institutions have acquired an interest in CKD through both these routes.

Financial Data

Tables 1–22, which follow Chapter 3, give detailed information on the financial circumstances of CKD Ltd over the last 5 years (i.e. 19x1–19x5). Chapter 3 discusses the meaning of this information and looks at the underlying structure of the main financial statements (especially those contained in Tables 1–4).

In addition to reviewing the recent history of CKD (in so far as this can be gleaned from financial statements) we also need to set the scene for the future. This is done in section 2.3.

2.3 Projections for 19x6

In this section we will outline CKD's plans for 19x6.

Sales Forecast for 19x6

During 19x6 Trevor Sand anticipates that the company will sell the following quantities of manufactured kitchen units at the specified prices shown in Fig. 2.2.

Product line	Units	Price (each) £	Revenue £
A	18,500	110	2,035,000
B	30,000	78	2,340,000
C	10,000	140	1,400,000
D	13,500	115	1,552,500
E	17,000	130	2,210,000
			£9,537,500

Figure 2.2 *Forecast sales for 19x6*

Alice Gunton's estimate of sales revenue from the design service for 19x6 is £2,251,000 (which will amount to 19 per cent of total sales revenue for CKD in 19x6 if the forecasts are realized).

Production Costs

CKD employs a standard costing system, and deliberations between Philip Randall and Malcolm Sand have produced a schedule of cost standards for 19x6 (Fig. 2.3).

	Product				
	A	**B**	**C**	**D**	**E**
Direct material	30.25	4.69	17.50	7.20	16.00
Direct labour	19.90	9.58	27.25	15.53	16.72
Direct cost	50.15	14.27	44.75	22.73	32.72
Variable manufacturing overheads	5.97	2.65	5.45	4.80	3.30
Variable cost	56.12	16.92	50.20	27.53	36.02
Fixed manufacturing overheads (@ 180% of direct labour cost)	35.82	17.24	49.05	27.95	30.09
Total standard cost per unit	**91.94**	**34.16**	**99.25**	**55.48**	**66.11**

All figures in £s

Figure 2.3 *Manufacturing cost standards for 19x6*

Variable overheads consist largely of labour-related costs, and the total budget for 19x6's variable manufacturing overheads is £365,500 made up as shown in Fig. 2.4.

	£
Indirect labour	231,500
Sundry materials	60,000
Power	20,000
Heating	15,000
Maintenance	39,000
	£365,500

Figure 2.4 *Variable manufacturing overheads budget, 19x6*

The fixed manufacturing overheads are budgeted as shown in Fig. 2.5.

	£
	£
Depreciation	210,000
Leasing and hiring	405,000
Canteen	170,000
Training	50,000
Rates and insurance	234,500
Salaries	1,490,000
	£2,559,500

Figure 2.5 *Fixed manufacturing overheads budget, 19x6*

In summary, the costs of producing the goods required by the sales forecast are shown in Fig. 2.6:

		A	B	C	D	E	TOTAL
Product line							
Units		18,500	30,000	10,000	13,500	17,000	
Direct material	£	559,625	140,700	175,000	97,200	272,000	1,244,525
Direct labour	£	368,150	287,400	272,500	209,655	284,240	1,421,945
Direct costs	£	927,775	428,100	447,500	306,855	556,240	2,666,470
Variable overheads	£	110,445	79,500	54,500	64,800	56,100	365,345
Variable costs	£	1,038,220	507,600	502,000	371,655	612,340	3,031,815
Fixed overheads	£	662,670	517,200	490,500	377,325	511,530	2,559,225
TOTAL	£	1,700,890	1,024,800	992,500	748,980	1,123,870	5,591,040

Figure 2.6 *Product cost of sales estimates, 19x6*

It is not expected that there will be any significant net change in inventory levels between the beginning and end of 19x6.

Standards have not yet been developed for other categories of cost (e.g. relating to clerical or distribution activities), but Malcolm Sand is keen to pursue the possibility of extending cost standards beyond the manufacturing area.

Design Department Costs

The cost of design services in 19x6 is expected to amount to a total of £1,246,360. Details are given in Fig. 2.7.

	£
	£
Salaries	375,000
Depreciation	18,360
Marketing (see Fig. 2.13)	720,000
Consumables	42,000
Utilities	26,000
Outside services	65,000
	£1,246,360

Figure 2.7 *Cost estimates for design services, 19x6*

All the design department's costs are treated as being the cost of sales in the year in which they are incurred.

Marketing Plans

CKD has divided the UK into five sales areas as follows for its manufactured lines:
Area 1:   South-east England (including London)
Area 2:   South-west England and Wales
Area 3:   Midlands
Area 4:   Northern England
Area 5:   Scotland and Northern Ireland

Area	Number of salesmen	Salaries	Expenses	Total cost
1	7	101,500	16,800	118,300
2	7	91,000	15,000	106,000
3	4	52,000	6,000	58,000
4	5	65,000	8,200	73,200
5	7	91,000	19,500	110,500
TOTAL	30	£400,500	£65,500	£466,000

Figure 2.8 *Budgeted selling expenses, 19x6*

The number of salesmen, and their expected salaries and expenses for 19x6, are given in Fig. 2.8.

The sales forecast can be broken down by area (Fig. 2.9) and by customer category (Fig. 2.10).

Product line	Customer category							
	Dept. stores		Builders' merchants		DIY outlets		TOTAL	
	Units	£	Units	£	Units	£	Units	£
A	6,000	660,000	9,000	990,000	3,500	385,000	18,500	2,035,000
B	5,900	460,200	11,500	897,000	12,600	982,800	30,000	2,340,000
C	6,800	952,000	3,000	420,000	200	28,000	10,000	1,400,000
D	3,100	356,500	6,000	690,000	4,400	506,000	13,500	1,552,500
E	2,000	260,000	10,500	1,365,000	4,500	585,000	17,000	2,210,000
TOTAL (£)		2,688,700		4,362,000		2,486,800		9,537,500

Figure 2.10 *Sales forecast by customer categories & product*

Promotional plans for 19x6 include advertising by product line as outlined in Fig. 2.11.

Product line	Area												
	1		2		3		4		5		TOTAL	
	Units	£	Units	£	Units	£	Units	£	Units	£	Units	£
A	4,000	440,000	3,000	330,000	3,500	385,000	3,800	418,000	4,200	462,000	18,500	2,035,000
B	13,000	1,014,000	6,000	468,000	2,000	156,000	2,600	202,800	6,400	499,200	30,000	2,340,000
C	1,600	224,000	1,500	210,000	3,800	210,000	1,600	532,000	1,600	224,000	10,000	1,400,000
D	4,100	471,500	2,800	322,000	1,000	115,000	4,600	529,000	1,000	115,000	13,500	1,552,500
E	6,500	845,000	4,000	520,000	1,500	195,000	3,500	455,000	1,500	195,000	17,000	2,210,000
TOTAL (£)		2,994,500		1,850,000		1,061,000		2,136,800		1,495,200		9,537,500

Figure 2.9 *Sales forecast by area and product, 19x6*

Product line	Advertising budget £
A	15,000
B	36,000
C	20,000
D	15,000
E	40,000
Full range	14,000
	£140,000

Figure 2.11 *19x6 advertising budget*

Products B and E will be featured in exhibitions/trade shows at an estimated cost of £12,000.

A special mailing shot relating to product E will be made to builders' merchants during 19x6 at a probable cost of £5,000.

Advertising and promotional activities are undertaken on a national (rather than regional) basis for manufactured product lines.

Total budgeted marketing costs for 19x6 are as summarized in Fig. 2.12.

			£
Salaries:	Marketing	134,500	
	Salesmen	400,500	535,000
Advertising			140,000
Depreciation:	Fixtures and fittings 20%		15,240
	Motor vehicles 60%		70,500
Motor vehicles' standing charges			6,200
Bad debts			30,000
Printing			115,000
Travelling			35,400
Running costs of motor vehicles			42,500
			£989,840

Figure 2.12 *19x6 marketing budget*

Turning to the design services context, Alice Gunton proposes to spend the following on marketing activities during 19x6 (see Fig. 2.13), and the costs will become part of the cost of sales for design services.

	£
Market research study	12,000
Advertising	633,000
Promotion via exhibitions	60,000
Literature/printing	15,000
TOTAL	£720,000

Figure 2.13 *Marketing budget for design services, 19x6*

Distribution

The existing warehouse facilities are adequate for the current scale of operations (covering all categories of inventory).

Payroll costs constitute the largest element in the 19x6 budget, and mainly relate to goods inwards, internal stock movements, and order assembly/despatch activities, plus the clerical costs associated with procurement and inventory recordkeeping.

Fig. 2.14 gives the distribution budget.

	£
Payroll	390,440
Depreciation: Equipment	70,000
Fixtures and fittings	38,100
Freight charges	156,260
Packaging materials	43,200
TOTAL	£698,000

Figure 2.14 *Distribution budget for 19x6*

Administration

Various costs that apply to other areas, including legal costs, recruitment costs, telephone costs, are budgeted under the Administration Department for reasons of convenience. This department is under Malcolm Sand's control and the budget for 19x6 is given in Fig. 2.15.

	£
Salaries	698,230
Depreciation: Fixtures and fittings	22,860
Office equipment	73,440
Motor vehicles	47,000
Insurance	24,000
Motor vehicles' standing charges	3,600
Stationery and postage	83,000
Telephone	51,000
Motor vehicles, running costs	19,500
Legal costs	12,000
Recruitment costs	10,000
Maintenance	35,000
	£1,079,630

Figure 2.15 *Administration budget for 19x6*

Financial matters

The company is due to make the first repayment of £360,000 on the 12 per cent loan on 1 January 19x6. The anticipated financial costs for 19x6 are shown in Fig. 2.16.

	£
Interest on debt capital	232,800
Audit fee	27,500
Bank charges	4,000
	£264,300

Figure 2.16 *Financial budget for 19x6*

It will be necessary for new clear-cut policies to be established for the following:
- cash management (including the use to which cash surpluses should be put from time to time);
- the management of debtors and creditors;
- the management of inventories of all types;
- capital expenditure;
- the balance of debt and equity.

As we proceed through the book we will deal with each of these themes. This will enable us to produce, by the end, an integrated financial plan that includes projected balance sheet, profit and loss account, funds flow statement, and value added statement, plus a series of ratio benchmarks.

Capital Assets

CKD Ltd plans to acquire new fixed assets and to dispose of some older ones during 19x6. The acquisitions are planned as in Fig. 2.17.

	£
New plant and machinery	400,000
New fixtures and fittings	350,000
New office equipment	50,000
New motor vehicles	140,000
TOTAL	£940,000

Figure 2.17 *Proposed capital expenditure for 19x6*

Old plant and machinery costing £200,000 (WDV £60,000) will be sold for scrap for approximately £20,000. Old fixtures and fittings costing £250,000 (WDV £100,000) will be sold for an estimated £55,000.

2.4 Summary

This chapter has introduced Contemporary Kitchen Designs Ltd. The book will go on to discuss the themes laid out in this chapter, and the data relating to CKD will be used to illustrate the approaches to financial analysis that managers might find useful.

Since our main concern is with the future, we have used this chapter to provide a range of projections into 19x6 covering expected sales and budgeted costs. Before we can develop an integrated financial plan we need to look in more detail at ways of developing suitable policies for managing cash, debtors, creditors and inventory, as well as raising and spending capital funds. We turn to these matters in Part 2 (Chapters 4–8), and include a summary of CKD's plans and underlying assumptions in Chapter 15.

Our next step, however, is to gain a greater understanding of CKD's financial circumstances via a detailed review of the years 19x1–19x5.

Chapter 3
————A Commentary on CKD Ltd————

3.1 Financial Data for Last Five Years

CKD Ltd has been operating for nearly 20 years, but we will confine our attention to the details of the last five years (19x1 to 19x5).

Tables 1–4 (pp. 38–42) will be referred to a good deal as we progress through the book, so it is important that we give them an adequate introduction at this point. Subsequent tabulations within this chapter will look in greater detail at particular items summarized in Tables 1–4, and subsequent chapters will offer fuller analysis.

There are four principal financial statements given in summary form in Tables 1–4. These are:

1. The balance sheet (pp. 38–9)
2. The profit and loss account (p. 40)
3. The funds flow statement (p. 41)
4. The value added statement (p. 42)

Of these four the last is a recent addition, and there is no formal requirement that value added statements be produced. The first two, the balance sheet and profit and loss account, have been the cornerstone of financial reporting for a long time and, along with the third, the funds flow statement, are formally required.

The Balance Sheet

In essence this lists, at a given point in time, the resources of an enterprise and the claims against those resources. The resources are easy to envisage, especially since many (including machinery and finished stock available for sale) are tangible objects. Claims, in contrast, are intangible and typically represent legal rights. Thus, for example, a supplier who has provided materials but who has not yet been paid has a claim against the enterprise amounting to the value of the goods he has supplied. Other claims relate to the provision of capital: those who lend money to an enterprise have a claim reflecting the sum loaned, and the conditions on which it was lent. And the owners—whether shareholders (as in a limited company) or partners or proprietors in an unincorporated business—have a claim on the resources of the business in so far as these exceed the sum of the claims by other parties.

It is apparent, therefore, that, in total:

$$\text{Resources} = \text{Claims}$$

Since 'claims' encompasses those of both owners (and lenders) and suppliers, we can distinguish their respective interests by separating out ownership and lenders' claims and calling them 'capital'. Thus:

$$\text{Resources} = \text{Claims} + \text{Capital, or}$$
$$\text{Resources} - \text{Claims} = \text{Capital}$$

It is this relationship that the balance sheet seeks to portray, and it is helpful to think of it as a 'snapshot' of an enterprise's financial position at a point in time. In other words, an enterprise's balance sheet on 31 December 19x0, would differ from that on 30 December 19x0, and also from that on 1 January 19x1, since transactions will be taking place continually, and a balance sheet at any given date will include the impact of all transactions up to that date.

In Table 1 (pp. 38–9) we see that Resources consist of two categories of assets: fixed assets and current assets. The former are long-lived items that are necessary to facilitate the activities of the business, including plant, furniture, vehicles, and premises. Such items are not held directly for trading purposes (i.e. machinery is not held for resale: it is intended to produce finished goods which are held for resale). However, from time to time fixed assets that are no longer required will be sold (or scrapped) and will consequently disappear from the balance sheet. Similarly, newly-acquired fixed assets, such as new cars for the salesforce, will be added to the sum for the appropriate category of asset in the balance sheet.

Fixed assets are of value in that they provide services of one kind and another over long periods of time. A problem arises whenever a balance sheet has to be produced in that most fixed assets will have some 'service potential' remaining, but this will be less than was present when the assets were new. For example, an item of plant might be expected to provide service at a constant rate over 20 years. A balance sheet produced at the end of 10 years might reflect this in the following way:

Initial cost of plant   £10,000
Expected useful life   20 years
Annual depreciation = $£10,000/20$ = £500
∴ Balance sheet value after 10 years = £10,000 − (10 × £500) = £5,000.

'Depreciation' is simply an attempt that financial analysts make to spread the initial cost of a long-lived asset over its expected useful life. It has nothing to do with an asset's secondhand value in the marketplace other than by pure coincidence.

The annual depreciation for fixed assets of all categories will be treated as a cost (to be charged against revenue) year by year: in the above example, a charge of £500 for this item of plant will be made each year against revenue in the profit and loss account. But in the balance sheet it is usually found that the initial cost of fixed assets is shown, with *cumulative* depreciation to date being deducted to give the *written down value* (WDV). Again, using the above example, the relevant entry in the balance sheet would be:

Initial cost   £10,000
Depreciation to date:
(10 years @ £500)   5,000
                                _____
Written down value   £ 5,000

Within Table 1 you can see a summary, year by year, of the initial cost, cumulative depreciation, and written down values of the various categories of CKD's fixed assets. Over time the picture changes and we can seek to understand these changes by reference to Tables 5, 6, and 7 (pp. 43–5)

If we focus on plant and machinery we see (Table 1) that on 31 December 19x1, CKD had plant originally costing £1,000,000 which had been depreciated to the extent of £400,000, giving a written down value of £600,000. Table 6 gives the basis of depreciation: 10 per cent of the original cost is written off each year, so the depreciation charge in 19x1 for plant was:

$$10\% \text{ of } £1,000,000 = £100,000$$

From Table 5 it can be seen that disposals and acquisitions of plant took place as follows:

Disposals		*Acquisitions*	
19x4	£400,000	19x1	£400,000
		19x3	£600,000
		19x5	£800,000.

Whenever fixed assets are sold the proceeds should be compared with the written down value of the assets in question, with any difference being either a gain or a loss on disposal. This is demonstrated for CKD in Table 7. Staying with plant, it is shown that the plant disposed of in 19x4 had an initial cost of £400,000 and had been depreciated by £300,000. The WDV of £100,000 was greater than the £50,000 proceeds of sale, so the difference (£100,000 − £50,000) will be shown in the profit & loss account for 19x4 (Table 2) as a *loss on disposal*.

Other details of the acquisition, depreciation, and disposal of CKD's fixed assets over the years 19x1–19x5 can be seen in Tables 5 to 7 and these details are reflected in the balance sheets (Table 1) as well as in supporting statements (Tables 2–4).

Turning to current assets requires us to shift our focus to trading matters. A simple cycle can be illustrated (see Fig. 3.1) to demonstrate the relationships among current assets.

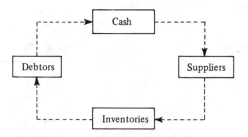

Figure 3.1 *Current asset flow*

Starting with cash, this is used to pay suppliers (which is intended to include all suppliers of goods and services, as suggested by the inputs in Fig. 1.4). In a manufacturing enterprise the inputs are combined to produce finished goods which can be sold, but this is only one of the categories of inventory (or stock) that exists: others are inventories of raw materials, work-in-progress and consumable items (which will cover stationery, spare parts for machinery, and so on).

As finished goods are sold this asset is converted into another: sums due from customers (i.e. debtors). And as debtors pay for the goods they have bought so the cash balance is replenished.

Within Table 1 the various current asset balances as at 31 December for each of the last five years are portrayed. It is CKD's policy to invest surplus cash in short-term securities (shown in the balance sheet as 'Investments') in much the same way that an individual might put spare cash into a building society account. In this way a modest return can be generated without irrevocably committing funds to alternative uses. In 19x3, 19x4, and 19x5 CKD was in a cash surplus position (as shown by the balances in the cash account among current assets), while in 19x1 and 19x2 there was a cash deficit (as shown by the overdraft among current liabilities).

It is clear that the Investment balances of £50,000 in 19x1 and 19x2 were poorly synchronized with the cash position, although by 19x5 the position was under better control.

Sums due from debtors increased considerably from 19x1 to 19x5:

19x1	£733,560
19x2	£860,710
19x3	£1,356,270
19x4	£1,701,860
19x5	£1,930,080

This is an increase of 163 per cent, whereas sales only increased by 85 per cent over the five years. On the face of it this warrants further investigation, and we will return to it in future chapters.

In every business there will be *prepayments* whenever the periods over which the services for which payments in advance are made fail to coincide with the enterprise's financial year. Taking the payment of rates as an example, if CKD's rates for the period 1 April 19x1 to 31 March 19x2 were £20,000 there would be a prepayment of £5,000 at CKD's financial year end (31 December 19x1) relating to the portion of the rates payment (25 per cent) attributable to the period 1 January 19x2 to 31 March 19x2. Supposing that the rates for the fiscal year 1 April 19x2 to 31 March 19x3 were £24,000, we would have the following picture:

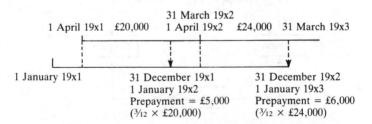

The prepayment is a current asset in that it represents benefits paid for in advance but not yet received. It is a straightforward matter to calculate the charge for rates for CKD's financial year ending on 31 December 19x2: this is made up of $(3/12 \times £20,000) + (9/12 \times £24,000) = £23,000$ and this amount would appear in the profit and loss account as an expense to be charged against revenue earned during 19x2.

Coming back to inventories, Fig. 3.2 shows that these have almost doubled in total over the five years from 19x1. We will discuss in later chapters how significant this might be, and how financial analysis can help in inventory management. For the present, however, we can see from Table 8 (p. 46) the movements in inventories over the five years with which we are concerned. The details will be picked up later.

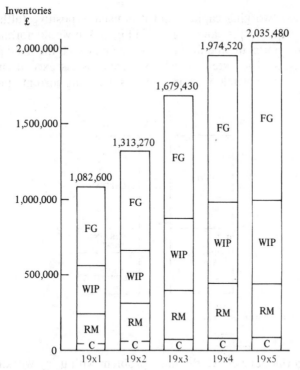

Figure 3.2 *Inventory levels, 19x1–19x5*
FG = Finished goods
WIP = Work in progress
RM = Raw materials
C = Consumables

What about the claims against CKD's resources? If we deal first with current liabilities (which are sums payable in the short-term by the enterprise) we can see that these consist of a bank overdraft in 19x1 and 19x2 and various creditors of which the most significant group is trade creditors, suppliers of goods and services necessary to facilitate trading activities. Tax is invariably paid in arrears, so most enterprises—unless they are operating at a loss—will have the Inland Revenue as a creditor.

In limited companies there will tend to be a lag between the proposal of a dividend to shareholders, its approval at an annual general meeting, and the actual payment of the dividend. During this period the sum will appear among creditors' balances within current liabilities.

Finally in the case of CKD we have *accruals*. These are the opposite of prepayments and represent benefits received for which payment is made in arrears. Electricity can be taken as a good example: an enterprise will consume electricity and only receive an invoice after the end of the period during which consumption took place. When financial statements are being prepared at 31 December each year, it is necessary to estimate the amounts that will be payable for inputs consumed within the year but which have not yet been invoiced—these are the accruals.

As a general proposition we can argue that current liabilities are much easier to manage than are current assets, but it is often helpful in financial analysis to consider the two categories together, at least as an initial indicator of financial condition. This is illustrated in Table 9 (p. 46). The difference between current assets and current liabilities is termed 'working capital' and it is usually positive (although it can be negative). The reason for this name is given in Fig. 3.3: it would normally be expected that the long-term capital in an enterprise would finance all the fixed assets and some of the current assets. The extent to which current assets exceed current liabilities measures the extent to which long-term capital is financing current operations; hence, 'working' capital.

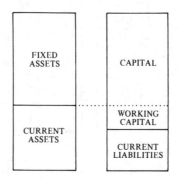

Figure 3.3 *The derivation of working capital*

From a managerial perspective the main problem with using working capital as an indicator of financial position is that it is a residual left over from two aggregations. One can argue that it is the specific elements within these aggregations (e.g. cash, trade creditors) that need to be monitored and managed rather than the residual 'working capital', but, as we shall see, broad indicators are needed to draw attention to discrepancies that will lead to more detailed investigation.

Moving on to consider the claims of those who have provided capital for the business, we can identify two categories. In the first place there is the ownership category—shareholders' funds. This is made up of the issued share capital plus capital reserves and revenue reserves. Table 1 shows us that the share capital was £1,000,000 in 19x1 and 19x2, but increased to £2,400,000 in 19x3 and then to £3,000,000 in 19x5. The capital reserve started at £423,680 but decreased to £23,680 in 19x3. As will be explained later, capital reserves arise from certain specific non-trading activities and can only be used for legally-specified purposes. The reduction in 19x3 of £400,000 was due to a scrip (or bonus) issue of shares, which explains part of the increase in share capital in 19x3 (see Table 10, p. 47).

Revenue reserves result from trading activities and represent the cumulative undistributed profits of an enterprise.

	Revenue reserve (opening)		Retained earnings for year		Revenue reserve (closing)
19x1	£391,650	+	£150,500	=	£542,150
19x2	£542,150	+	£285,560	=	£827,710
19x3	£827,710	+	£335,960	=	£1,163,670
19x4	£1,163,670	+	£466,860	=	£1,630,530
19x5	£1,630,530	+	£321,170	=	£1,951,700

Figure 3.4 *Calculation of revenue reserves*

Taking the data from Tables 1 and 2, we can construct Fig. 3.4 which illustrates for each year the relationship between revenue reserves and retained earnings. For example, Table 1 shows the revenue reserves at 31 December 19x3 to be £1,163,670. This closing balance for 19x3 must be the opening balance for 19x4, and if we add to it the retained earnings for 19x4, given in Table 2 as £466,860, we arrive at the closing balance of £1,630,530 shown in CKD's balance sheet for 31 December 19x4 in Table 1.

In overall terms shareholders' funds have increased from £1,965,830 in 19x1 to £4,975,380 in 19x5, an increase of over 150 per cent.

The second category of capital is made up of long-term loans. From Table 1 we can see that a loan of £1,200,000 existed in 19x1, at an annual interest rate of 10 per cent. In 19x3 this was renegotiated and increased to £1,800,000 at an interest rate of 12 per cent. During the following year, 19x4, a further loan was obtained at 15 per cent which caused the debt almost to double from £1,200,000 in 19x1 to £2,200,000 in 19x5. As a proportion of shareholders' funds, however, debt has decreased as shown in Fig. 3.5.

19x1	(£1,200,000 ÷ £1,965,830) × 100 = 61%
19x2	(£1,200,000 ÷ £2,251,390) × 100 = 53%
19x3	(£1,800,000 ÷ £3,587,350) × 100 = 50%
19x4	(£2,200,000 ÷ £4,054,210) × 100 = 54%
19x5	(£2,200,000 ÷ £4,975,380) × 100 = 44%

Figure 3.5 *Debt as a proportion of equity*

Table 10 offers a summary of the capital claims on the resources of CKD over the period 19x1–19x5, and Table 11 (p. 48) offers a concise summary of the assets (or resources) and claims (or capital plus liabilities) of CKD over the same period.

The Profit and Loss Account

This statement seeks to match the revenue generated during a specified time period with the expenses incurred in generating that revenue. It is, therefore, representing a *flow* of economic events over a period and hence is analogous to a cinefilm, by comparison with the snapshot analogy given for the balance sheet taken at a point in time.

In its simplest form we can argue that:

$$\text{Revenue} - \text{Expense} = \text{Profit}$$

This emphasizes the fact that profit is a residual. Since revenue is not usually too difficult to ascertain, the main focus of attention in measuring profit (or loss) for a period inevitably falls upon expenses. As we saw in our earlier discussion of fixed assets, for example, the way in which depreciation is calculated is wholly arbitrary, but the amount that is charged as depreciation expense in a period has a significant influence on reported profit for that period. (If you doubt the arbitrariness of depreciation charges just consider that there are several ways, all equally acceptable, of measuring it; that the analyst will be free to determine the method he or she will use; the estimated length of life of the asset; the expected residual value, if any, at the end of the asset's expected useful life; and so on. One can see that the outcome is necessarily arbitrary.) This type of problem arises in connection with many expense items because the practice of reporting on an annual, quarterly or monthly basis means that long-lived assets must be depreciated, accruals (e.g. for utilities) must be made, and various other items must be 'adjusted' to fit a time span that is not their natural one.

Table 2 summarizes CKD's profit and loss accounts for years 19x1–19x5. The conventional format involves, firstly, matching the sales revenue with the 'cost of sales'. This latter figure is not the same as 'cost of production' because it will usually be found that stock levels differ between the beginning and the end of a financial period. If stocks were increasing then it follows that the cost of production would be greater than the cost of sales, and vice versa when stocks are decreasing. To the extent that goods have been manufactured *but not yet sold* they will be an *asset* (and appear among current assets in the balance sheet). But the cost of goods sold during a period needs to be set against the revenue of that period to determine the gross profit.

The sales revenue generated in 19x1 (Table 2) totals £5,950,000. This was attributable, in part, to the sale of kitchen fittings manufactured by CKD and, in part, to the fees received for CKD's design services. In Table 12 (p. 50) we can see the breakdown of the total, which includes the following:

Manufactured lines:	A	£810,000	
	B	£975,000	
	C	£1,437,500	
	D	£1,140,000	
	E	£1,470,000	
			£5,832,500
Design services			£117,500
TOTAL SALES REVENUE FOR 19x1			£5,950,000

Similar breakdowns are given for subsequent years. By taking 19x1 as a base year we can derive *index numbers* (with 19x1 = 100) to see the pattern of growth in sales revenue over time. For total sales revenue this is given in column 1 of Fig. 3.6, and the indices for the constituent elements are given in columns 2 and 3.

	Total sales	Sales of manufactured products	Sales of design services
19x1	100	100	100
19x2	120	116	305
19x3	160	147	812
19x4	180	160	1,183
19x5	185	157	1,596

Figure 3.6 *Pattern of sales, 19x1–19x5*

For total sales (by value) there has been continuous growth, but at a decreasing rate from 19x3 onwards, while for the sales of manufactured items this same broad pattern applies but at significantly lower rates. The growth in the sales of design service, in contrast, is startling, although it is important to recognize that this activity was only introduced in 19x0.

Further attention will be paid to revenue aspects in later chapters. However, it does need to be emphasized at this point that the indices portrayed in Fig. 3.6 beg the question about the value of the pound (£): in so far as this declines over time due to inflation, the indices will be overstating the real rate of change. One way to counter this is to use inflation-adjusted figures, and we will deal with this in Chapter 8.

The build up of the cost of sales is provided by Tables 13 to 16 (pp. 50–3). Taking the cost of manufactured sales first, it is shown in Tables 13–15 how the relevant figures are calculated. Since the details will be discussed at length later in the book it is not proposed to delve deeply into these data at this stage, but the links between the data in Tables 13–15 can be briefly outlined.

From Table 13(a) it can be seen that the total manufactured cost of sales for 19x5 is £5,528,100. This is made up of direct material and direct labour inputs totalling £2,632,450 and variable and fixed overheads of £2,895,650. All these figures are given as aggregates, but in Table 14 we are shown the elemental unit costs for each product line. From this data, plus the details of units sold given in Table 12, we can construct Fig. 3.7 which deals with direct material costs.

Product line	Units sold in 19x5	Direct material cost per unit £	Total direct material cost £
A	18,500	29.26	541,310
B	27,500	4.69	128,975
C	13,500	17.82	240,570
D	13,800	5.86	80,868
E	13,750	16.39	225,337
			1,217,060

Figure 3.7 *Direct material element in cost of sales*

By means of similar calculations it is a straightforward task to relate the unit cost data for direct labour, variable and fixed overheads (from Table 14) to the aggregate data given in Table 13(a).

The details of manufacturing overheads are provided by Table 15, and these, along with direct manufacturing costs, are summarized in Table 13(b). This latter table shows clearly that the costs of manufacture in each year (e.g. £5,586,630 in 19x5) differ from the cost of sales in each year (e.g. £5,528,100 in 19x5) by the change in inventory. In all years from 19x1 to 19x2 the inventory increased, so the cost of manufacturing in all cases exceeded the cost of sales.

One of the major distinctions between supplying goods, on the one hand, and supplying services, on the other, is that it is not possible to hold inventories of services. It follows that the costs of supplying services during a particular time period closely approximate to the costs incurred in running the service operation during that period. (The differences that arise will be due to partially completed assignments carried over from one period to another, and invoiced to the client as sales of the second period.) In the case of CKD we have made the slightly simplifying assumption that there are no carryovers from one year to another, hence the cost of providing design services year by year becomes the corresponding cost of sales. Table 16 gives the details.

By combining the cost of sales data from Table 13(a), for manufactured items, and Table 16, for design services, we can reconcile the total figures given in Table 2, as shown in Fig. 3.8.

	Manufacturing cost of sales £	+	Design services cost of sales £	=	Total cost of sales £
19x1	3,489,700		734,800		4,224,500
19x2	4,113,400		813,200		4,926,600
19x3	5,334,500		948,700		6,283,200
19x4	5,724,800		1,022,500		6,747,300
19x5	5,528,100		1,076,400		6,604,500

Figure 3.8 *Component cost of sales figures*

When we match the cost of sales with sales revenue (as in Table 17 on p. 54) we can see the way in which gross profit is generated by each of the two main activities (manufacturing and design services).

	Manufacturing gross profit £	+	Design services gross profit £	=	Total gross profit £
19x1	2,342,800		(617,300)		1,725,500
19x2	2,668,100		(454,700)		2,213,400
19x3	3,231,500		5,300		3,236,800
19x4	3,595,200		367,500		3,962,700
19x5	3,603,650		799,350		4,403,000

Figure 3.9 *Components of gross profit*

As Fig. 3.9 demonstrates, design services were a drain on profits until 19x3 when they made a modest margin of £5,300. By 19x5 design services were making 18 per cent of CKD's gross profit while generating 17 per cent of the sales revenue.

Once the gross profit figure (which is a primary indicator of trading performance) has been determined, the next stage in Table 2 involves the deduction of a variety of expenses. These relate to marketing, distribution, administration, and financial aspects of CKD's operations. Some details are given in Table 18 (p. 55) of the constituent elements of each expense category. Each item of expense is categorized in Table 18 as either 'fixed' or 'variable', and Table 19 (p. 56) summarizes all expenses in this manner. The meaning of this classification is given more fully later in the book.

Net operating profit is determined by deducting the various expenses listed in Table 18 from the gross profit as shown in Table 2. This is a more refined indicator of trading performance than is the gross profit figure, but certain transactions that are not principally concerned with the manufacturing and marketing of kitchen fittings and designs need to be accounted for to convert the net operating profit into net profit before tax. In the context of CKD we have two examples of these transactions: one is the interest earned on short-term investments (in 19x1, 19x2, and 19x4); and the other is the gains/losses made on the disposal of fixed assets in all years except 19x2 (the details are given in Table 7). Both sets of transactions are reflected in Table 2.

The net profit before tax is often taken as a key indicator of overall business performance, with opinions varying as to the need to allow for the impact of taxation. It is clearly the case that taxes have to be paid, which means that the profit available for distribution as dividends or for retention within the business is the *net of tax* amount. It follows that net profit after tax is, logically, a more appropriate overall performance indicator. The tax rules will be known, and managers should really seek to allow for these to produce as good an after-tax profit as they are reasonably able.

Table 2 shows that the tax rate varies from 40 per cent in 19x1 and 19x2, to 45 per cent in 19x3 and 19x4, and then to 50 per cent in 19x5. Such changes should be allowed for in decision-making.

As noted in the previous paragraph, after-tax profits are available for distribution or retention. CKD has consistently proposed dividends at a rate of 10 per cent of the nominal value of issued share capital from 19x1 to 19x4, but increased this to 15 per cent in 19x5. Retained earnings—which are added to the revenue reserves in the balance sheet, as shown in Fig. 3.4—are what remain after all the above deductions have been made.

The Funds Flow Statement

There are many ways in which 'funds' might be defined. Perhaps the most important point is to think of funds as representing *purchasing power*, and then they can be defined in a way that suits a particular purpose. For instance, if there is a shortage of cash within an enterprise, an appropriate way to define funds might well be in terms of cash itself. This is the tightest (and, as a result, the most limiting) operational definition of funds. On the other hand, a broader definition (which echoes Fig. 3.1) is *working capital*: this is, in fact, the most usual definition of funds, and whenever the expression 'funds' is used without further elaboration it can generally be assumed that a working capital definition is being used.

Table 9, as we have already noted, summarizes CKD's funds flow (using the working capital definition), and Table 3 expands on this. If funds are equivalent to purchasing power the aims of a funds flow statement are to show, for a given period of time, where funds came from and the uses to which they were put. The difference between the inflow and outflow of funds is the net funds flow for the period.

Let us reflect a little on the clues that the balance sheet and profit and loss account give us regarding the flow of funds through an enterprise. The balance sheet tells us something about an enterprise's financial position by listing its resources and the claims against those resources at a point in time. Purchasing power is provided whenever new claims are created on the part of the providers of capital (e.g. a new share issue, or a new loan) or when fixed assets are sold. Such transactions are primarily concerned with financing questions. In addition, from the profit and loss account, we can see how much purchasing power has been generated from trading operations. This gives us three main sources of funds:
1. Funds from operations;
2. Funds from sale of fixed assets;
3. Funds from share issues and loans.

Table 3 lists the amounts CKD received from each of these sources during the five years from 19x1 to 19x5. We can see that the total inflow ranged from £695,300 in 19x1 to £2,660,140 in 19x5.

The outflow of funds can be accounted for by listing the purchase of new fixed assets, the repayment of loans, and payments for taxation and dividends. In the case of CKD, as Table 3 shows, there were no loan repayments during the years in which we are interested, but there were substantial outlays on:
• acquisition of fixed assets;
• payment of taxation;
• payment of dividends.

In 19x1 there was a net outflow of funds of £50,700 but each of the remaining years had a net inflow of funds. The significance of this will be picked up in the next few chapters.

As a footnote it might be helpful even in this introductory chapter to comment on the derivation of funds from operations. If we look at the data in Table 3 for 19x3 we see that funds from operations consisted of:

Net profit before tax	£1,047,200
Plus depreciation	399,800
Less gain on sale	(40,000)
	£1,407,000

It is necessary to add back the depreciation charge for the year because this *does not use funds*. When depreciation charges are shown they merely represent an attempt to spread an asset's initial cost over an estimate of its years of useful life. As such, they are simply entries in books of account rather than a flow of funds. (The flow of funds takes place, of course, when a new asset is purchased.) In a similar way, the funds flow from the sale of assets is given by the proceeds from the sale itself, i.e. the amount realized: any gain (or loss) on disposal needs to be deducted from (or added back to) the net profit figure since it only appears there in the first place to allow the books to balance; it does not represent a flow of funds.

The Value Added Statement

Two key issues underlie the value added statement. Firstly, it is recognized that an enterprise literally *adds value* to the materials and services (inputs) that it buys: this is evidenced by the ability of most enterprises to sell their output for more than the cost of the inputs contained in that output. The added value is, in fact, wealth, and the second key issue is the recognition (as suggested by Fig. 1.3) that a number of different interest groups have the right to share in the wealth that the enterprise has created.

From Table 4 we can see the value added by CKD's activities over the five years 19x1–19x5. This is given by deducting from the sales revenue figure the cost of bought-in materials and services. We have seen in Tables 13,15, 16 and 18 the categories of bought-in items that need to be accounted for which include:
• raw material and components
• utilities
• fees for professional services
• stationery, printing, postage
• hire and lease charges
• advertising
• financial charges (e.g. rates, audit, bank charges)
and so on. The resulting value added represents the wealth that has been created by the efforts of those who are engaged in the enterprise's activities. As such it needs to be distinguished from profit, although the two can be reconciled. The primary difference is the exclusion of labour costs from the list of bought-in items that form the basis of the value added calculation. 'Labour' (for value added purposes) is a

participant in the distribution of wealth rather than (as in the profit and loss account) a charge against revenue.

It is also necessary to distinguish value added, which essentially results from trading activities, and funds flow, which results from a combination of trading and financing activities.

The participation in value added, as given in Table 4, is relatively straightforward. Payments to employees are made up of salaries, wages, and associated employment costs (e.g. national insurance contributions, superannuation contributions). The total figure for each year is arrived at as shown in Fig. 3.10.

(All figures in £s)

	19x1	19x2	19x3	19x4	19x5
Direct labour	1,020,200	1,130,370	1,427,280	1,515,990	1,415,390
Indirect labour	141,055	200,232	278,949	273,337	227,520
Manufacturing salaries	820,069	1,141,614	1,286,478	1,328,863	1,433,759
Design salaries	150,525	192,010	236,500	282,500	329,750
Marketing salaries	208,720	264,650	366,690	432,690	512,560
Distribution salaries	144,210	191,330	256,780	317,790	368,340
Administration salaries	281,050	344,020	473,100	565,490	658,710
TOTAL	2,765,829	3,464,226	4,325,777	4,716,660	4,946,032

Figure 3.10 *Wages and salaries*

All other figures in Table 4 can be found in Tables 2 and 3, and Fig. 3.11 illustrates the relative magnitude of each participant's share of the added value created by CKD over the five years.

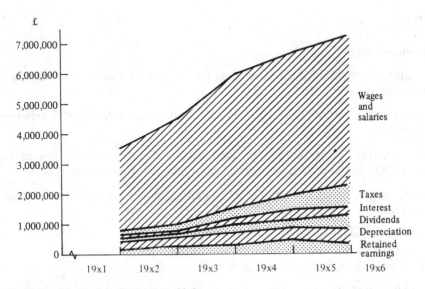

Figure 3.11 *Constituent elements of value added*

We will return to the notion of value added as a performance measure in a later chapter.

Ratios

It is difficult to assess any financial data when it is presented in isolation. Thus the statement that CKD made a profit in 19x3 of £575,960 is not terribly meaningful. To some extent this is because one needs to specify carefully which measure of profit one is using (e.g. gross, net operating, net before tax, net after tax), but mainly it is due to the absence of any benchmark against which to judge the profit figure. It is much more helpful to relate the profit to the investment that had to be made to earn it or, in some circumstances, to the sales revenue that helped generate it.

As a general rule *relative* figures are much more useful than are *absolute* figures, and Tables 20–2 (pp. 57–9) give a series of relative measures derived from data on CKD given in earlier tables. The measures we have included in these tables are by no means exhaustive: many variations are available and managers should feel free to specify which ratios they consider to be most helpful to them. However, the emphasis in Tables 20–2 is on the financial condition of CKD as represented by tests of liquidity (Table 20), tests of profitability (Table 21), and tests of financial structure (Table 22). Future chapters will discuss each of these in some detail, and we will also consider operating ratios at a later stage.

3.2 Summary

Within this chapter we have reviewed the recent history of CKD Ltd by means of four key financial statements: the balance sheet, profit and loss account, funds flow statement, and value added statement. As well as looking at the general issues underlying these statements we have related the discussion to the specific circumstances of CKD Ltd.

3.3 Exercises

Review questions

1. Identify the main financial statements that have been discussed in this chapter, and explain their basic roles.

2. Justify the assertion (given in 'the accounting equation') that Resources = Claims.

3. How can one distinguish between fixed assets and current assets? Give examples from CKD Ltd and from any organization in which you have worked.

4. What do you understand by the term 'depreciation'? Why is it charged against revenue?

5. Is there any relationship between:
   (a) written down value and market value? or
   (b) depreciation charges and cash flows?

6. Explain the relationships among current assets and current liabilities by means of 'the trading cycle'.

7. Is the practice of dividing time into arbitrary periods (e.g. financial years) in order to produce financial reports helpful to the effective management of an enterprise?

8. Distinguish between trading and financing activities. Use data from CKD Ltd to illustrate your answer.

9. What impacts does inflation have upon an organization's financial position and financial performance?

10. How do you think 'funds' should be:
    (a) defined?
    (b) measured?

11. In what ways are:
    (a) funds statements;
    (b) value added statements;
    useful to managers?

12. Do you consider *relative* figures to be more helpful to management than *absolute* figures? Justify your answer by reference to data from CKD Ltd.

CKD Ltd

TABLE 1: Balance Sheets as at 31 December 19x1–19x5

TABLE 2: Profit and Loss Accounts for years to 31 December 19x1–19x5

TABLE 3: Funds Flow Statements for years to 31 December 19x1–19x5

TABLE 4: Value Added Statements for years to 31 December 19x1–19x5

TABLE 1 *Balance sheet as at 31 December 19x1–19x5*

	19x1				19x2		
	Cost	Dep.	WDV		Cost	Dep.	WDV
Fixed assets							
Plant and machinery	1,000,000	400,000	600,000		1,000,000	500,000	500,000
Land and buildings	2,100,000	630,000	1,470,000		2,400,000	678,000	1,722,000
Fixtures and fittings	720,000	380,000	340,000		720,000	416,000	304,000
Office equipment	154,000	108,800	45,200		229,000	154,600	74,400
Motor vehicles	220,000	160,000	60,000		220,000	215,000	5,000
	4,194,000	1,678,800		2,515,200	4,569,000	1,963,600	2,605,
Current assets							
Cash			—				—
Investments			50,000				50,000
Debtors			733,560				860,710
Prepayments			38,000				41,500
Inventories:							
Consumables	47,200				56,640		
Raw materials	195,600				254,280		
Work-in-progress	316,000				347,600		
Finished goods	523,800		1,082,600		654,750		1,313,270
				1,904,160			2,265,
Current liabilities							
Overdraft			602,500				50,000
Creditors:							
Trade	332,030				939,200		
Taxation	166,000				257,040		
Dividends	100,000				100,000		
Accruals	53,000		651,030		73,250		1,369,490
				1,253,530			1,419,
Net current assets				650,630			845,
Net total assets				£3,165,830			£3,451,
Financed by:							
Share capital (£1 shares)	1,000,000				1,000,000		
Capital reserve	425,680				423,680		
Revenue reserve	542,150				827,710		
Shareholders' funds			1,965,830				2,251,390
Long-term loans:							
10%	1,200,000				1,200,000		
12%	—				—		
15%	—		1,200,000		—		1,200,000
				£3,165,830			£3,451,

	19x3				19x4				19x5		
	Cost	Dep.	WDV		Cost	Dep.	WDV		Cost	Dep.	WDV
	,600,000	660,000	940,000		1,200,000	480,000	720,000		2,000,000	680,000	1,320,000
	,400,000	726,000	1,674,000		3,000,000	786,000	2,214,000		3,000,000	846,000	2,154,000
	,170,000	234,500	935,500		1,170,000	308,000	862,000		1,170,000	381,500	1,088,500
	229,000	200,400	28,600		509,000	302,200	206,800		409,000	304,000	105,000
	290,000	207,500	82,500		290,000	280,000	10,000		330,000	282,500	47,500
	,689,000	2,028,400		3,660,600	6,169,000	2,156,200		4,012,800	6,909,000	2,494,000	4,415,000

	54,600			451,880			478,600	
	—			—			400,000	
	1,356,270			1,701,860			1,930,080	
	72,800			64,200			83,700	
70,800			80,240			82,670		
322,740			361,860			352,080		
474,000			537,200			553,100		
811,890	1,679,430		995,220	1,974,520		1,047,630	2,035,480	
		3,163,100			4.192,460			4,927,860
	—			—			—	
657,610			1,047,560			842,910		
471,240			578,340			771,170		
240,000			240,000			450,000		
67,500	1,436,350		85,150	1,951,050		103,400	2,167,480	
		1,436,350			1,951,050			2,167,480
		1,726,750			2,241,410			2,760,380
		£5,387,350			£6,254,210			£7,175,380
,400,000			2,400,000			3,000,000		
23,680			23,680			23,680		
,163,670			1,630,530			1,951,700		
		3,587,350			4,054,210			4,975,380
—			—			—		
,800,000			1,800,000			1,800,000		
—	1,800,000		400,000	2,200,000		400,000	2,200,000	
		£5,387,350			£6,254,210			£7.175,380

TABLE 2 *Profit and loss accounts for years to 31 December 19x1–19x5*

	19x1		19x2		19x3		19x4		19x5	
	£	£	£	£	£	£	£	£	£	£
Sales revenue		5,950,000		7,140,000		9,520,000		10,710,000		11,007,500
Cost of sales		4,224,500		4,926,600		6,283,200		6,747,300		6,604,500
Gross profit		1,725,500		2,213,400		3,236,800		3,962,700		4,403,000
Marketing expenses	410,050		490,870		708,420		804,720		896,170	
Distribution expenses	274,150		335,800		486,610		558,000		636,830	
Administrative expenses	478,300		580,880		787,450		960,290		1,072,500	
Financial expenses	166,500		168,250		247,120		304,490		305,160	
		1,329,000		1,575,800		2,229,600		2,627,500		2,910,660
Net operating profit		396,500		637,600		1,007,200		1,335,200		1,492,340
(Loss)/gain on disposal	15,000		—		40,000		(50,000)		10,000	
Interest earned	5,000		5,000		—		—		40,000	
		20,000		5,000		40,000		(50,000)		50,000
Net profit before tax		416,500		642,600		1,047,200		1,285,200		1,542,340
Tax @ 40%	166,000		257,040							
Tax @ 45%					471,240		578,340			
Tax @ 50%									771,170	
Net profit after tax		250,500		385,560		575,960		706,860		771,170
Dividends proposed (10%)	100,000		100,000		240,000		240,000			
Dividends proposed (15%)									450,000	
Retained earnings		150,500		285,560		335,960		466,860		321,170

TABLE 3 *Funds flow statements for years to 31 December 19x1–19x5*

	19x1		19x2		19x3		19x4		19x5	
	£	£	£	£	£	£	£	£	£	£
SOURCES OF FUNDS										
A. Operations										
Net profit before tax	416,500		642,600		1,047,200		1,285,200		1,542,340	
Add: Depreciation	263,800		284,800		399,800		427,800		497,800	
Loss on sale	—		—		—		50,000		10,000	
Deduct: Gain on sale	15,000		—		40,000		—		20,000	
		665,300		927,400		1,407,000		1,763,000		2,030,140
B. Proceeds from sale		30,000		—		105,000		50,000		30,000
C. Financing										
New share capital	—		—		1,000,000		—		600,000	
New debt	—		—		600,000		400,000		—	
		—		—		1,600,000		400,000		600,000
TOTAL SOURCES		695,300		927,400		3,112,000		2,213,000		2,660,140
USES OF FUNDS										
A. Acquisition of assets										
Plant and machinery	400,000		—		600,000		—		800,000	
Land and buildings	—		300,000		—		600,000		—	
Fixtures and fittings	—		—		750,000		—		—	
Office equipment	—		75,000		—		280,000		—	
Motor vehicles	80,000		—		170,000		—		120,000	
		480,000		375,000		1,520,000		880,000		920,000
B. Taxation		166,000		257,040		471,240		578,340		771,170
C. Dividends		100,000		100,000		240,000		240,000		450,000
TOTAL USES		746,000		732,040		2,231,240		1,698,340		2,141,170
FUNDS FLOW DURING YEAR		(50,700)		195,360		880,760		514,660		518,970

TABLE 4 *Value added statements for years to 31 December 19x1–19x5*

	19x1		19x2		19x3		19x4		19x5	
	£	£	£	£	£	£	£	£	£	£
Value added:										
SALES TO CUSTOMERS	5,950,000		7,140,000		9,520,000		10,710,000		11,007,500	
LESS: BOUGHT IN										
MATERIALS AND SERVICES	2,383,871		2,628,374		3,531,223		4,004,340		3,745,328	
VALUE ADDED		3,566,129		4,511,626		5,988,777		6,705,660		7,262,172
Applied as follows:										
TO EMPLOYEES:										
Wages, salaries, pensions, etc.	2,765,829		3,464,226		4,325,777		4,716,660		4,946,032	
TO GOVERNMENT: Taxes	166,000		257,040		471,240		578,340		771,170	
TO PROVIDERS OF CAPITAL:										
Interest	120,000		120,000		216,000		276,000		276,000	
Dividends	100,000		100,000		240,000		240,000		450,000	
TO PROVIDE FOR ASSETS:										
Depreciation	263,800		284,800		399,800		427,800		497,800	
TO PROVIDE FOR THE FUTURE:										
Retained earnings	150,500		285,560		335,960		466,860		321,170	
		3,566,129		4,511,626		5,988,777		6,705,660		7,262,172

Summaries of Movements and Balance Sheet Items 19x1–19x5

TABLE 5: Summary of Fixed Assets Movements

TABLE 6: Depreciation Policies

TABLE 7: Losses/Gains on Disposal of Fixed Assets

TABLE 8: Inventory Movements (Manufacturing)

TABLE 9: Summary of Working Capital Changes

TABLE 10: Summary of Capital Movements

TABLE 11: Summary of Assets and Liabilities

TABLE 5 *Summary of fixed assets movements* (All figures in £s)

	19x1	19x2	19x3	19x4	19x5
Plant and equipment					
Disposals (at cost)	—	—	—	400,000	—
Acquisitions (at cost)	400,000	—	600,000	—	800,000
Depreciation for year	100,000	100,000	160,000	120,000	200,000
Land and buildings					
Disposals (at cost)	—	—	—	—	—
Acquisitions (at cost)	—	300,000	—	600,000	—
Depreciation for year	42,000	48,000	48,000	60,000	60,000
Fixtures and fittings					
Disposals (at cost)	—	—	300,000	—	—
Acquisitions (at cost)	—	—	750,000	—	—
Depreciation for year	36,000	36,000	73,500	73,500	73,500
Office equipment					
Disposals (at cost)	—	—	—	—	100,000
Acquisitions (at cost)	—	75,000	—	280,000	—
Depreciation for year	30,800	45,800	45,800	101,800	81,800
Motor vehicles					
Disposals (at cost)	60,000	—	100,000	—	80,000
Acquisitions (at cost)	80,000	—	170,000	—	120,000
Depreciation for year	55,000	55,000	72,500	72,500	82,500
Total depreciation for year	263,800	284,800	399,800	427,800	497,800
Capital expenditure	480,000	375,000	1,520,000	880,000	920,000

TABLE 6 *Depreciation policies*

PLANT AND MACHINERY				*10% Historical cost at year end*
e.g.	19x1	Op. bal.	300,000	
		P & L	100,000	*10% yr. end figure of £1,000,000*
	19x1	Cl. bal.	£400,000	

LAND AND BUILDINGS				*2% Historical cost at year end*
e.g.	19x1	Op. bal.	588,000	
		P & L	42,000	*2% yr. end figure of £2,100,000*
	19x1	Cl. bal.	£630,000	

FIXTURES AND FITTINGS				*Rates varying between 5% and 8% of historical cost at year end*
e.g.	19x1	Op. bal.	344,000	
		P & L	36,000	*5% yr. end figure of £720,000*
	19x1	Cl. bal.	£380,000	

OFFICE EQUIPMENT				*20% Historical cost at year end*
e.g.	19x1	Op. bal.	78,000	
		P & L	30,800	*20% yr end figure of £154,000*
	19x1	Cl. bal.	£108,800	

MOTOR VEHICLES				*25% Historical cost at year end*
e.g.	19x1	Op. bal.	150,000	
		Disposal	(45,000)	
		P & L	55,000	*25% yr. end figure of £220,000*
	19x1	Cl. bal.	£160,000	

Op. bal = opening balance
Cl. bal. = closing balance

TABLE 7 *Losses/gains on disposal of fixed assets* (All figures in £s)

	19x1	19x2	19x3	19x4	19x5
Plant and machinery					
Cost				400,000	
Acc. dep'n				300,000	
WDV				100,000	
Proceeds				50,000	
(Loss)/gain				(50,000)	
Land and buildings	—	—	—	—	—
Fixtures and fittings					
Cost			300,000		
Acc. dep'n			255,000		
WDV			45,000		
Proceeds			75,000		
(Loss)/gain			30,000		
Office equipment					
Cost					100,000
Acc. dep'n					80,000
WDV					20,000
Proceeds					10,000
(Loss)/gain					(10,000)
Motor vehicles					
Cost	60,000		100,000		80,000
Acc. dep'n	45,000		80,000		80,000
WDV	15,000		20,000		—
Proceeds	30,000		30,000		20,000
(Loss)/gain	15,000		10,000		20,000
Summary					
Cost of disposals	60,000	—	400,000	400,000	180,000
Acc. dep'n	45,000	—	335,000	300,000	160,000
WDV	15,000	—	65,000	100,000	20,000
Proceeds	30,000	—	105,000	50,000	30,000
Net (loss)/gain	15,000	—	40,000	(50,000)	10,000

TABLE 8 *Inventory movements (manufacturing)*   (All figures in £s)

	19x1	19x2	19x3	19x4	19x5
Opening inventory (RM + WIP + FG)	976,280	1,035,400	1,256,630	1,608,630	1,894,280
Inputs during year (DM + DL + V.o/h. + F.o/h.)	3,548,820	4,334,630	5,686,500	6,010,450	5,586,630
	4,525,100	5,370,030	6,943,130	7,619,080	7,480,910
Closing inventory (RM + WIP + FG)	1,035,400	1,256,630	1,608,630	1,894,280	1,952,810
C.O.G.S.	3,489,700	4,113,400	5,334,500	5,724,800	5,528,100

Year-end balances	19x1	19x2	19x3	19x4	19x5
Raw materials	195,600	254,280	322,740	361,860	352,080
WIP	316,000	347,600	474,000	537,200	553,100
Finished goods	523,800	654,750	811,890	995,220	1,047,630
	1,035,400	1,256,630	1,608,630	1,894,280	1,952,810
Consumables	47,200	56,640	70,800	80,240	82,670
Inventory total	1,082,600	1,313,270	1,679,430	1,974,520	2,035,480

△ Inventory total	+59,120	+221,230	+352,000	+285,650	+58,530
of which: V.o/h.	4,349	14,086	26,385	19,047	3,477
F.o/h.	30,609	90,434	169,798	128,493	25,479
DM + DL	24,162	116,710	155,817	138,110	29,574
	59,120	221,230	352,000	285,650	58,530

TABLE 9 *Summary of working capital changes*   (All figures in £s)

	19x0	19x1	19x2	19x3	19x4	19x5
Current assets	1,213,590	1,904,160	2,265,480	3,163,100	4,192,460	4,927,860
Current liabilities	512,260	1,253,530	1,419,490	1,436,350	1,951,050	2,167,480
Working capital	701,330	650,630	845,990	1,726,750	2,241,410	2,760,380
△ Working capital	N/A	(50,700)	195,360	880,760	514,660	518,970

TABLE 10 *Summary of capital movements*   (All figures in £s)

	19x1	19x2	19x3	19x4	19x5
Share capital					
Opening balance	1,000,000	1,000,000	1,000,000	2,400,000	2,400,000
New issues	—	—	1,000,000	—	600,000
Scrip issue	—	—	400,000	—	—
Closing balance	1,000,000	1,000,000	2,400,000	2,400,000	3,000,000
Capital reserve					
Opening balance	423,680	423,680	423,680	23,680	23,680
Scrip issue	—	—	(400,000)	—	—
Closing balance	423,680	423,680	23,680	23,680	23,680
Revenue reserve					
Opening balance	391,650	542,150	827,710	1,163,670	1,630,530
Retained profits	150,500	285,560	335,960	466,860	321,170
Closing balance	542,150	827,710	1,163,670	1,630,530	1,951,700
Owners' equity	1,965,830	2,251,390	3,587,350	4,054,210	4,975,380
Loan capital					
10%/12% loan*					
Opening balance	1,200,000	1,200,000	1,200,000	1,800,000	1,800,000
Additions	—	—	600,000	—	—
Closing balance	1,200,000	1,200,000	1,800,000	1,800,000	1,800,000
15% Loan					
Opening balance	—	—	—	—	400,000
Additions	—	—	—	400,000	—
Closing balance	—	—	—	400,000	400,000
TOTAL LONG TERM DEBT	1,200,000	1,200,000	1,800,000	2,200,000	2,200,000
TOTAL CAPITAL EMPLOYED	3,165,830	3,451,390	5,387,350	6,254,210	7,175,380

*Renegotiated from 10% to 12% in 19x3

TABLE 11 *Summary of assets and liabilities*   (All figures in £s)

	19x1	19x2	19x3	19x4	19x5
Fixed assets					
Historical cost	4,194,000	4,569,000	5,689,000	6,169,000	6,909,000
Depreciation	1,678,800	1,963,600	2,028,400	2,156,200	2,494,000
WDV	2,515,200	2,605,400	3,660,600	4,012,800	4,415,000
Current assets					
Cash	—	—	54,600	451,880	478,600
Investments	50,000	50,000	—	—	400,000
Debtors	733,560	860,710	1,356,270	1,701,860	1,930,080
Prepayments	38,000	41,500	72,800	64,200	83,700
Inventories	1,082,600	1,313,270	1,679,430	1,974,520	2,035,480
TOTAL	1,904,160	2,265,480	3,163,100	4,192,460	4,927,860
TOTAL ASSETS	4,419,360	4,870,880	6,823,700	8,505,260	9,342,860
Long term claims					
Share capital	1,000,000	1,000,000	2,400,000	2,400,000	3,000,000
Capital reserve	423,680	423,680	23,680	23,680	23,680
Revenue reserve	542,150	827,710	1,163,670	1,630,530	1,951,700
Owners' equity	1,965,830	2,251,390	3,587,350	4,054,210	4,975,380
Loan capital	1,200,000	1,200,000	1,800,000	2,200,000	2,200,000
Capital employed	3,165,830	3,451,390	5,387,350	6,254,210	7,175,380
Current liabilities					
Overdraft	602,500	50,000	—	—	—
Trade creditors	332,030	939,200	657,610	1,047,560	842,910
Taxation	166,000	257,040	471,240	578,340	771,170
Dividends	100,000	100,000	240,000	240,000	450,000
Accruals	53,000	73,250	67,500	85,150	103,400
TOTAL	1,253,530	1,419,490	1,436,350	1,951,050	2,167,480
TOTAL CLAIMS	4,419,360	4,870,880	6,823,700	8,205,260	9,342,860

Summaries of Trading Results 19x1–19x5

TABLE 12 *Summary of revenue*

Product line	19x1			19x2			19x3			19x4			19x5		
	No.	Unit price	Revenue	No.	Unit price	Revenue	No.	Unit price	Revenue	No.	Unit price	Revenue	No.	Unit price	Revenue
		£	£		£	£		£	£		£	£		£	£
A	9,000	90	810,000	11,000	95	1,045,000	15,750	100	1,575,000	18,000	105	1,890,000	18,500	105	1,942,500
B	15,000	65	975,000	18,000	68	1,224,000	22,500	70	1,575,000	26,500	70	1,855,000	27,500	75	2,062,500
C	12,500	115	1,437,500	12,500	124	1,550,000	13,750	130	1,787,500	15,000	140	2,100,000	13,500	140	1,890,000
D	12,000	95	1,140,000	14,500	100	1,450,000	19,700	105	2,068,500	16,250	110	1,787,500	13,800	110	1,518,000
E	14,000	105	1,470,000	13,750	110	1,512,500	13,000	120	1,560,000	13,500	125	1,687,500	13,750	125	1,718,750
TOTAL			5,832,500			6,781,500			8,566,000			9,320,000			9,131,750
Index (19x1=100)			100			116			147			160			157
Design services															
Revenue (£)			117,500			358,500			954,000			1,390,000			1,875,750
Index (19x1=100)			100			305			812			1,183			1,596

TABLE 13(a) *Summary—Manufacturing cost of sales*   (All figures in £s)

	19x1	19x2	19x3	19x4	19x5
VARIABLE COSTS					
Direct material (at St.)	721,550	892,620	1,104,610	1,258,000	1,217,060
Direct labour (at St.)	1,020,200	1,130,370	1,427,280	1,515,990	1,415,390
Prime cost	1,741,750	2,022,990	2,531,890	2,773,990	2,632,450
Variable overhead (at St.)	217,490	281,730	376,930	380,950	347,710
Total variable cost	1,959,240	2,304,720	2,908,820	3,154,940	2,980,160
Fixed overheads					
Absorbed	1,530,460	1,808,680	2,425,680	2,569,860	2,547,940
TOTAL MFCT. COST OF SALES	3,489,700	4,113,400	5,334,500	5,724,800	5,528,100
Fixed overhead absorption rate	150% DL£	160% DL£	170% DL£	170% DL£	180% DL£

TABLE 13(b) *Summary—Total manufacturing costs*   (All figures in £s)

	19x1	19x2	19x3	19x4	19x5
Prime costs:					
Direct materials	725,306	952,809	1,160,545	1,320,526	1,232,479
Direct labour	1,040,606	1,186,891	1,527,162	1,591,574	1,429,545
Variable overheads	221,839	295,816	403,315	399,997	351,187
Fixed overheads	1,561,069	1,899,114	2,595,478	2,698,353	2,573,419
TOTAL	3,548,820	4,334,630	5,686,500	6,010,450	5,586,630
Less: COS	3,489,700	4,113,400	5,334,500	5,724,800	5,528,100
△ Inventory	59,120	221,230	352,000	285,650	58,530

TABLE 14 *Unit cost analysis*

Product cost standards	19x1	19x2	19x3	19x4	19x5
	£	£	£	£	£
Product line A:					
DM	23.96	27.92	27.62	29.46	29.26
DL	19.17	20.01	20.09	20.62	19.51
Vo/h	4.79	5.79	6.03	5.89	5.36
Unit VC	47.92	53.72	53.74	55.97	54.13
Fo/h	28.75	32.13	34.16	34.86	35.12
Unit TC	76.67	85.85	87.90	90.83	89.25
Product line B:					
DM	3.73	3.96	4.24	4.23	4.69
DL	8.94	8.49	9.09	8.59	9.39
Vo/h	2.24	2.49	2.73	2.45	2.66
Unit VC	14.91	14.94	16.06	15.27	16.74
Fo/h	13.42	13.62	15.44	14.59	16.90
Unit TC	28.33	28.56	31.50	29.86	33.64
Product line C:					
DM	14.78	16.81	16.84	19.49	17.82
DL	24.35	25.22	25.48	28.05	26.72
Vo/h	4.35	5.14	5.46	5.70	5.34
Unit VC	43.48	47.17	41.78	53.24	49.88
Fo/h	36.52	40.17	43.22	47.54	48.11
Unit TC	80.00	87.34	91.00	100.78	97.99
Product line D:					
DM	3.62	4.15	5.33	6.02	5.86
DL	11.01	11.71	14.82	16.12	15.23
Vo/h	2.58	3.21	4.17	4.33	4.22
Unit VC	17.21	19.07	24.32	26.47	25.31
Fo/h	16.52	18.69	25.24	27.43	27.41
Unit TC	33.73	37.76	49.56	53.90	52.72
Product line E:					
DM	15.84	17.74	18.28	16.70	16.39
DL	19.79	19.81	20.31	17.37	16.39
Vo/h	3.96	4.54	4.87	4.01	3.28
Unit VC	39.59	42.09	43.46	38.08	36.06
Fo/h	29.69	31.78	34.52	29.40	29.51
Unit TC	69.28	73.87	77.98	67.48	65.57

DM   = Direct material
DL   = Direct labour
Vo/h = Variable overhead
VC   = Variable cost
Fo/h = Fixed overhead
TC   = Total cost

TABLE 15 *Summary of manufacturing overheads* (All figures in £s)

	19x1	19x2	19x3	19x4	19x5
*Variable overheads**					
Indirect labour	143,882	210,092	298,738	286,669	229,780
Sundry materials	34,860	38,572	47,433	51,302	54,734
Power	10,460	11,156	13,791	14,654	15,283
Heating	9,023	10,284	12,826	14,103	15,016
Maintenance	23,614	25,712	30,527	33,269	36,374
	221,839	295,816	403,315	399,997	351,187
Fixed overheads†					
Depreciation P & M	83,000	83,000	122,000	95,000	157,500
,, L & B	28,000	32,000	32,000	40,000	40,000
Leasing and hiring	330,000	330,000	370,000	390,000	440,000
Canteen	125,000	130,000	140,000	147,500	160,000
Consultants' fees	—	—	300,000	—	—
Training	—	—	150,000	495,490	122,160
Rates and insurance	175,000	182,500	195,000	201,500	220,000
Salaries	820,069	1,141,614	1,286,478	1,328,863	1,433,759
TOTAL	1,561,069	1,899,114	2,595,478	2,698,353	2,573,419
TOTAL MFCT. OVERHEADS	1,782,908	2,194,930	2,998,793	3,098,350	2,924,606
*Included in COS	217,490	281,730	376,930	380,950	347,710
†Absorbed into GOS	1,530,460	1,808,680	2,425,680	2,569,860	2,547,940
Included in inventory	34,958	104,520	196,183	147,540	28,956
TOTAL MFCT. OVERHEADS	1,782,908	2,194,930	2,998,793	3,098,350	2,924,606

TABLE 16 *Design cost data* (All figures in £s)

		19x1	19x2	19x3	19x4	19x5
Salaries	FC	150,525	192,010	236,500	282,500	329,750
Depreciation OE 20%	FC	6,160	9,160	9,160	20,360	16,360
Advertising	FC	523,264	544,408	616,880	618,634	623,699
Consumables	VC	17,621	19,519	23,267	29,823	31,148
Utilities	VC	12,357	15,412	18,372	19,451	19,784
Outside services	VC	24,873	32,691	44,521	51,732	55,659
*TOTAL Cost of sales		734,800	813,200	948,700	1,022,500	1,076,400

*Assuming no opening or closing W-I-P.
FC = Fixed cost
VC = Variable cost

TABLE 17 *Trading summaries*

	19x1	19x2	19x3	19x4	19x5
	£	£	£	£	£
Total sales revenue	5,950,000	7,140,000	9,520,000	10,710,000	11,007,500
Cost of sales	4,224,500	4,926,600	6,283,200	6,747,300	6,604,500
Gross profit	1,725,500	2,213,400	3,236,800	3,962,700	4,403,000
Index of sales revenue (19x1=100)	100	120	160	180	185
Manufacturing	£	£	£	£	£
Sales revenue	5,832,500	6,781,500	8,566,000	9,320,000	9,131,750
Cost of sales	3,489,700	4,113,400	5,334,500	5,724,800	5,528,100
Gross profit	2,342,800	2,668,100	3,231,500	3,595,200	3,603,650
% Total sales revenue	98%	95%	90%	87%	83%
Design	£	£	£	£	£
Sales revenue	117,500	358,500	954,000	1,390,000	1,875,750
Cost of sales	734,800	813,200	948,700	1,022,500	·1,076,400
Gross profit/(loss)	(617,300)	(454,700)	5,300	367,500	799,350
% Total Sales Revenue	2%	5%	10%	13%	17%

TABLE 18 *Expense summaries (1)* (All figures in £s)

		19x1	19x2	19x3	19x4	19x5
Marketing		410,050	490,870	708,420	804,720	896,170
Salaries	FC	208,720	264,650	366,690	432,690	512,560
Advertising	FC	60,640	65,270	108,050	115,730	115,000
Dep'n F&F 20%	FC	7,200	7,200	14,700	14,700	14,700
" MV 60%	FC	33,000	33,000	43,500	43,500	49,500
MV Standing charges	FC	4,000	4,400	4,800	4,960	5,440
Bad debts	VC	14,960	18,700	26,180	29,170	29,900
Printing	VC	44,600	50,750	84,740	97,320	100,120
Travelling	VC	16,930	21,160	25,390	28,440	29,530
MV Running costs	VC	20,000	25,740	34,370	38,210	39,420
Distribution		274,150	335,800	486,610	558,000	636,830
Salaries	FC	144,210	191,330	256,780	317,790	368,340
Dep'n F&F 50%	FC	18,000	18,000	36,750	36,750	36,750
" P&M	FC	17,000	17,000	38,000	25,000	42,500
" L&B	FC	14,000	16,000	16,000	20,000	20,000
Freight charges	VC	62,650	71,250	103,410	122,070	131,560
Packing materials	VC	18,290	22,220	35,670	36,390	37,680
Administration		478,300	580,880	787,450	960,290	1,072,500
Salaries	FC	281,050	344,020	473,100	565,490	658,710
Dep'n F&F 30%	FC	10,800	10,800	22,050	22,050	22,050
" OE 80%	FC	24,640	36,640	36,640	81,440	65,440
" MV 40%	FC	22,000	22,000	29,000	29,000	33,000
Insurance	FC	10,000	12,000	16,000	18,000	18,500
MV Standing charges	FC	2,500	2,750	3,000	3,100	3,400
Rates	FC	20,000	24,000	26,000	29,000	30,000
Stationery & Postage	VC	24,470	27,140	52,270	55,490	52,270
Telephone	VC	25,100	28,870	38,900	43,930	60,200
MV Running costs	VC	10,000	12,730	16,790	19,340	18,270
Legal costs	VC	5,240	10,170	14,320	12,760	18,560
Recruitment costs	VC	26,630	32,280	38,430	49,270	61,310
Maintenance (OE) costs	VC	15,870	17,480	20,950	31,420	30,790
Financial		166,500	168,250	247,120	304,490	305,160
Interest	FC	120,000	120,000	216,000	276,000	276,000
Audit fee	FC	20,000	22,000	25,000	25,750	26,250
Bank charges & interest	VC	26,500	26,500	6,120	2,740	2,910
TOTAL EXPENSES		1,329,000	1,575,800	2,229,600	2,627,500	2,910,660
(Gain) Loss on Disposal		(15,000)	—	(40,000)	50,000	(10,000)
Interest earned		(5,000)	(5,000)	—	—	(40,000)
NET TOTAL		1,309,000	1,570,800	2,189,600	2,677,500	2,860,660

FC = Fixed cost
VC = Variable cost

TABLE 19 *Expense summaries (2)*   (All figures in £s)

	19x1	19x2	19x3	19x4	19x5
Manufacturing C. of S.					
Variable	1,959,240	2,304,720	2,908,820	3,154,940	2,980,160
Fixed	1,530,460	1,808,680	2,425,680	2,569,860	2,547,940
TOTAL	3,489,700	4,113,400	5,334,500	5,724,800	5,528,100
Design					
Variable	54,851	67,622	86,160	101,006	106,591
Fixed	679,949	745,578	862,540	921,494	969,809
TOTAL	734,800	813,200	948,700	1,022,500	1,076,400
Marketing					
Variable	96,490	116,350	170,680	193,140	198,970
Fixed	313,560	374,520	537,740	611,580	697,200
TOTAL	410,050	490,870	708,420	804,720	896,170
Distribution					
Variable	80,940	93,470	139,080	158,460	169,240
Fixed	193,210	242,330	347,530	399,540	467,590
TOTAL	247,150	335,800	486,610	558,000	636,830
Administration					
Variable	107,310	128,670	181,660	212,210	241,400
Fixed	370,990	452,210	605,790	748,080	831,100
TOTAL	478,300	580,880	787,450	960,290	1,072,500
Financial					
Variable	26,500	26,250	6,120	2,740	2,910
Fixed	140,000	142,000	241,000	301,750	302,250
TOTAL	166,500	168,250	247,120	304,490	305,160
Summary:					
Variable costs	2,325,331	2,737,082	3,492,520	3,822,496	3,699,271
Fixed costs	3,228,169	3,765,318	5,020,280	5,552,304	5,815,889
TOTAL COSTS	5,553,500	6,502,400	8,512,800	9,374,800	9,515,160

Summary of ratios based on 19x1–19x5 data

TABLE 20: Tests of Liquidity and Financial Stability

TABLE 21: Tests of Profitability and Efficiency

TABLE 22: Tests of Financial Structure

TABLE 20 *Tests of liquidity and financial stability*

Name of ratio	Formula	State result as	19x1	19x2	19x3	19x4	19x5
1. Current ratio	$\dfrac{\text{Current assets}}{\text{Current liabilities}}$	Ratio	1.52:1.0	1.59:1.0	2.20:1.0	2.15:1.0	2.27:1.0
2. Acid-test ratio	$\dfrac{\text{Monetary current assets}}{\text{Current liabilities}}$	Ratio	0.62:1.0	0.64:1.0	0.98:1.0	1.10:1.0	1.30:1.0
3. Working capital turnover	$\dfrac{\text{Sales}}{\text{Working capital}}$	Times	9.14	8.43	5.51	4.78	3.98
4. Inventory turnover	$\dfrac{\text{Cost of sales}}{\text{Average stock}}$	Times	3.47	3.59	3.72	3.27	2.87
5. Debtors to sales ratio	$\dfrac{\text{Debtors}}{\text{Sales}} \times 100$	%	12.3%	12.1%	14.3%	15.9%	17.5%
6. Debtors days (collection period)	$\dfrac{\text{Debtor}}{\text{Sales}} \times 365$	Days	45	44	52	58	64
7. Creditors turnover ratio	$\dfrac{\text{Creditors}}{\text{Purchases}} \times 100$	%	13.9%	35.7%	18.6%	26.2%	22.5%
8. Creditors days (payment period)	$\dfrac{\text{Creditors}}{\text{Purchases}} \times 365$	Days	51	130	68	95	82

TABLE 21 *Tests of profitability and efficiency*

Name of ratio	Formula	State results as	19x1	19x2	19x3	19x4	19x5
1. Return on investment (after interest and tax)	Net profit after tax / Total net assets	%	7.91%	11.17%	10.69%	11.30%	10.75%
2. Return on investment (after tax before interest)	Net profit after tax but before interest / Total net assets	%	11.69%	14.65%	14.70%	15.71%	14.59%
3. Gross profit ratio	(Gross profit / Sales) × 100	%	29.0%	31.0%	34.0%	37.0%	40.0%
4. Gross profit ratio (manufacturing)	Gross profit (man.) / Sales (man.)	%	40.16%	39.34%	37.72%	38.57%	39.46%
5. Gross profit ratio (design)	Gross profit (design) / Sales (design)	%	−525.36%	−126.83%	0.55%	26.43%	42.61%
6. Net profit ratio (before interest and taxation)	Net profit before interest and tax / Sales	%	9.02%	10.68%	13.27%	14.58%	16.52%
7. Net profit ratio (after tax and before interest)	Net profit after tax and before interest / Sales	%	6.22%	7.08%	8.32%	9.18%	9.51%
8. Net profit ratio (after interest and tax)	Net profit after interest and tax / Sales	%	4.21%	5.40%	6.05%	6.60%	7.01%
9. Capital investment turnover	Sales / No. of shares in issue	Times	1.88	2.07	1.77	1.71	1.53
10. Earnings per share	Net profit after tax / No. of shares in issue	£	£0.25	£0.38	£0.24	£0.29	£0.26
11. Payroll to value added ratio	Total payroll costs / Value added	%	77.6%	76.8%	72.2%	70.3%	68.1%
12. Value added to payroll ratio	Value added / Payroll	£	£1.29	£1.30	£1.38	£1.42	£1.47
13. Value added to investment	Value added / Total net assets	£	£1.13	£1.31	£1.11	£1.07	£1.01

TABLE 22 *Tests of financial structure*

Name of ratio	Formula	Result stated as	19x1	19x2	19x3	19x4	19x5
1. Debt-Equity ratio	Long + short term debt / Shareholders' equity	%	91.7%	55.5%	50.2%	54.3%	44.2%
2. Debt ratio	Total debt / Total assets	%	40.8%	25.6%	26.3%	26.8%	23.5%
3. Times interest earned ratio	Profit before interest and taxation / Interest cost	Times	3.71	5.36	5.53	5.79	6.35
4. Dividend payout	Dividend payment / Profit after tax	%	39.9%	25.9%	41.6%	33.9%	58.3%
5. Cash flow to debt ratio	Funds generated by operations / Total debt	%	36.9%	74.2%	78.2%	80.1%	92.3%

Part 2

Analysing Overall Financial Performance

Chapter 4

———————Evaluation of Performance———————

4.1 Introduction

In Chapter 1 we discussed the role of financial analysis in business enterprises and examined the aims, origins and limitations of financial analysis as a tool for management. We saw that financial analysis aims to help managers in controlling their enterprise's performance. It does this by providing them with a system and set of procedures for analysing and understanding financial indicators of performance.

In this and the three subsequent chapters we shall be concerned with aspects of the evaluation of company performance using the information provided in Chapter 3 about Contemporary Kitchen Designs Limited (hereafter CKD Ltd). In this chapter we present a general overview of performance evaluation as an element of the control process in organizations. We also examine the concepts underlying performance evaluation and some of the problems associated with it. In the subsequent chapters we shall be more specific, examining in turn liquidity, profitability and capital structure in Chapters 5, 6 and 7 respectively. In Chapter 12 we return to the theme of control.

4.2 The Control Process

In everyday usage, the word *control* has a variety of senses: it can mean to direct; to regulate; to restrain; or alternatively, to dominate or to command. In the organizational setting, control is best understood in terms of the idea of *regulation*. Regulation can be thought of as an extremely broad process. It exists to ensure that what ought to be done is done, and to detect when it is not done. Regulation thus seeks to bring about intended or desired outcomes by exercising a positive influence on events and leaving as little as possible to chance.

To ensure order and ultimately the long-run survival of an enterprise it is crucial that control be exercised. We term this form of control *management control*, and the set of procedures and systems instituted by management to help them exercise this control is known as the *management control system*. More formally, a management control system can be defined as a set of policies, procedures and associated information processing designed to help managers influence organizational activities in the following ways:
- by clearly defining objectives and other inputs;
- by measuring progress in achieving those objectives;
- by evaluating the enterprise's performance;
- by indicating the means of corrective action.

Fig. 4.1 illustrates the control process. This figure helps to illustrate the idea of control as a process incorporating the four stages outlined above: it expands on the simple

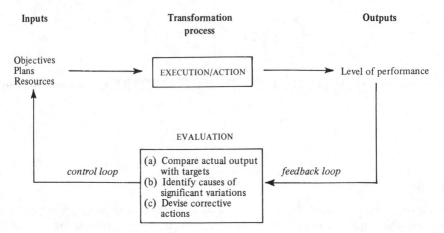

Figure 4.1 *The control process*

input/output model shown in Fig. 1.4 of Chapter 1 (p. 6). This model develops the earlier model by adding a feedback loop, an evaluation function and a control loop. The feedback loop is the flow of information about the level of performance. This information is then evaluated by reference to targets and plans, variations are investigated, and appropriate corrective action is initiated via the control loop. Let us examine these four aspects of control in more detail.

Defining Objectives

Objectives can be regarded as the end results which management should be achieving. As such, management must not only understand the enterprise's objectives but should also be fully committed to their attainment. Plans provide the means to these ends and are facilitated via the allocation of resources, as discussed in Chapter 1 (pp. 6–7).

As far as performance evaluation is concerned, clear objectives are very important: without them there is no benchmark against which to assess actual results. However, establishing objectives for an organization is difficult on account of the complexity and diversity of organizations and the people making them up. Recall that in Chapter 1, section 1.2, we identified the range of constituents in a commercial enterprise whose different interests must be served. Often, simplistic objectives such as profit maximization are attributed to organizations, though clearly for many organizations *survival* may be the critical objective.

Moreover, even when objectives are established it is not at all clear that they become or remain the *real* objectives of the organization. This arises because individuals and groups inside and outside the enterprise have their own aims and objectives which impact on the way in which the enterprise develops. For example, the department-orientation of many enterprises often encourages departmental objectives to take the place of corporate objectives, instead of reinforcing them. However, this is an enduring aspect of corporate life. The lesson for the manager is that he or she must recognize, understand, and accept the inevitable sub-optimization which results from the fact that organizations are complex, multi-purpose systems.

Nonetheless, for pragmatic reasons, an attempt must be made to comprehend objectives (and specify if possible) so that the enterprise's performance may be evaluated from appropriate points of view. Specific factors to be considered in this regard include details of markets and products, growth and expansion opportunities, risk, financial performance and requirements, personnel strength, and the overall direction of the industry and economy. Once the overall objectives have been established, sub-goals of a more operational nature can be determined, the collective values of which will secure attainment of the major objectives.

If we consider the expansion of CKD Ltd into the kitchen design business as an example, we might hypothesize that the following scenario took place in the planning stages. Firstly, someone associated with the company identified that a market existed for a kitchen design service. Preliminary research work would then have begun to evaluate the size and future potential of the market. This would have involved an examination of, *inter alia*, the existing competition, profit potential of the market, initial finance needed to begin trading, availability of and access to qualified staff. Based on the preliminary findings (clearly good in this case) the board of CKD Ltd would have given approval for more intensive market research, resulting in a final proposal for board consideration. The final proposal document would have incorporated a business plan detailing the return expected from investing in the expansion and including projected operating results for, say, the first five years' trading.

At that stage the board would have approved the expansion proposal and a decision would have been made, based on the proposal and any modifications imposed by the directors, that the new division should earn a net of tax return on its investment of, say, 16 per cent within a specified period of time. From that starting point the company would then have begun the detailed budgetary planning phase making up the budgets for specific areas of activity (e.g. sales and expenses by product line, finance and cash flow) to ensure that the overall objective would be achieved.

The main point to note about this process is that it should be *reflexive*. That is, it may be necessary to revise the main organizational objectives as individual operating budgets are prepared, and likewise operating budgets may need revision in the light of financial constraints. Thus, formulating a set of coherent objectives and interrelated budgets is not a one-way process from the top down, but rather a critical, iterative process involving many changes and revisions. In summary, therefore, we see that the manager will usually move from a vague statement of objectives to a more precise and specific set of measures of performance for the organization. In later chapters the budgeting process is examined in much greater detail: Chapter 9 focuses on budgetary planning and Chapter 11 on budgetary control.

Measuring Progress

Probably the single most important control concept is the idea that it is information which provides the basis for all control. We can think of this information in two senses: *feedback* control and *feed-forward* control. Feedback control is illustrated in Fig. 4.1 above.

Feedback control occurs where actual outputs of an enterprise or part of an enterprise (e.g. the production department) are measured and compared with the stated objectives. The resulting analysis and evaluation forms a basis for deciding on corrective action required and it is this flow of corrective information that allows an activity to be controlled.

However, in dynamic organizational environments the delays in receiving feedback information may be excessive. Feed-forward control is an attempt to minimize the loss of control which can result from these delays. In feed-forward control the manager predicts what outputs are expected to be at some future time—he or she anticipates outcomes. Where the predicted outcomes differ from plan, control actions are implemented ahead of time in a way that aims to minimize the anticipated differences. One of the serious difficulties with the feed-forward control model is that it is very difficult to predict outcomes in complex organizations. Nonetheless, there will be cases—particularly when the time span is short—where feed-forward control will be effective.

In helping to establish, co-ordinate and administer a control system (whether of feedback or feed-forward design), the manager, in conjunction with his financial colleagues, must focus attention on devising, compiling and constantly improving an adequate and up to date system of reports. If the reports are inadequate then the actions based on them will also tend to be inadequate. Reports have the following principal uses:

1. They highlight deviations from plan in order that corrective action may be taken before serious problems develop. This is the most constructive and fruitful use of control data.
2. They spotlight things that have gone wrong, permitting management to remedy the situation and cut losses in the most efficient manner.
3. They help managers determine exactly how and why variations from plan have arisen, and may suggest steps that should be taken to prevent their recurrence. This is highly constructive, as mistakes cannot always be avoided, but they need not be repeated.
4. They pinpoint those responsible for failure.

An example of such an information system in a manufacturing enterprise might be one that is designed to identify and report the presence of material wastage. The observation that wastage is occurring constitutes feedback information to the manager, telling him or her that output (i.e. performance) is off-target by reference to some predetermined standard. The job of the manager is then to take corrective action by considering an improved input-factor combination.

It should be clear at this stage that the subject area of management accounting described in Chapter 1 is especially concerned with providing such information.

Evaluation of Enterprise Performance

At the outset it is important not to underestimate the difficulties associated with the evaluation of an enterprise's performance, in whole or in part. The measurement of progress and the evaluation of performance are closely related. An effective information and reporting system is a prerequisite for effective performance evaluation: in fact, the evaluation is essentially an extension of the measurement process.

There are two important stages in the evaluation process.

Selecting the Unit/Process/Model for Evaluation

In Chapter 1 we saw that performance measurement is concerned with the efficiency

and effectiveness of converting inputs into outputs. However, for obvious practical reasons it is necessary to consider efficiency and effectiveness from two points of view:
- the organization as a whole; and
- the constituent segments and activities of the organization, such as geographical areas, product lines, or departments.

These two issues are addressed in greater depth in Chapter 9 where we discuss the criteria for segmenting an organization's operations into suitable units for analysis, but the general case can be made here in relation to CKD Ltd, where it is clear that it will be necessary to evaluate the Design division and the Manufacturing division separately.

Within each division there are a number of issues to be evaluated separately, such as the working capital requirements, liquidity position, and the financing structure. (Concerning the latter issue, for example, it is apparent that the capital finance requirements for the Manufacturing division will be greater than for the Design division.) The analysis can then be extended in depth to consider the more specific areas, such as sales and costs.

In approaching the evaluation in this way the expectation is that the analysis of the divisions will assist in constructing a picture of the effectiveness of the organization as a whole.

Selecting the Relevant and Appropriate Performance Measures

Performance measures should be chosen which provide useful information for control purposes. Therefore, a measure should tell us something about the level of achievement of goals or targets. Unfortunately, this is often not done and the careless choice of measures can lead to spurious analysis and inappropriate recommendations for action.

We can illustrate this by considering a fairly common error made in popular financial news commentary. A news report might state that 'XYZ Ltd, one of Britain's largest industrial companies, reported a record profit for 1987 of £754m'. Very often the intention is to convey the idea that XYZ Ltd had a successful year's trading, and it is possible that useful information of a sort is thus conveyed. One might make the reasonable assumptions that XYZ Ltd is not a loss-making company, that it is not in liquidation, and that it may continue in operation for the foreseeable future. But there is little else to be gleaned from the simple statement that £754m profit was earned.

The quality of the information can be improved in a variety of ways. One immediate improvement would be to define clearly the term 'profit'. For example, the information that CKD Ltd earned a net profit before taxation for the year ended 31 December 19x2 of £642,600 is more informative because profit is defined more precisely as being 'before tax'. If we know that the profit for the previous year, 19x1, was £416,500 the quality of our information is further improved: we now know that profit is increasing and at what rate. The information that the total investment of capital in CKD in 19x2 was £3,451,390 enables us to establish that the pre-tax profit of £642,600 represents a pre-tax return on the invested capital of 18.6 per cent (£3,451,390). We now have a measure of performance which is helpful in comparing alternative uses of those funds.

The central lesson to be taken from this is that financial analysis is essentially about comparison. One technique widely used in performance evaluation to make such comparisons is *ratio analysis*. This idea will be examined in more detail, but it is worth stressing again that while this book is primarily concerned with exploring aspects of financial analysis, in keeping with the systems approach by which one looks at the enterprise in total, we shall as far as possible make explicit the linkages between financial and non-financial measures.

In analysing an enterprise's financial performance, management is concerned with the relationships between financial amounts rather than the absolute value of those amounts. This was shown earlier with the example of CKD Ltd's 19x2 profit before taxation. It was apparent that, by itself, the profit figure means little; but when related to the previous year's profit, it begins to have significance because it helps to indicate a trend. In fact, the analysis of financial statements is only possible when the figures are expressed as percentages or ratios.

A great many ratios can be computed, as we will show, but caution must be exercised. Ratios can often hide information, by aggregation, for example. But if ratios are used carefully it should be possible to pinpoint precisely those areas of activity requiring managerial attention.

This is made possible by working down a ratio pyramid. The apex is the return on investment (ROI). It is common to see ROI expressed in a variety of ways: in some cases profit before taxation is used, in others profit after taxation; in some cases the value of the investment is in book terms (i.e. WDV) and in other cases in market value terms. This should not present any difficulty provided those using the ratio are aware of the method by which it has been calculated. We have chosen to use the net profit *after* taxation but *before* deducting the fixed interest charge (e.g. £120,000 in year 19x1: see Table 18, page 55). We use the book value of the investment given as the total net assets identifiable on the balance sheets. The ratio is expressed as:

$$\frac{\text{Net profit after taxation but before fixed interest}}{\text{Investment (net total assets)}} \times 100$$

This is the *primary ratio*. It can tell us something about the profitability of an investment. In the case of CKD this ratio has already been computed for the five years 19x1 to 19x5 (see Table 21, p. 58). They are:

19x1	11.7%
19x2	14.6%
19x3	14.7%
19x4	15.7%
19x5	14.6%

Over the five year period we can see that CKD has increased its return on the capital invested. Although this provides management with useful information, in its present form it is still not as useful as it might be. For example, management has no way of judging if 14.6 per cent in year 19x2 is a satisfactory return. To form a view about that they must compare it with the expected return for that year. The expected return will have been set as an objective based on management's overall plans for the business. But, taking a very simple case, management might have decided that an alternative use of the capital funds would be to invest them in the shares of another furniture manufacturer. If they know that an after-tax return of 30 per cent is available from investing in such a company, then there would be some basis for questioning CKD Ltd's investment yielding 14.6 per cent. Of course, business decisions are never as simple as this but the comparison does help to illustrate the decision process involved.

The primary ratio (ROI) is composed of two *secondary ratios*: the margin on sales and the capital turnover ratio. These are given below (calculation of the ratios is deferred until Chapter 6):

$$\frac{\text{Net profit}}{\text{Sales}} \quad \text{and} \quad \frac{\text{Sales}}{\text{Investment}}$$

The relationship between the primary and secondary ratios is simple and direct as follows:

$$\frac{\text{Net profit}}{\text{Investment}} = \frac{\text{Net profit}}{\text{Sales}} \times \frac{\text{Sales}}{\text{Investment}}$$

It will be appreciated that if ROI is off target, the reason may be found in a low profit on sales percentage or a low ratio of sales to capital employed, or both. However, it may be necessary to investigate the *tertiary ratios* (i.e. those constituting the secondary) in order to identify precisely the area of discrepancy.

Net profit itself reflects the relationship between the gross profit rate, sales and overheads, whereas the investment base is composed of both working capital and fixed assets. From these relationships the following tertiary ratios can be readily computed:

$$\frac{\text{Gross profit}}{\text{Sales}} \qquad \frac{\text{Sales}}{\text{Overheads}}$$

$$\frac{\text{Sales}}{\text{Working capital}} \qquad \frac{\text{Sales}}{\text{Fixed assets}}$$

The process of disaggregating ratios into their component parts can be continued further until the reasons for particular levels of performance are fully known and attended to. In the same way that the secondary ratios were broken down into tertiary ratios, each of the tertiary ratios can be broken down into their elemental parts, and so on. A pyramid is illustrated in Fig. 4.2.

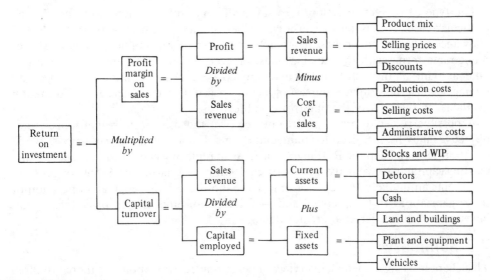

Figure 4.2 *Constituents of return on investment*

One important skill in financial analysis lies in being able to use ratio analysis effectively. In many instances a manager will be called upon to analyse and comment upon the activities of organizations where he or she does not have access to the detailed supporting schedules to the accounts, or to details of all the underlying transactions. This might happen, for example, where a manager is called upon to make a credit rating decision about a potential customer, or when making a preliminary assessment on the attractiveness of a prospective acquisition. The necessary skill involves being able to determine which ratios are applicable, whether their value is acceptable, and interpreting the significance of changes over time. If more detailed analysis is then required to identify or confirm explanations, then so be it, but the initial analysis should reduce the effort required. This ability only comes by gaining familiarity with and experience of financial statements, and an understanding of the ways in which financial statements seek to reflect the enterprise's underlying activities.

In subsequent chapters we will become more familiar with ratio analysis. Before doing that a word of warning is in order. Financial analysis is not a precise art and there are many difficulties of measurement and interpretation. Because of this it is advisable that ratios are used in conjunction with other measures, such as budgets, standards, market shares, employee turnover rates, and so forth. Again, it is variations and changes in these measures, rather than their absolute size, that are usually of greatest managerial significance.

Corrective Action

The whole point of financial analysis is to aid the control effort of the organization, hence analysis and evaluation must result in action to modify performance in accordance with plans and objectives. Information without action is curiosity, not control. Calculating ratios can assist in this task to the extent that it helps to identify problem areas in need of management attention. Ratio analysis enables control to be specific, since it can be related to the individuals responsible for the 'wrong' ratio values.

The type of corrective action necessary will vary with the circumstances of each particular case. It may be that in a case where material cost exceeds the budgeted allowance, the manager has to search for alternative suppliers or attempt to renegotiate terms with the existing ones, or even revise the organization's plans to take account of the extra cost. There are no general prescriptions available: the manager must determine courses of action based upon the specific information available, in the light of the enterprise's objectives.

A possible risk in appraising performance over the short term is that longer term objectives may be sacrificed for immediate gains. For example, it may be possible in the short term to keep the ROI high by a delay in replacing capital equipment (i.e. the existing capital base will have a low written down value). However, in the longer term this seems an unlikely strategy for improving the overall efficiency and operation of the organization. In Chapters 13 and 14 the topic of efficient and profitable capital investments is considered in greater detail.

4.3 Summary

This chapter has provided an overview of performance evaluation and there are three important ideas to be taken from it. The first is that performance evaluation should be understood as a part of the control process. Secondly, financial analysis is only one aspect of performance evaluation and must never be considered in isolation. Thirdly, ratio analysis, the main technique used in financial analysis, derives its usefulness from providing measures for comparison, not from providing absolute measures.

4.4 Exercises

Review Questions

1. What do you understand the concept of control to mean in business enterprises? Consider three possible interpretations and argue for the one with which you have least sympathy.

2. Explain why financial managers and other users of financial information must be cautious when using ratios. Are there any situations in which extreme caution must be exercised?

3. Discuss why financial information relating to an enterprise is compared with the past performance of the same enterprise and the performance of other enterprises. What difficulties exist in comparisons with other enterprises?

4. Information is a term which is often used loosely. Define what you understand the term to mean.

5. The return on investment and the return on sales ratios are related. Explain how these ratios relate to each other.

6. To what extent do you think financial and accounting related ratios adequately capture measures of organizational performance? Develop a performance evaluation model which you feel adequately captures measures of performance for CKD Ltd.

7. How important is precision in performance evaluation?

8. What implications can be drawn from the content of this chapter for the design of management control systems in medium-sized enterprises?

9. Why is it necessary to divide business into segments/activities?

10. In what ways will concepts of control differ in service enterprises as compared with manufacturing enterprises?

4.5 Further Reading

Abramson, R., & W. Halset (1979), *Planning for Improved Enterprise Performance; A Guide for Managers and Consultants*, Geneva: International Labour Organization.
A good practical guide to improving various aspects of enterprise performance.
Tucker, S.A. (1961), *Successful Managerial Control by Ratio Analysis*, New York: McGraw Hill.
An excellent book and still of value after 25 years.

Van Horne, J. (1983), *Financial Management and Policy*, New Jersey: Prentice-Hall International Inc. (6th edition)
  A renowned textbook with a strong managerial emphasis.

See also the recommended reading in Chapter 10 (pp. 204–205).

Chapter 5

——————Liquidity Assessment——————

5.1 Introduction

This chapter examines the very important question of liquidity in business enterprises. Liquidity is important because companies that do not remain liquid can be forced out of business by trade creditors and other providers of finance. It is a concern which in times of economic hardship assumes special significance for business managers. Liquidity refers to an enterprise's ability to meet its current financial obligations as they arise, and thereby remain solvent.

Liquidity must be distinguished from profitability. Profitability is a measure of *operating performance* whereas liquidity is a measure of *financial condition*. It is possible for an enterprise to be profitable and yet unable to pay its current obligations. An instance where this can arise is when an enterprise underestimates the level of permanent capital needed to finance the planned level of activity in its business. In many such cases it is common in the initial stages for an enterprise to make profitable sales and to show promising signs of growth. When it then becomes apparent that the enterprise has not properly planned the level and/or mix of finance necessary (to extend credit to customers and hold adequate levels of stock) it can find itself unable to maintain this level of activity and service. The resulting scenario is often bleak: sales may decline; suppliers may withdraw trade credit facilities; and assets not owned

	LIQUID	ILLIQUID
PROFITABLE	Cell 1	Cell 2
UNPROFITABLE	Cell 3	Cell 4

Figure 5.1 *Profitability versus liquidity*

by the company (e.g. leased or rented assets) may be impounded, ultimately forcing the enterprise into liquidation.

In Fig. 5.1, using a two by two matrix, the most desirable and least desirable situations for companies to be in are illustrated. Clearly, the strongest companies will be located in cell 1 where both profitability and liquidity are being achieved. Companies located in cell 4 are unsuccessful and corporate failure is imminent— enterprises cannot survive when they are unprofitable *and* illiquid. Companies die by going into liquidation; and it is worth noting that this is not necessarily a voluntary action.

A question does arise as to whether it is preferable to be located in cell 2 or cell 3. In general, the answer is that being located in cell 2 poses a more serious threat to the enterprise. While profitability is obviously important, it is liquidity which holds the key to initiating change in the enterprise. Thus, if the company is liquid though unprofitable it will generally be in a position to revise its strategy (perhaps by developing new products). If the company is profitable but illiquid it may find that it is forced out of business before it gets the chance to correct the problem.

In recent years the failure to maintain the delicate balance of resources necessary to meet financial obligations as they become due has caused may business failures. It may again be stressed that it is *not* correct to say that illiquidity is the cause of these failures; rather, the cause will usually be found in poor management of the enterprise's resources (e.g. poor reliability of products, poor marketing) which can then result in a critically illiquid position. For that reason the emphasis in this chapter is on the evaluation of the use of liquid resources, bearing in mind that such an evaluation must always be seen in the context of the company's total resources. Ultimately it is the effective management of resources that will improve an enterprise's liquidity.

5.2 Liquid Resources

In Chapter 2, Fig. 2.2, we introduced the idea of enterprises existing on the funds circulating within them. This model is developed in Fig. 5.2 by expanding it to incorporate all the fund flows (both long term and short term) through a business.

Fig. 5.2 illustrates the distinction between current funds flow (sometimes called operating funds flow) and long term funds flow. The longer term funds are usually

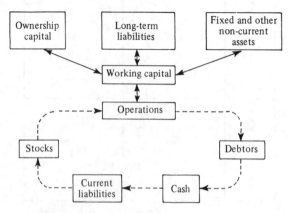

Figure 5.2 *Long and short term flow of funds*

defined as those funds which remain in the company for longer than four years, and short term funds as those funds which flow continuously through the company and consequently have a realization period of less than one year. A third category known as medium term funds is sometimes used to refer to finance with a life of one to four years. The various alternative sources of short and medium term funds are discussed in section 5.3 of this chapter and the sources of long term funding are considered in Chapter 7.

The two-way flow signs on the longer term flows of funds in Fig. 5.2 indicate that transactions occur in both directions: e.g. long term liabilities to banks are repaid and additional lending may be sought; similarly, owners' capital may be increased during the life of the company and dividend payments made.

Fig. 5.3 sets out the forms of finance used by CKD Ltd in each of the years 19x1 to 19x5. It is important to realize that our information only gives us a *point estimate* (i.e. at each year end) of the types and amount of finance used. There may be many movements on these balances during the year which are hidden from our view.

	19x1 £	19x2 £	19x3 £	19x4 £	19x5 £
Short term:					
Bank overdraft	602,500	50,000	—	—	—
Trade creditors	332,030	939,200	657,610	1,047,560	842,910
Taxation	166,000	257,040	471,240	578,340	771,170
Medium/long term:					
Loan capital	1,200,000	1,200,000	1,800,000	2,200,000	2,200,000
Long term:					
Share capital	1,000,000	1,000,000	2,400,000	2,400,000	3,000,000
Capital reserve	423,680	423,680	23,680	23,680	23,680
Revenue reserve	542,150	827,710	1,163,670	1,630,530	1,951,700
Total funds	4,266,360	4,697,630	6,516,200	7,880,110	8,789,460

Figure 5.3 *Finance employed by CKD Ltd*

We have excluded the proposed dividend from the listing of finance available in Fig. 5.3 on the grounds that it is usually paid very shortly after the year end and does not really form a source of funding on a continuing basis. Taxation, on the other hand, is not paid until some time after the year end (i.e. the Inland Revenue provides a period of grace during which time the precise liability can be calculated and paid) and on that basis this does provide a source of funding for a reasonable period of time.

Clearly, managing liquidity involves managing the level of *all* funds. For practical purposes though, a distinction is usually made between the management of long term and short/medium term finance. The management of the longer term finance is referred to as *capital structure management* and discussed in detail in Chapter 7. The management of short/medium term finance is referred to as *liquidity management*. The fundamental distinguishing feature is that management of long term finance (as far as most small and medium-sized businesses are concerned) has the longer planning horizon. For example, a company may decide that, given its expected growth over the next five years, it requires long term finance of £1 million to support the projected expansion. The company can then arrange to acquire this finance and, other things being equal, the financial structure will remain as planned for the duration of the planning period (five years in this case).

On the other hand, sales, purchases, cash receipts and payments cause the short term liquid funds to change daily and it is the management of these shorter term funds (including cash), which we commonly refer to as liquidity management. It seems appropriate to retain the distinction here; therefore the examination of longer term financial arrangements is deferred to Chapter 7.

5.3 Sources of Short and Medium Term Finance

Short Term Finance

Short term finance is typically required to cover short term trading needs, especially where companies experience seasonal variations in liquidity. For example, sales in retail stores are often depressed during the summer months, yet a given store may wish to maintain its full range of product lines. In that situation, short term finance will be used to finance the temporary decline in internally-generated liquid resources. Some of the main sources of such finance are examined below.

Bank Overdraft

The bank overdraft is generally the cheapest and most flexible form of bank borrowing available. Interest is charged only on the daily balance outstanding. Ideally, a bank overdraft should only be used to finance very short term cash shortages (say, up to three months). The great benefits of the overdraft are the cost, the ease of negotiation and the flexibility. Provided the customer is creditworthy, an overdraft can generally be renewed as required. A significant drawback is that an overdraft is usually repayable on demand and banks are cautious of customers who try to use an overdraft as a cheap form of long term borrowing.

Short Term Loans

The definition of a short term loan varies. Banks often use the term to refer to loans of up to three years' duration. This may raise some confusion, given our earlier definition for medium term finance. We use short term here to mean term loans of approximately one year's duration or less. These loans are provided by banks for more specific purposes than general liquidity shortages. They are often provided to finance expensive stock items. In the retail motor trade, for example, where such loans are common, they are known as stocking loans: the bank or finance company agrees to finance the dealer's stock of vehicles until they are sold.

Short term loans are more expensive than overdraft facilities but they are often continuous: the loans revolve for each new stocking period.

Debt Factoring

An increasing number of small and medium-sized companies are turning to debt factoring as a way of improving cash flow and liquidity. In 1984 the Association of British Factors reported a 37 per cent increase in business among the eight leading factoring companies. Factoring involves an ongoing arrangement between a trader and a factoring company whereby the latter purchases the trade debtors of a client, initially paying up to 80 per cent of the value of the debt and then assuming responsibility for collecting the debt, and also providing a sales ledger accounting service. The consideration for this service is an interest charge (usually 2–4 per cent over the current base rate) on the monies provided and a service fee (varying from 0.5–2.5 per cent of turnover).

The benefit of using the service is that it can release thousands of pounds tied up in trade credit earlier than would normally occur. Thus cash flows will be more predictable, resulting in better management. A second benefit is that the factoring company may be able to carry out the sales ledger administration and debt collection more cheaply and more efficiently than the client.

A variation on factoring debts is *invoice discounting*. This is a means of generating cash by selling to an invoice discounting company a selection of debtors' invoices. A proportion of the value of the invoice is paid immediately by the discount company. As and when amounts due from debtors are received by the company, remittances are made to the discount company. Unlike factoring, the discount company does not take control of the collection of amounts due from debtors. This is a costly form of finance but it can prove worthwhile as an emergency standby source of funds.

Bills of Exchange

A bill of exchange is a negotiable document involving an agreement by one party to pay another a sum of money at a fixed date in the future (traditionally 90 days, though this can vary). It is similar in concept to a post-dated cheque. Bills of exchange are widely used by exporting companies; the exporter arranges for the purchaser to 'accept' a bill of exchange which means that the purchaser will pay the amount at a fixed future date. The benefit from the point of view of liquidity is that bills of exchange are negotiable instruments and can be discounted with banks for cash as soon as they have been accepted. The cost of bill discounting is competitive with bank overdraft and it has the added advantage that the cost is fixed on the date the bill is discounted: it is not affected by subsequent changes in the market rates of interest.

Trade Credit

Trade credit is one of the most obvious short term forms of finance. Trade credit (normally 30 days) is provided by the suppliers of goods and services to an enterprise. It is widely believed that it is advantageous to take long credit from suppliers. It is considered to be a form of 'free' financing, but this is not necessarily true. To benefit from trade credit will normally mean foregoing cash discounts. At 2.5 per cent for settlement within 30 days, to take advantage of trade credit costs approximately 34 per cent per annum. Taking extended credit can also have an adverse effect on the commercial relationship with suppliers; it can result in a poor credit rating and ultimately even a refusal to extend any credit.

Medium Term Finance

Medium term finance usually has a one to four year repayment period. It is used by companies to buy assets such as plant and machinery which have a corresponding lifespan, or to provide a proportion of permanent working capital. There are two main sources of medium term finance.

Medium Term Loan

Medium term loans are provided by financial institutions such as the commercial or merchant banks and finance companies. The loans are designed to give the company a form of guaranteed finance over an agreed period. Although the interest rates are higher than on overdrafts, the borrower does have the benefit of knowing precisely what the repayment demands are and this will help in liquidity management.

Industrial Hire Purchase

Industrial hire purchase is a method of paying for plant and machinery, or other commercial assets, by instalments. It is a simple, convenient and readily available form of medium term finance. Hire purchase finance is costly; interest rates are high and usually fixed when the agreement is made. The terms typically require an initial deposit, with the balance being paid in fixed regular payments over the period of the agreement. The principal benefit of hire purchase is that it relieves pressure on working capital by freeing funds that might otherwise be tied up in fixed assets.

5.4 Tests of Liquidity

It is difficult to exaggerate the importance of liquidity; the entire cycle of stock into sales, debtors into cash, and cash to creditors is concerned with the central question of liquidity. This cycle is known as the *cash conversion cycle* and it is measured as the number of days taken for cash to complete the operating cycle set out in Fig. 5.2. It is calculated as follows:

1. Average number of days inventory is held (inventory days)
Less:
2. Average number of days credit taken from suppliers (creditors' days)
Plus:
3. Average number of days credit given to customers (debtors' days).

We examine the calculation of each of these measures, along with other ratios, later in this section. However, it will be helpful to have in advance some intuitive understanding of the cash conversion cycle. As the calculations later in this section will show, the cash conversion cycle in CKD Ltd based on the 19x1 figures is as follows:

	Days
Inventory days	105
Less: Creditors days	(51)
Add: Debtors days	45
Cash conversion cycle	99

If operations are being managed effectively, the cash conversion cycle will approximate closely to a target level. Inventory will move quickly through the business from raw material into work-in-progress into finished goods; sales will then generate revenue by which profit and working capital—and hence liquidity—are maintained and improved; but if liquidity is stretched, bankruptcy or liquidation can follow. An enterprise must therefore monitor its cash conversion cycle continuously: the longer the cycle becomes, the higher the risk that the enterprise will face a liquidity crisis.

For example, criticism is regularly made of trade union negotiators that in seeking wage increases, they fail to comprehend the implications of their demands on an enterprise's cash flow. Wages and salaries are clearly a very significant drain on cash flow and unplanned increases may affect a company's ability to pay its other liabilities (there is little scope for managing suitable payment dates for payroll). If, as a consequence, creditors lose confidence in the enterprise's ability to pay they may cease to extend credit, thereby putting a further strain on what may already be a serious cash situation. Furthermore, sales may be lost if the company's liquidity position prevents the extension of credit to its customers, and this can add impetus to a downhill slide.

This section introduces some of the main tests of liquidity, using the information presented for CKD Ltd at 31 December 19x1. The subsequent section analyses and evaluates the company's liquidity position over years 19x1 to 19x5. (To familiarize yourself with the financial information in the Tables following Chapter 3, you should check the sources of the information used below.)

There are five chief tests of liquidity.

Current (or working capital) ratio 19x1

$$\frac{\text{Current assets}}{\text{Current liabilities}} = \frac{1,904,160}{1,253,530} = 1.52$$

This indicates the company's ability to meet current liabilities as they become due, and is of importance to suppliers of short term funds, such as banks and trade creditors. The ratio tells us that CKD's current assets are 1.5 times the value of its current liabilities. On that basis, we might take some comfort that it can meet its current liabilities without too much strain on resources.

It is difficult to say what the ratio should be, though benchmarks of 2.0 and 2.25 are sometimes suggested. If it is too low it can lead to financial difficulty but, by the same token, if it is too high it means that capital is idle and inefficient. What we regard as more important is that the manager understands the significance of the nature and proportion of each element of current assets and current liabilities. For example, a company having a high percentage of cash is more liquid than one with a high percentage in inventories, even though they both have the same working capital ratio.

In a managerial sense, therefore, the current ratio is of limited value since each item within both current assets and current liabilities has a separate significance that is lost in the overall ratio. Also, from the outsider's point of view, its value is limited: it may not be appropriate, for example, to treat stock as being a liquid asset.

Due to the above criticisms, some analysts prefer to use a more stringent test of liquidity:

Acid test (or quick assets) ratio 19x1

$$\frac{\text{Quick assets}}{\text{Current liabilities}} = \frac{783,560}{1,253,530} = 0.62$$

Quick assets are defined as current assets less stock. The ratio gives a more immediate measure of liquidity since it assumes a worst possible scenario—that none of the stock can be sold. However, the above formulation of the ratio should not be taken too literally. Rather, the point to understand is that the ratio tries to give a measure of liquidity assuming all current liabilities fall due immediately. Thus, depending on the information available and the organization being analysed, it may (and often will) be more appropriate for the manager to assess what resources can be realized immediately in cash, rather than to rely on a simplistic rule of thumb such as current assets less stock. In fact, in many instances stock will have an immediate realizable value.

Inventory turnover ratio

$$\frac{\text{Cost of sales}}{\text{Average stock}} = \frac{3,489,700}{1/2(976,280 + 1,035,400)} = 3.47$$

This ratio measures the speed with which stock is turned over. It provides information, therefore, on the efficiency of stock management and can indicate whether capital is locked up in unnecessarily large volumes of stock. It may thus be a vital warning signal. A number of points concerning the above calculation should be borne in mind. Firstly, as calculated above, the stock turnover ratio is very crude: we have made no attempt to distinguish between the different categories of stock, such as raw material, work-in-progress and finished goods. This is done so as not to confuse at this early stage. Secondly, it is calculated using only the cost of sales for the Manufacturing division (because no stock is held by the Design division). Thirdly, the figure for stock excludes the amounts for consumables (which are not held for resale).

A variation is to show the average turnover period. In terms of months this is given by:

$$\frac{\text{Average stock}}{\text{Cost of sales}} \times 12 \quad \frac{1,005,840}{3,489,700} \times 12 = 3.46 \text{ months}$$

and shows that the average stock item has a 'shelf life' of 3.46 months, or approximately 105 days.

Debtors to sales ratio 19x1

In most commercial and industrial organizations, goods are supplied on credit (usually 30 days). Extending credit to suppliers is a use of a company's capital resources. We can assess the management of this resource by calculating the debtors to sales ratio. (Note that the sales figure in this ratio should strictly be credit sales if the relationship between debtors and sales is to be meaningful.) The ratio is:

$$\frac{\text{Debtors}}{\text{Sales}} \times 100 = \frac{733,560}{5,950,000} \times 100 = 12.32\%$$

We see that in 19x1, debtors at the year end represented 12.32 per cent of the annual credit sales. By itself the ratio tells us very little, but when compared with the same ratio at other points in time it is possible to assess trends. Generally speaking, the lower the percentage the more efficient the management of debt collection. It is more useful to show this ratio in terms of months or days rather than as a percentage. This gives the formula:

$$\frac{\text{Debtors}}{\text{Sales}} \times 12 = \text{Average collection period in months}$$

or:

$$\frac{\text{Debtors}}{\text{Sales}} \times 365 = \text{Average collection period in days}$$

amounting to 1.47 months or 45 days.

Creditors turnover ratio 19x1

This ratio measures the amount of credit taken from suppliers. The ratio is given by the formula:

$$\frac{\text{Creditors}}{\text{Purchases}} \times 100 = \frac{332,040}{2,383,871} \times 100 = 13.93\%$$

For purchases we use the amount for bought in materials and services in the value added statements (Table 4, page 42). Companies will generally prefer this percentage to be high, indicating that they are taking long periods of often costless credit from their suppliers. However, it is as well to note that if too long a period of credit is taken it may reflect badly on the credit rating of the company and ultimately result in a restriction of credit from suppliers. Again, as with the debtors to sales ratio, it is more useful to express this ratio in terms of months or days taken to pay suppliers, rather than as a percentage. This is expressed as follows:

$$\frac{\text{Creditors}}{\text{Purchases}} \times 12 = \text{Average payment period in months}$$

or:

$$\frac{\text{Creditors}}{\text{Purchases}} \times 365 = \text{Average collection period in days}$$

amounting to 1.6 months or 51 days.

Within the short term, the five measures of liquidity given above are the most important. They enable management to identify over-trading (i.e. allowing the level of business to expand with an inadequate financial base) and over-capitalization (i.e. the situation in which an unnecessarily high degree of liquidity/working capital exists for a given level of trading activity). These are two of the most serious difficulties which liquidity management tries to overcome.

5.5 Analysis of Liquidity in CDK Ltd

In approaching the analysis of any aspect of company activity, it is helpful to proceed in four stages as outlined below:

Stage 1: Form a preliminary overview of the area of interest. (With liquidity, this might be the general structure of financing in the business.)

Stage 2: Calculate important ratios and identify particular changes in ratio values for further investigation.

Stage 3: Carry out detailed investigation into selected items to identify reasons for large or unusual changes in ratios.

Stage 4: Relate stage 3 back to stage 1, to get a fuller understanding of the general trajectory of the firm and make appropriate recommendations for action.

Each of these stages is examined below in relation to CKD Ltd.

Stage 1 - Overview

It is helpful to set the analysis of CKD's liquidity position in the context of the company's development during the past five years. At the end of 19x1, CKD Ltd employed the following mix of finance to support its operations:

	£	£
Finance from shareholders:		
Share capital	1,000,000	
Capital reserve	423,680	
Revenue reserve (accumulated profit)	542,150	
		1,965,830
Finance from bankers:		
Loan capital	1,200,000	
Bank overdraft	602,500	
		1,802,500
Total finance		£3,768,330

These monies are financing a range of assets as follows:

	£
Fixed assets (property, equipment, etc.)	2,515,200
Current assets (debtors, stocks, etc.)	1,904,160
Total	£4,419,360

The shortfall in funding for the assets (£4,419,360 − £3,768,330 = £651,030) is made up for by the company's current liabilities outstanding (excluding bank overdraft) which are:

	£
Trade creditors	332,030
Taxation	166,000
Dividends	100,000
Accruals	53,000
Total	£651,030

This is nothing more than another way of looking at the company's balance sheet.

It is clear that during the five years 19x1 to 19x5, the company traded profitably and generated funds from operations. This helped to eliminate the need for overdraft finance by 19x3. The profits also helped to expand the base of operations. For example, sales increased dramatically over the five years and the company invested in additional fixed assets during each of the five years.

In 19x3, CKD Ltd raised additional long term finance: £1m from shareholders and £0.6m from its bankers. Along with the internally generated funds (i.e. profit), these funds were used to finance the company's expansion. We suggest, therefore, that the analysis and evaluation of the liquidity of CKD must be set in the context of what is clearly a fast growing and dynamic company.

Stage 2 - Analysis of Important Ratios

Above we suggested that there are five chief measures which help to guide the analysis of liquidity. These measures, together with the cash conversion cycle, are produced in Fig. 5.4 for each of the five years of trading.

	19x1	19x2	19x3	19x4	19x5
Current ratio	1.52	1.59	2.20	2.15	2.27
Acid test	0.62	0.64	0.98	1.10	1.30
Inventory turnover	3.47	3.59	3.72	3.27	2.87
Debtors' days	45	44	52	58	64
Creditors' days	51	130	68	95	82
Cash conversion cycle (in days)	99	16	82	74	109

Figure 5.4 *Summary of important liquidity measures*

Data from Table 1 (pp. 38–9) indicate that from 19x1 to 19x5, both the current ratio and the acid test ratio increased in each year. Given that we now know that the purpose of these two ratios is to assess the company's ability to meet its current liabilities, we might be tempted to conclude that the company's liquidity has improved consistently. As we shall see, while such a conclusion may be valid, it does not necessarily follow from the observed increases in the ratios.

Calculating the ratios is only a stage in the analysis process: we cannot leave it at that. The important thing for the manager to understand is why particular ratios changed, and so any further unusual changes must be investigated. The task is essentially to gain an understanding of the general and particular events that helped to improve or diminish the company's performance or position: to discover what story the ratios tell.

The summary of ratio values in Fig. 5.4 highlights a number of changes of interest for analysis: between 19x2 and 19x3 the current ratio and the acid test ratio increased significantly; between 19x3, 19x4 and 19x6 the inventory turnover worsened; the trend in the collection period for debtors is rising each year; and the variability in credit taken from suppliers is noticeable. Of course, the manager may also select additional changes for investigation, but for illustrative purposes the next section focuses attention on those changes identified above.

Stage 3 - Detailed Investigation

We can begin to construct the detailed analysis by examining changes in the composition of the items making up the ratios which require further examination. The best way to do this is to use the funds flow statement, which identifies the change in working capital (or other appropriate definition of funds) from one period to another by setting out the sources and applications of funds making up that change.

We shall be referring to funds flow statements (Table 3, page 41) and to the balance sheets (Table 1, pages 38–9) for the periods 19x1 to 19x5 and the reader should

iliar with these. An additional statement setting out the changes in the
of working capital between 19x1 and 19x5 is produced in Fig. 5.5 to
analysis.

...ponent of working capital	Increase (decrease) 19x1–x2 £	Increase (decrease) 19x2–x3 £	Increase (decrease) 19x3–x4 £	Increase (decrease) 19x4–x5 £
Cash	—	54,600	397,280	26,720
Investments	—	(50,000)	—	400,000
Debtors	127,150	495,560	345,590	228,220
Prepayments	3,500	31,300	(8,600)	19,500
Inventories	230,670	366,160	295,090	60,960
Bank overdraft	552,500	50,000	—	—
Trade creditors	(607,170)	281,590	(389,950)	204,650
Taxation	(91,040)	(214,200)	(107,100)	(192,830)
Dividends	—	(140,000)	—	(210,000)
Accruals	(20,250)	(5,750)	(17,650)	(18,250)
Net change	195,360	880,760	514,660	518,970

Figure 5.5 *Changes in components of working capital*

We now proceed to investigate the changes in ratios identified for further
examination.

Increases in Current Ratio and Acid Test Ratio

Reasons for the increases in these two ratios are considered together. In Table 1 (pp.
38–9) it can be seen that current assets of £2.26m in 19x2 increased to £3.16m in 19x3,
whereas current liabilities increased only marginally from £1.42m to £1.44m over the
same period. What this indicates is that the requirement for working capital increased
by almost £900,000. There are two main reasons for this; debtors increased by
£495,560 (£1,356,270 – £860,710) and inventories increased by £366,160 (£1,679,430
– £1,313,270), a total increase of £861,720. Of course, the changes in the other
components of current assets and liabilities also affect the level of working capital
required but, as is evident from examining the listing of current liabilities, the
increases and decreases in the constituent elements net down to an almost negligible
change of only £16,860 (£1,419,490 – £1,436,350).

It is now of interest to establish how the additional working capital was funded. The
answer to this question is to be found in the funds flow statement for 19x3 in Table 3
(page 41). There, the sources of funds for the year ended December 19x3 are shown to
total £3,112,000 and, having deducted the applications of £2,231,240, the net funds
flow of £880,760 remaining represents the additional funds invested in working
capital.

While the funds flow statement explains the sources of the increase in working
capital, it does not tell us whether the relationship of the components of working
capital to each other is optimal. To do this the manager must examine the constituents
in more detail (i.e. cash, stocks, debtors and creditors). As a start, the acid test shows
that in 19x3 CKD Ltd is more liquid than at the previous year end, and that the trend
improves up to 19x5. (The sources of this improved liquidity can be identified in the
funds flow statements.) However, whether the level of this ratio (1.0 to 1.3) is optimal

for CKD Ltd can only be determined by a still more detailed analysis of the actual average cash inflows and outflows on a daily, weekly or monthly basis in the company.

There are indications in CKD Ltd that the management of liquid resources is taken very seriously. In particular, the existence of the short term investments, where CKD Ltd invests surplus cash funds, suggests that cash flow planning is undertaken. Cash flow planning is vitally important in the modern enterprise, and even in small and medium sized businesses it demands daily attention from management.

The key to managing cash is planning. Companies should plan the timing of cash flows (receipts and payments) for different planning horizons. Depending on the business, a short term horizon might be daily, weekly or monthly and the medium term horizon would cover periods of up to one year ahead. For periods of longer than one year the plan will probably be more general than specific, but that does not diminish the importance of preparing such a plan.

The objective in preparing the cash flow plan is to assess as early as possible the expected level of cash balances at future dates, so that plans can be made either to invest surplus cash or to arrange borrowing (or more permanent financing) where shortages are expected. Thus for each planning period a statement will be prepared beginning with the opening cash balance. To this will be added the anticipated receipts of cash (from debtors and other sources). Expected payments to suppliers and expense payments will be subtracted, leaving an estimated closing balance of cash. By examining the movements in the cash balances over several periods, the company will be able to assess the level of cash balances which are surplus to immediate requirements; or, alternatively, the borrowing arrangements which need to be made to cover any shortages.

Decrease in Inventory Turnover

In each of the five years 19x1 to 19x5 CKD Ltd has increased its holding of inventory. From 19x1 to 19x3 the rate of stock turnover is reasonably static, but between 19x3 and 19x5 the rate of turnover decreased from 3.72 times to 2.87 times. This decrease is a cause for management concern. There are two things which management must do to gain a fuller understanding of the reasons for the decrease. Firstly, management must decide on the desirable and realistic rate of stockturn in their business. This can be determined in the light of factors such as the nature of the manufacturing process, the range of products, the type of business, and the current industry trading conditions. Secondly, management must carry out a detailed analysis of the holdings of each category of inventory (raw materials, work-in-progress and finished goods) to establish the specific reasons why the ratio differs from the desired level. The manager should pay particular attention to slow-moving or obsolete items included in the valuation of inventory, as these will result in an unrealistically high ratio.

The increase in the ratio can be explained by examining the components of the ratio–sales and inventory.

Debtors' Collection Period

The credit extended to debtors has increased gradually over the five year period. In 19x1 the collection period was 45 days and by 19x5 it has crept up to 64 days. If it is assumed that CKD Ltd has the usual credit policy of extending 30 days' credit from the end of the month in which the goods were purchased, then a 45–50 day collection period would seem acceptable. While 64 days' collection period is not an immediate critical problem, it is nonetheless a signal which management should investigate.

There are a number of factors which can cause the collection period to increase. It may be that debtors are taking advantage of slack collection procedures by delaying payment, or that one or more larger debts are overdue, causing a bias in the ratio. In these cases the system of credit control operating within CKD Ltd needs to be improved. This might involve assigning someone to the task of credit control, improving follow-up procedures for late payments, or developing an efficient reporting system to highlight late payers, depending on where the weakness exists. Typically such a report should set out a listing of the debtors' balances on the basis of age of balance. An example of such a report appears in Fig. 5.6.

Debtors' balances	30 days or less £	30 to 60 days £	60 to 120 days £	Over 120 days £
Debtor A and Co.	2,000	500	—	—
Debtor B and Co.	1,000	—	250	—
Debtor C and Co.	—	—	—	3,000

Figure 5.6 *Aged listing of debtors*

A more worrying reason for the collection period deteriorating is the presence of debtors who are unable, for whatever reason, to pay the amounts due. Management can identify slow payers and doubtful accounts from the aged analysis of debtors. Strict follow-up collection procedures should begin as soon as a debtor is identified as entering into either of these categories. If a debtor becomes insolvent and is liquidated it may be that CKD Ltd will receive no payment for the debt; in such cases it is necessary to write off the debt, thus incurring a loss. However, management can and should reduce the risk of incurring bad debts by exercising strict vetting approval before accepting customers on a credit basis.

If debt collection is a difficult problem for a company it may be worth considering the benefits of using the services of a factoring company (discussed in section 5.3). The decision to use factoring would be based on an analysis of the costs saved (administrative and financial) versus the cost of factoring.

Variability in Credit Taken From Suppliers

Although there were some estimation difficulties in relation to the calculation of the credit period taken from suppliers (i.e. using bought in materials and services as a proxy measure for purchases), there is an unusual level of variability in the ratio which is worthy of investigation—particularly between the years 19x1 and 19x2. At 31 December 19x2, creditors' balances were £607,170 higher than at the previous year end, and represented approximately 130 days' purchases. This change provides the key to understanding the change in financial position between these two years.

The explanation seems reasonably clear in this case; CKD Ltd delayed paying creditors in order to reduce its overdraft, which stood at £50,000 at 31 December 19x2 compared with £602,500 at the previous year end. It would seem, therefore, that the company either voluntarily gave priority to repaying the overdraft or perhaps was requested to do so by its bankers. The amount does vary in later periods and in 19x4 it appears that CKD Ltd is taking 95 days' credit from suppliers. This seems dangerously high from the point of view of maintaining good relationships with suppliers. Furthermore, it seems unusual in view of the fact that the company is holding a large cash balance. The reasons for this continuing variability in creditors' days are not immediately clear from the financial statements and further investigative work into the underlying figures needs to be undertaken.

Stage 4 - General Summary and Advice to CKD Ltd

In this chapter we have concentrated on the analysis of liquidity only in CKD Ltd. For that reason the analysis is partial. In Chapter 7 it will be necessary to combine the analysis of the different aspects of performance, effectiveness and financial position in order to develop a considered proposal advising CKD Ltd on matters of financial policy.

In the meantime, there are a number of tentative general observations that can be made, given the analysis in this chapter. The first is that CKD's working capital position and its liquid position are strong. The company is therefore in a strong position to resource further growth (assuming that market conditions are favourable). This is facilitated not only by the availability of cash of £478,600 and marketable investments of £400,000, but also by the fact that the company has the capacity to raise short term finance if required. At present there is none. Secondly, the management of working capital in the company seems to have been good. This has been particularly evident in the company's ability to raise finance of the appropriate size and term as and when required: for example, CKD Ltd has avoided using a short term overdraft facility for any significant length of time, preferring to raise more permanent finance in the form of share capital and long term debt.

However, in examining aspects of their working capital management, we identified certain issues for further investigation—the decreasing inventory turnover and the increasing collection period for debtors. Despite the overall appearance of company strength and the absence of immediately critical problems, these issues should be investigated in greater detail.

5.6 Summary

This chapter has examined liquidity management and stressed the importance of maintaining liquidity as a prerequisite for enterprise survival. It is not an understatement to say that managing liquid resources is probably the single most important key to survival. If a company is liquid, there is some chance that other problems may be resolved in time: where the opposite is the case this becomes all the more difficult.

The most important idea for the manager to take from this chapter is that liquidity management involves the *continuous monitoring* of current and anticipated future cash inflows and outflows.

5.7 Exercises

Review Questions

1. What is insolvency?

2. Why does an enterprise have to invest in working capital? How should an enterprise determine the size of this investment?

3. What ratios would you use to measure an enterprise's liquidity position?

4. It is generally argued that liquidity is a more critical variable in business enterprises' survival than profitability. Examine a business of your choice where the emphasis might be reversed.

5. Identify certain industries that rely heavily on trade credit to finance assets. Consider the importance of trade credit in the financing of large versus small enterprises.

6. You have taken up an appointment as financial manager with a medium-sized manufacturer of children's clothing (turnover approx. £5m p.a.). There are no cash budgeting, planning or review procedures in operation at the time of your appointment. Write a paper to the board of directors explaining the main features of a new system which you have been requested to design.

7. What factors should CKD Ltd take into account when deciding on its inventory-holding policy? Discuss these factors in relation to each of the main categories of inventory.

8. Discuss the benefits (financial and otherwise) to an enterprise from factoring its debts.

9. Consider some of the disadvantages of an enterprise relying too heavily on its bank overdraft as a source of short term finance.

10. The current ratio is related to an enterprise's ability to pay its short term liabilities. What additional information would you require before concluding the appropriateness or otherwise of a specific current ratio value?

Problems

1. Independent Packaging Ltd's assets and liabilities at 31 December 19x7 are as follows:

Assets		£	Liabilities	£
Cash at bank		4,200	Trade creditors	18,300
Quoted investments		1,400	Current portion of	
Debtors		12,400	long term debt	6,220
Inventory		16,800	Taxation liability	3,900
Plant and equipment			Sundry current liabilities	2,800
Cost	45,600		Long term debt	46,000
Depreciation	13,680	31,920	Equity shares	20,000
Property			Retained earnings	24,700
Cost	60,000			
Depreciation	4,800	55,200		
		£121,920		£121,920

Determine Independent Packaging's net investment in working capital. What additional information would you require to be able to comment on the appropriateness of this level of investment?

2. Clifden (Ireland) Ltd manufactures a range of household electrical appliances mainly for export. It reported the following information for the past two years.

	19x7	*19x6*
Annual credit sales	£6,500,000	£4,200,000
Average debtors' balance	£1,500,000	£575,000

(a) Calculate the average debtor payment period for each year.
(b) Calculate the debtors' turnover ratio.
(c) Calculate the average debtors' payment period for 19x7 on the assumption that the 19x6 debtors' turnover ratio was maintained in 19x7.
(d) What factors might have caused the change in the debtors' turnover ratio over the two year period?

3. Morris Tools Ltd and Green Machinery Ltd are both manufacturers operating in the machine tool industry. The profit and loss accounts and balance sheets for each for the year 19x7 are presented below:

Profit and loss accounts	*Morris Tools* £	*Green Machinery* £
Turnover	4,000,000	2,000,000
Cost of goods sold	3,200,000	1,600,000
Gross profit	800,000	400,000
Operating expenses	250,000	130,000
Interest charges	65,000	40,000
Profit before taxation	485,000	230,000
Taxation (@ 50%)	242,500	115,000
Profit after taxation	£242,500	£115,000

Balance sheets	*Morris Tools* £	*Green Machinery* £
Fixed Assets (net of depreciation)	1,000,000	500,000
Current Assets		
Stock and work in progress	800,000	600,000
Debtors	552,500	376,000
Cash and bank balances	80,000	40,000
	1,432,500	1,016,000
Current Liabilities		
Creditors	450,000	300,000
	282,500	116,000
Accrued expenses	732,500	416,000
Net Current Assets	700,000	600,000
NET TOTAL ASSETS	£1,700,000	£1,100,000
Financed by		
Share capital (£1 shares)	800,000	400,000
Revenue reserves	400,000	350,000
Shareholders' funds	1,200,000	750,000
Long term loan	500,000	350,000
	£1,700,000	£1,100,000

(a) Calculate the current ratio, the acid-test ratio, the inventory turnover ratio, the debtors' payment period and the creditors' payment period for each company.
(b) Estimate the cash conversion cycle for each.
(c) Comment on the differences in ratio values between each company.

4. As general manager of Garland Wholesale Sports Ltd you have been concerned for some time to tighten the inventory control policy so as to reduce the length of time that stock is held by the company. At the present time stock is held on average for approximately 75 days and you wish to reduce this to 60 days. Under the old policy the average stock holding was £1,240,000. Sales are expected to continue at their present level of £6,000,000 p.a. The cost of goods sold is expected to continue at 75 per cent of sales.
(a) Calculate the average stock outstanding if the new inventory control policy is established.
(b) Garland Wholesale currently incurs carrying and financing costs on its stock of 20 per cent of average stock. How much will be saved by reducing the holding period from 75 to 60 days?
(c) Assume that in achieving the reduction in holding time Garland will lose purchase discounts amounting to 0.4 per cent of its £3,000,000 annual material purchases. Ordering costs are also likely to increase by £6,000. Would you recommend that Garland adopts the new inventory control policy?

5. Caprice Marketing Ltd, an enterprise operating in a highly seasonal industry, is estimating its cash requirements for the first quarter of 19x8. The following schedule of sales and purchase information is available:

	Sales £	Purchases £
November	80,000	120,000
December	160,000	30,000
January	40,000	20,000
February	40,000	60,000
March	80,000	90,000
April	110,000	60,000
May	90,000	40,000

Sales are made on two month credit terms. All purchases must be paid for in the month following purchase. Monthly salaries amount to £18,000 and the annual rent of £24,000 is paid half-yearly in advance. The bank balance on 1 January 19x8 is £56,000 overdrawn.
(a) Prepare a cash budget for the first quarter of 19x8.
(b) Consider ways in which Caprice might control the seasonality of its cash requirements.

5.8 Further Reading

Clarkson, G.P.E., & B.J. Elliot (1983), *Managing Money and Finance*, Aldershot: Gower. (3rd edition by A. Johnson)
· This is a very comprehensive guide to the management of money and finance. In particular, it contains a number of good chapters on management of cash.
Garbutt, D. (1985), *How to Budget and Control Cash*, Aldershot: Gower.

In this carefully structured manual the author liberates the subject from conventional accounting procedures and presents it in a fresh, practical way.

Holmes, F.G., & J.C.R. Hewgill (1975), *Cash Flow Crisis*, London: British Productivity Council.

This book adopts a case-study approach to examine a cash crisis in a medium-sized business shortly after going public.

Hutson, T.G., & J. Butterworth (1983), *Management of Trade Credit*, Aldershot: Gower. (3rd edition)

With over 40 years of relevant experience, the authors demonstrate how companies of all sizes can improve their management of trade credit.

Bank of England (1983), *Money for Business*, London: Bank of England and City Communications Centre.

This is a useful and up-to-date guide on the sources of finance available to small and medium-sized businesses.

Ray, G.H. & P.J. Hutchinson (1983), *The Financing and Financial Control of Small Enterprise Development*, Aldershot: Gower.

A book reporting empirical research into the financial control and the development of small businesses up to the time of public flotation.

Chapter 6
—Analysis of Profitability and Value Added—

6.1 Introduction

Measures of profitability and value added are quite closely related. Both are measures of wealth creation and the calculation of each is derived from the income and expenditure arising from an enterprise's trading activities during an accounting period. The distinction between the two concepts is at the level of the analysis of those incomes and expenditures; profit measures the residual (i.e. revenue minus costs) available to shareholders, whereas value added measures the residual (called *value added*, i.e. costs less bought-in materials and services) available to a wider interest group entitled to share in the wealth of the enterprise (see Fig. 1.3, p. 5). Note, however, that the same accounting measurement concepts are used in producing both the profit and loss statement and the value added statement.

It would be helpful in introducing this chapter to be able to offer a generally accepted definition of 'profit'. Unfortunately, profit is a concept that cannot easily be defined. One simple way to define it is to say that profit is equal to revenue minus costs. However, this definition raises a range of further questions which it is equally difficult to answer. For example, what is revenue? What is cost? How are they measured?

To take only one of these questions, that concerning cost, consider the following problem: assume that you began business as a grain dealer on 1 January and purchased 1 ton of grain for resale at a cost of £150. Later, you sold the grain for £200. Further, assume that when you then replace the ton of grain in order to continue your trade, it has increased in price to £160 per ton. What is the profit on your first transaction?

The most likely calculation for you to perform would be the following:

Sale of grain	£200
Less: Cost of grain	£150
Profit on transaction	£50

The accounting basis for this type of profit calculation is known as the *historical cost basis* of accounting. That is, the historical cost of the goods sold is subtracted from the sales income to give the profit on the transaction. This is the most common basis used in accounting, but it is not the only basis which can be used.

You may have reckoned that, although you received £200 cash from your customer, you had to pay out £160 to purchase more grain and stay in business. Therefore, after the replacement transaction, only £40 cash remains. Thus, using a *replacement cost basis* of accounting (as opposed to historical cost basis) your profit calculation appears as follows:

Sale of grain	£200
Less: Replacement cost of grain	£160
Profit on transaction	£40

From the foregoing it is clear that the calculation of accounting profit can be a fairly confused area. Note also that there are many more complications of measurement (e.g. depreciation, valuation of inventory) than the example discussed above. Accountants have 'solved' this dilemma as far as the day to day practice of accounting is concerned by defining what is called *accounting profit*. What accountants have done is to specify a set of detailed rules which, when followed, produce a measure of accounting profit. This is not the only approach which can be taken and it is still a subject of considerable controversy within the accounting profession. The more familiar and public aspect of this controversy is the ongoing debate about the correct way to account for the effects of inflation (see Chapter 8 for a discussion of this theme).

If this seems a somewhat over-critical view of accounting, particularly to those who have always understood accounting to be the last word in objective measurement, it is helpful to remind ourselves of the difficulties which the measurement of profit has caused accountants in the past. One well-documented example surrounded the attempted takeover of Pergamon Publishing Company by Leasco Inc in 1968. Chalmers Impey (Pergamon's auditors) initially certified the profits for 1968 as £1.503 million. A subsequent audit by Price Waterhouse on the same period's activities certified a £60,000 loss. Approximately half the difference was attributable to the method of valuing stocks of books and journal back-issues, while the remainder related to the treatment of profits on transfers between affiliated companies. A city correspondent wrote at the time: 'A simple soul might reckon that you cannot have two independent experts coming up with different profit figures from the same set of accounts; he would be wrong.'

There were a number of similar incidents during the 1960s resulting in severe criticism of the accounting profession. Since that time the profession has gone a considerable way towards standardizing many of its conventions in order to achieve consistency and uniformity in financial measurement and reporting. These standardized conventions relate only to financial reports for external publication, although many of them are also applied where information is for internal use. Some of the important ones are considered in the next section, and in the Appendix (pp. 291–5).

6.2 Conventions in Accounting

It is important that management should be aware of the principles and conventions that underlie accounting, since these are of general application for preventing chaos in recording and reporting financial affairs. In Chapters 1 and 3 we have discussed some of these conventions (though without specifying that they were such). Here the main conventions are formally listed and briefly outlined.

The Business Entity Convention

This distinguishes the enterprise from its proprietors, and enables the accounting system to deal with the effect of financial events on the business, rather than on the persons associated with it.

The Going Concern Convention

The going concern concept assumes that the enterprise will continue in operational existence for the foreseeable future. This means in particular that the profit and loss account and the balance sheet assume no intention or necessity to liquidate or curtail significantly the scale of the operation. Thus, the assets and liabilities of the enterprise can be valued on the basis that the enterprise is a continuing business. If such an assumption is not appropriate for an enterprise then its assets and liabilities may have to be valued on an alternative basis; for example, on the basis that the company will be sold off piecemeal (a break-up basis).

The Accounting Period Convention

This assumption postulates that the financial aspects of the activities of the company may be allocated to arbitrary time periods. For example, when reporting externally, it is common for enterprises to report on the activities for the previous year, while for internal purposes the period will differ depending on the type of business: accounting statements may be prepared on a monthly, weekly or even daily basis in certain businesses. In Chapter 3 we saw that measuring the performance of industrial and commercial activity in arbitrary accounting periods gives rise to many practical problems of measurement.

The Monetary Measure Convention

Only those events that can be expressed in monetary terms are recorded. This provides a common base, but it does mean that valuable information is excluded from accounting systems. As a result, the information requirements of some groups cannot be met by accounting information, as was seen in Chapter 1.

The Historical Cost Convention

The most common (though not the only) basis for valuation is the historical cost basis. This states that the value of all assets equals the amount of money exchanged for them. Profit is the difference between revenue and the corresponding historical cost associated with generating that revenue.

The Materiality Convention

This concept is adopted to avoid excessive and expensive detail. For example, it would be absurd to attempt to account for every sheet of paper used. It is easier (and sufficiently accurate for most purposes) to assume that a ream of paper is used up at the time it is issued from the stationery store.

The Consistency Convention

The consistency concept requires that there be a consistency of accounting treatment of like items within each accounting period, and from one period to the next. For example, it would not be consistent to charge depreciation on assets in one year and not in another.

The Prudence Convention

This principle concerns financial caution, and usually means that profit is, if anything, understated rather than overstated. For instance, it is customary practice to provide for foreseeable losses but not to anticipate gains.

The Matching Convention

The matching concept requires that we match revenues period by period with the cost of earning those revenues. In Chapter 3 we examined the problem of matching as it arises in the attempt to write off the cost of fixed assets over the accounting periods expected to benefit from their use, via depreciation charges.

The Duality Convention

The duality convention is the backbone of double-entry book-keeping. It means that every financial event affects an enterprise in two ways: an increase in assets may mean a corresponding increase in liabilities, and a decrease in liabilities may mean a decrease in assets.

Seen in the light of these principles, or conventions, accounting statements fail to convey an accurate and complete story of company affairs. As far as internal/ management reporting is concerned this is not necessarily so serious: because there is no legal or other requirement to follow, accountants can produce whatever form of information they consider useful in particular circumstances, ignoring conventions if they so wish. Nevertheless, to some degree the conventions outlined above do tend to be observed by the producers of internal management accounting information.

The failure to convey the complete enterprise picture is more serious as far as external reporting is concerned. Here the conventions must be observed. Furthermore, there are a number of other conventions, plus legal and professional rules, with which information for external consumption must comply.

6.3 Tests of Profitability

In Chapter 5, we saw that tests of liquidity largely relate to the balance sheet. Tests of profitability, on the other hand, are more concerned with the profit and loss account or income statement. A distinction should be made at this point between profit and profitability. Profit is an absolute measure—a stated monetary amount. Profitability is a relative measure; it is calculated by relating profit to some base; for example, as a percentage of capital employed. A number of possible bases are examined below.

Extending the analysis then involves examining the components of profit (i.e. revenues and costs) and the composition of the bases.

In this section we shall examine some of the main tests of profitability using the information presented for CKD Ltd for 19x1. Following that, we will use these ratios in analysing the profitability of CKD Ltd's Design division from 19x1 to 19x5.

Gross Profit Ratio

$$\frac{\text{Gross profit}}{\text{Sales}} = \frac{£1,725,500}{£5,950,000} \times 100 = 29.0\%$$

This is a particularly important indicator of profitability, showing the profit potential *before* charging financial, administrative, and selling expenses. The figure of 29 per cent represents the average mark-up on products sold and raises the important topic of price-fixing and profit margins.

Net Profit Ratios

There are a number of alternative net profit ratios in use. The difference between them relates to the definition of net profit used. Below, we examine three measures in common use:

1.
$$\frac{\text{Net profit before interest and taxation}}{\text{Sales}} = \frac{£536,500}{£5,950,000} \times 100 = 9.02\%$$

2.
$$\frac{\text{Net profit after taxation and before interest}}{\text{Sales}} = \frac{£370,500}{£5,950,000} \times 100 = 6.22\%$$

3.
$$\frac{\text{Net profit after taxation}}{\text{Sales}} = \frac{£250,500}{£5,950,000} \times 100 = 4.21\%$$

These ratios are considered by some to be the most important measures of performance, but (as was emphasized in Chapter 3) profitability might more usefully be measured by reference to the investment required to generate the profit.

As with the gross profit ratio, the net profit ratios direct attention to the price-fixing and profit margins, but *after* allowing for the marketing, distribution and administrative expenses and, depending on the precise definition of the ratio, either before or after the interest expense and taxation charge. Again, for the ratio to be meaningful it must be related to variations in volume.

Return on Total Investment Ratio

$$\frac{\text{Net profit after taxation and before interest}}{\text{Investment (net total assets)}} = \frac{£370,500}{£3,165,830} \times 100 = 11.69\%$$

This is the most important measure of performance as it indicates the comparative efficiency with which the whole company is run. In other words, it measures the earning power of the total permanent investment in the company. This is the primary ratio discussed in Chapter 4, and can be computed by multiplying the capital investment turnover by the net profit margin—as derived from the secondary ratios. This gives us:

Capital investment turnover:

$$\frac{\text{Sales}}{\text{Investment}} = \frac{£5,950,000}{£3,165,830} = 1.88 \text{ times}$$

Net profit ratio:

$$\frac{\text{Net profit after taxation and before interest}}{\text{Sales}} = \frac{£370,500}{£5,950,000} \times 100 = 6.22\%$$

that is:

Capital investment turnover	×	Profit rate	=	Return on investment
1.88	×	6.22%	=	11.69%

This shows quite clearly that performance (measured by ROI) can be improved by generating more sales per £1 of investment (i.e. by increasing the capital investment turnover), or by increasing the profit margin on each sale. A satisfactory ROI indicates an efficient use of funds, and this is of crucial interest to both management and shareholders.

Note that the return on investment ratio may also be calculated on an after interest and taxation basis. For the year 19x1 CKD Ltd's return on this basis would be calculated as follows:

$$\frac{\text{Net profit after interest and taxation}}{\text{Investment}} = \frac{£250,500}{£3,165,830} \times 100 = 7.9\%$$

6.4 Tests of Value Added

Our comments in Chapter 3 and earlier in this chapter have indicated that the value added statement supplements the profit and loss account. The value added concept sees the enterprise as a partnership among employees, shareholders, the government which is attempting to generate wealth, and other interest groups. Ratio measures associated with value added attempt to make inter-company and inter-period assessments of value added trends. It is appropriate to remind the reader here that value added is defined as:

Sales to customers	£xxx
Less: Bought in materials and services	£xxx
Value added	£xxx

Some of the chief tests of value added are calculated below using the information provided for 19x1 in CKD Ltd.

Payroll to Value Added Ratio

$$\frac{\text{Total payroll costs}}{\text{Value added}} = \frac{£2,765,829}{£3,566,129} \times 100 = 77.56\%$$

This ratio shows the proportion of value added which is consumed in wages and salaries. As a measure of return to employees this ratio might be compared across companies in the same industry. It is also helpful where one wishes to compare the relative returns between those providers of the different factors of production, e.g. capital and labour.

By reversing the payroll to value added ratio, it can become a measure of labour productivity.

Value Added to Payroll Ratio

$$\frac{\text{Value added}}{\text{Payroll}} = \frac{£3,566,129}{£2,765,829} \times 100 = 1.29$$

This ratio informs us that for each £1.00 expended on labour, £1.29 of value is added to the company. There are a number of possible modifications to this ratio depending on the detail required. It is possible, for example, to extend the analysis by calculating the value added per employee or the value added per employee hour worked. We do not wish to go into such detail here.

Value Added to Investment Ratio

$$\frac{\text{Value added}}{\text{Investment (net total assets)}} = \frac{£3,566,129}{£3,165,830} \times 100 = £1.13$$

This ratio is similar to the return on investment ratio; it is a measure of business efficiency and of the utilization of the enterprise's assets. When an enterprise is trading successfully this ratio should be growing. (Note that the ratio may also be rising where the old depreciated assets have not been replaced or modernized, so that a careful examination of the ratio is required before conclusions are drawn.)

Finally, a common analytical use of the value added statement (which is really an extension of payroll to value added ratio is to establish the relative percentage shares of the various participants in value added. Such an analysis simply presents the applications of value added from Table 4 (p. 42) in percentage terms rather than money terms. Fig. 6.1 illustrates such a presentation.

	19x1 £	19x2 £	19x3 £	19x4 £	19x5 £
Value added	3,566,129	4,511,626	5,988,777	6,705,660	7,262,172
	%	%	%	%	%
Value added	100	100	100	100	100
To employees	77.56	76.79	72.23	70.33	68.11
To government	4.65	5.70	7.86	8.62	10.62
To providers of capital:					
Interest	3.37	2.66	3.61	4.11	3.80
Dividends	2.81	2.22	4.01	3.60	6.20
To provide for assets	7.39	6.31	6.67	6.38	6.85
To retain in business	4.22	6.32	5.62	6.96	4.42
	100.00	100.00	100.00	100.00	100.00

Figure 6.1 *Statement showing relative shares of value added*

Fig. 6.1 is a helpful and easily understood statement. It shows how value added during a period has been applied. In this case the statement indicates that labour has been receiving a decreasing share of value added, while the Government's share in the form of taxation has increased from 4.65 per cent in 19x1 to 10.62 per cent in 19x5. Another interesting feature is the increasing share being applied to the providers of capital.

6.5 Analysis of Profitability in CKD Ltd

Our primary concern in this chapter is with the analysis of profitability and in this section we focus on the evaluation of profitability in CKD Ltd. Where appropriate, the analysis incorporates the additional insights which the value added statement offers, so far as the analysis of efficiency and wealth creation are concerned. As with the previous chapter on liquidity, we shall approach the analysis of profitability in four stages. In short, these stages are:

Stage 1: an overview of the area of interest;
Stage 2: selection of ratios for further investigation;
Stage 3: detailed investigation;
Stage 4: summary and general advice for corrective action.

Stage 1 - Overview

In a general way we can form an overview of profitability in CKD Ltd from the information in the profit and loss accounts presented in Table 2 (page 40). Clearly though, we must be mindful of the significance we attribute to what will be an

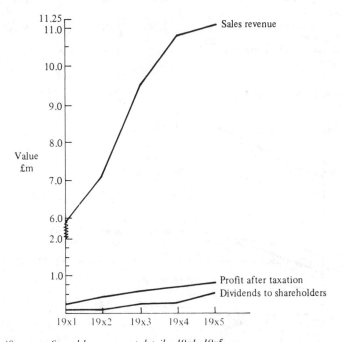

Figure 6.2 *Significant profit and loss account details, 19x1–19x5*

essentially cursory review, given our earlier warning about the danger of interpreting accounting information at face value.

If we inspect Table 2 it is possible to identify a number of signs suggesting profitability and successful company growth. The net profit after taxation is increasing each year (from an amount of £250,500 in 19x1 to £771,170 in 19x5); sales are growing (from £5.9m in 19x1 to £11m in 19x5); and dividends paid to shareholders are increasing each year. This is graphed in Fig. 6.2.

The initial signs therefore are good. Recognizing this will impact on the perspective which we adopt when extending the analysis. For example, our analysis will be future oriented. The analysis will also be diagnostic; it will have a primary emphasis on identifying the reasons for the success and promoting further growth. One can envisage the opposite emphasis in analysis where an enterprise's performance and profitability is in decline. There, the analysis would be directed at locating the causes of failure and developing strategies to eradicate them. We can see, therefore, the importance of this initial overview stage in helping to give direction to the task of financial analysis.

Stage 2 - Selection of Important Ratios

In the last section we examined the calculation of the chief measures which help guide the analysis of profitability and value added. A number of these are set out for each of the five years 19x1 to 19x5 in Fig. 6.3 to 6.6.

	19x1 %	19x2 %	19x3 %	19x4 %	19x5 %
Gross profit ratio	29.0	31.0	34.0	37.0	40.0
Net profit ratio (before interest and taxation)	9.02	10.68	13.27	14.58	16.52
Net profit ratio (after interest and taxation)	4.21	5.40	6.05	6.60	7.01
Return on investment (after taxation and before interest)	11.69	14.65	14.70	15.71	14.59
Return on investment (after interest and taxation)	7.91	11.17	10.69	11.30	10.75

Figure 6.3 *Important profitability ratios*

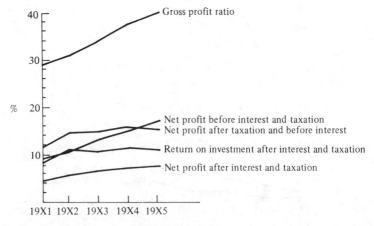

Figure 6.4 *Graph of profitability ratios, 19x1–19x5*

Payroll to value added ratio	77.56%	76.78%	72.23%	70.33%	68.11%
Value added to payroll ratio	£1.29	£1.30	£1.38	£1.42	£1.47
Value added to investment ratio	£1.13	£1.31	£1.11	£1.07	£1.01

Figure 6.5 *Important value added ratios*

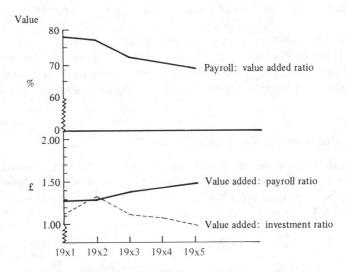

Figure 6.6 *Graphing of value added ratios, 19x1–19x5*

One unusual ratio shown in these Figures is the declining value added to investment ratio. The ratio indicates that although both value added and net investment are increasing in absolute terms (see Tables 1 and 4, pp. 38–9 and 42, for details), the net investment is increasing at a faster rate than value added, hence the declining ratio. It is important to interpret this very carefully. Ideally, the ratio would be rising, indicating that as the company expands, its ability to add value increases. However, it would be naïve to expect new investment to lead to increased value added in the short term. Thus, CKD Ltd should wait until the full benefit of new investment in 19x3, 19x4 and 19x5 is reflected in the operating results of the company before finally evaluating the changes in that ratio.

With the exception of the declining value added to investment ratio, one imagines that in today's harsh economic climate management would be pleased to report the generally increasing trends indicated above. However, increasing trends in themselves do not provide sufficient information for analysis purposes: before assessment can be made we need to develop a benchmark against which to compare the actual performance. To do this requires detailed understanding of the enterprise's objectives, the business risks, and the sources of profitability within the enterprise. It is only through understanding the critical factors contributing to the enterprise's profitability (among other things) that management will be able to develop appropriate and effective policy for the enterprise. This chapter, therefore, attempts to bring the reader closer to such an understanding.

At this point it should be clear that in terms of assessing the profitability of CKD Ltd, Figs 6.3 to 6.6 are only partial; the most obvious omission is the absence of an analysis segregating the two classes of business in which CKD Ltd is engaged. For although as a whole the company is operating in the kitchen furniture industry, one division of the business, the Manufacturing division, is capital-intensive while the Design division is labour-intensive. An analysis of the operation which does not separate these units would produce spurious results. Similarly, any attempt to use the same criteria for evaluating both divisions would be inappropriate. This type of analysis is termed *segmental analysis* and is the subject of special consideration in Chapter 10.

Nonetheless, it is important to introduce the ideas associated with profitability analysis at this stage. Therefore, in the next stage we follow through the analysis of profitability by examining the results for the Design division only. The same analytical tools are used for the Manufacturing division, as will be made clear in Chapter 10.

Stage 3 - Detailed Analysis: The Design Division

In Fig. 6.7 we summarize the profit and loss accounts for the Design division for each of the past five years. It also seems appropriate at this stage of the analysis to consider the projected performance for 19x6, and so these results are included in the final column of Fig. 6.7.

	19x1 £	19x2 £	19x3 £	19x4 £	19x5 £	19x6 £
Sales	117,500	358,500	954,000	1,390,000	1,875,750	2,251,000
Cost of sales:						
Salaries	150,525	192,010	236,500	282,500	329,750	375,000
Depreciation	6,160	9,160	9,160	20,360	16,360	18,360
Advertising	523,264	544,408	616,880	618,634	623,699	720,000
Consumables	17,261	19,519	23,267	29,823	31,148	42,000
Utilities	12,357	15,412	18,372	19,451	19,784	26,000
Outside services	24,873	32,691	44,521	51,732	55,659	65,000
Total	734,800	813,200	948,700	1,022,500	1,076,400	1,246,360
P or (L)	(617,300)	(454,700)	5,300	367,500	799,350	1,004,640
P or (L)%	(525.36)	(126.83)	0.55	26.43	42.61	44.63

Figure 6.7 *Summary profit and loss accounts - Design division*

We shall perform this analysis of the profitability of the Design division by examining in detail significant features of the statement in Fig. 6.7. Even without calculating ratios, many of the significant features of the Design division's performance are evident: losses reversing into rapidly improving profit; sales growing from £117,500 in 19x1 to £1,875,750 in 19x5; increasing salaries; and very large advertising expenditure.

Losses

Perhaps the first thing to observe is that the division suffered substantial losses in its first two years of operation, followed by rising profits in the three subsequent years. The division also expects to earn profit in the coming financial year.

It is not uncommon for businesses to incur losses in the early years of operation. These usually involve relatively large amounts of operating expense before generating acceptable levels of sales revenues. With CKD Ltd this was certainly the case. It can be seen from the above income statements that the division committed substantial funds to advertising in its first two years of operation which could not have been expected to result in an immediate payoff. The payoff is evident in the later years, with the rapid growth in sales from 19x3 to 19x5 and in 19x6 (projected).

This observation helps to reinforce a point raised earlier when we considered the accounting conventions of matching and periodicity. By splitting the activities of CKD Ltd into arbitrary periods (one year in this case) accounting statements can misrepresent the underlying structure of the business. In the present case, the Design division of CKD Ltd incurred advertising expenditure of £523,264 in 19x1 and £544,408 in 19x2, the benefit of which was not to be realized until later years. However, accounting convention required that such expenditure be written off in the accounting period in which it was incurred. Thus, the years 19x1 and 19x2 show substantial costs which are not matched with the revenues which they helped to generate. Thus the losses in the first two years do not fairly reflect the underlying potential or structure of the Design division. (The above also reinforces the importance of our continuing advice that periodic financial statements should not be examined in isolation.)

Revenues

The second striking feature of the statements is the dramatic growth in sales revenue over the five year period. Sales revenues have increased 16-fold from 19x1 to 19x5. The manager will be best placed to assess the reasons for this large growth from marketing and sales analyses available internally—the financial statements of themselves tell us little. However, we might make the reasonable inference here that this is an indication of the quality of the service provided by the Design division. The increase might also be taken as indicative of the success of the company's marketing and advertising policy.

Cost of Sales

A helpful guide towards assessing the level of costs is to compare the level of individual cost categories with revenues over time. For illustration purposes we do this for the two major components of cost—salaries and advertising—though the manager should do it for all costs. The calculation for each year is shown below in Fig. 6.8; but it should be remembered that as far as the early years are concerned the percentages warrant careful and informed interpretation.

	19x1	*19x2*	*19x3*	*19x4*	*19x5*	*19x6*
	%	%	%	%	%	%
Sales revenue	100	100	100	100	100	100
Salary costs	128	54	25	20	18	17
Advertising costs	445	152	65	45	33	32

Figure 6.8 *Summary of relationship between costs and sales*

The expectation in carrying out an analysis as set out in Fig. 6.8 is that significant variations in the relationship between the costs and revenues will not normally be present. Should they exist, however, the above method of analysis will enable management to focus their more detailed investigations on particular income and cost categories.

The consistent decrease in salary costs as a percentage of sales is encouraging. It seems that salary costs are beginning to settle at around 17–18 per cent of sales value. Also, as one would expect, the advertising cost is also decreasing as a percentage of sales. We can compare these costs with those of other established firms in the kitchen design business to assess their reasonableness but it does seem that, with a projected gross profit rate of 44.6 per cent for 19x6, the Design division is operating very successfully.

Net margin

It will have been observed that there is no statement disclosing the net profit for the Design division. The detailed information supporting the financial statements presented for CKD Ltd provides an analysis of costs split between the two divisions down to the gross profit level (see Tables 16 and 17, pp. 53 and 54). Of the remaining expenses, the distribution expense relates solely to the Manufacturing division, as does the marketing expense (note that marketing/advertising expense for the Design division is included as an expense in calculating gross profit: Table 16). The other two expense items, administration and finance, are not separated to show the portion relating to manufacture and the portion relating to design.

This is not unusual; it may well be that the management of CKD Ltd believes that the cost of preparing such analyses is excessive in relation to the possible managerial benefit. However, as analysts we may wish to give these expenses some attention. Consider finance, for example; no charge has been made to the Design division's cost of sales for interest on borrowings, but we know that finance was certainly required to fund the large advertising expenditure in the early years of operation before the division began to earn profit. It is also evident that the Design division uses office accommodation, though no charge appears in the cost of sales for rent or depreciation on buildings. Lastly, it is reasonable to assume that an element of the administration expenses relates to the Design division. It should be possible, therefore, for the financial analyst to make an assessment of the costs relating to each division (even very roughly) and extend the analysis of profitability to the net profit level.

The point we wish to make at this stage is that the analysis of the profitability of CKD Ltd is incomplete until these other costs have been assessed. Detailed analysis of these issues is deferred to Chapter 10.

Return on investment

Some readers may be wondering if it is possible to calculate the return on investment for the Design division. Again, this is difficult because CKD Ltd prepares its balance sheet for the whole company, not for each division, so information about funds tied up in the Design division is not immediately available.

We can specify the investment for illustration purposes. Taking fixed assets first, the Design division uses two offices representing an investment of, say, £25,000. There is also an investment in office equipment which we can estimate from the depreciation charged to the design section (i.e. 20 per cent of the total charge: see Table 16, page 53). This represents an investment in office equipment in 19x5 amounting to £21,000 (i.e. 20% × £105,000).

Moving on to consider other working assets and liabilities, assume that the behaviour of total debtors is representative of the behaviour of design debtors. On that basis the investment in debtors in 19x5 will be 60 days' sales revenue (Chapter 5, p. 85) amounting to £308,000 (i.e. £1,875,750 × 60/365). The main creditor in the Design division is for advertising: on the assumption that CKD Ltd takes 50 days' credit (see Chapter 5, p. 86), advertising creditors will amount to approximately £85,000 (i.e. £623,699 × 50/365) at 31 December 19x5. Finally, assuming a cash requirement of £100,000, we can estimate a total investment in the Design division of £369,000 made up as follows:

	£
Land and buildings	25,000
Office equipment	21,000
Debtors	308,000
Creditors	(85,000)
Cash	100,000
Approximate total investment	£369,000

The gross profit of £799,350 in 19x5 represents a return on this investment in excess of 200 per cent. The calculations are approximate, but it is evident that the adjustments required (including the costs not charged in calculating gross profit) would not materially alter the very high return. We can see, therefore, that it is possible in some instances to carry out a reasonably informed analysis of company performance from the financial data alone.

Stage 4 - General Summary and Advice to CKD Ltd

Two dangers always to be avoided in financial analysis are to reach conclusions and develop prescriptions too quickly. The blind use of ratio analysis can result in very serious detrimental consequences for an enterprise. As we have stressed before, ratios should be interpreted in the context of the enterprise's objectives and strategies. What is important about ratio analysis is not simply the size or direction of variations in ratio values, but rather knowing why variations have occurred.

Our examination of profitability in CKD Ltd has been carried out using only the information provided about the Design division. The examination has of necessity been more an overview than a detailed analysis. Analysing and understanding the nature of profitability in CKD Ltd as a whole and the relationship between the two divisions is a very complex task and the chapters in Part 3 of the book are devoted to providing a more detailed analysis.

It is premature to offer any prescriptive policy advice to the company on the basis of our analysis in this chapter. This very point is an important one for the manager to take: too often in business advice is offered (and accepted) on the basis of inadequate analysis.

6.6 Summary

This chapter has provided an introduction to the analysis of profitability and value added. It has concentrated on providing the manager with a set of tools with which he or she can begin to make sense of the profit and loss account and the value added statement. Using the information made available for the Design division of CKD Ltd, these tools have been applied to show how a preliminary analysis can be carried out. The process of analysis is developed in Part 3 of the book and the linkages between this and the later chapters are brought out.

6.7 Exercises

Review Questions

1. Should enterprises attempt to maximize profit?

2. Discuss the relationship between owners' equity and the net income (profit or loss) of an accounting period.

3. If an enterprise's return on investment is low and management wishes to improve it, discuss the immediate strategies for investigating and identifying the problem areas.

4. Compare and contrast the concept of profit with the concept of value added.

5. Explain when expenses and revenues are recognized under the accrual basis of accounting. How does this differ from the cash basis?

6. If accountants use different methods to calculate profit, how will this affect the analyst's attempt to assess the relative performance of different firms?

7. Explain the entity concept.

8. What are the problems associated with the concept of periodic (e.g. one month, one year) measures of profit?

9. What problems may be indicated by a net profit margin substantially above the industry average?

10. Profit margins can vary substantially from industry to industry. Discuss the reasons why this is so, giving relevant examples.

Problems

1. The following profit and loss account was prepared by Jean Jagger after her first year operating as a medical practitioner.

Jean Jagger Medical Practice
profit and loss account for the year to 30 June 19x8

	£	£
Income		
Professional services rendered	28,000	
Amounts due from patients	4,500	32,500
Bank loan		12,000
Total income		44,500

Expenses

Secretary's salary	5,200	
Accounts payable	2,100	
Personal clothing	1,200	
Insurance cost	800	
Light and heat	1,000	
Office equipment	400	
Loan payment (including £250 interest)	1,600	
Surgery expenses	450	
Car	4,800	17,550
Profit for first year		£26,950

Identify and explain the errors in the above statement. What information is needed to correct each error identified?

2. West Side plc is a large diversified company with headquarters in London. West Side is the holding company for four subsidiaries, each operating in different markets. The segments are domestic audio and visual equipment, toiletries and cosmetics, stationery and writing materials, and scientific instruments. The following information was obtained from the most recent published annual report:

Subsidiary	Turnover	Operating profit	Total net assets
	£m	£m	£m
Audio-visual	754.5	243.0	468.8
Toiletries & cosmetics	687.0	60.6	321.5
Stationery & writing materials	257.7	4.0	255.6
Scientific instruments	380.2	38.0	298.9

(a) Relate the annual profit to sales to assess which subsidiary was most successful in generating profit for a given £ of sales.
(b) Relate the annual profit to investment to assess which subsidiary was most successful in generating profit for a given £ of assets invested.
(c) Discuss the relationship one might expect to find between turnover and assets investment in each of these subsidiaries.

3. The following data is available for four medium-sized private enterprises in the printing industry:

	W	X	Y	Z
	£000	£000	£000	£000
Sales	2,000	1,000	1,500	2,500
Net profit after tax	300	50	225	300
Total assets	1,500	750	1,500	2,400
Shareholders' funds	1,000	5,000	1,400	1,000

(a) Calculate the asset turnover ratio, the net profit margin and the return on shareholders' funds for each enterprise.
(b) Evaluate each enterprise's performance by comparing it with the industry averages given below:

Asset turnover	1.4
Net profit margin	0.12
Return on shareholders' funds	0.25

4. On 1 January 1986 Leslie Cosgrave opened a small high quality fashion boutique. The first year's income statement has been prepared using the cash basis of accounting as follows.

Leslie Cosgrave - Boutique
Statement of cash receipts and payments for the year ended
31 December 1986

	£	£
Cash receipts		
Owner's capital	3,000	
Cash sales	21,000	
Receipts from customer accounts	8,500	
Interest on bank savings account	100	
		32,600
Cash payments		
Owner's withdrawals	3,200	
Wages to shop assistants	11,000	
Goods for resale	10,800	
Advertising	1,200	
Sundry expenses	900	
Rent	2,400	
		29,500
NET INCOME		£3,100

The following additional information was obtained from Leslie Cosgrave's records:

(i) At 31 December 1986 customers still owe £3,800 (due in one month) for clothes purchased.

(ii) Ms Cosgrave still owes one of her assistants £370 for overtime work during the Christmas week.

(iii) As at 31 December, Ms Cosgrave owed various suppliers £1,900 for supplies of clothes. An inventory count on the same day revealed £2,800 of supplies on hand. Ms Cosgrave has recently learnt that the 'cash basis' may not be the most appropriate method for preparing a statement of income.

(a) Prepare a brief memorandum to Ms Cosgrave explaining the matching principle.

(b) Using the matching principle, prepare a revised income statement for her first year of trading.

5. Morris Tools Ltd and Green Machinery Ltd are both manufacturers operating in the machine tool industry. The profit and loss accounts and balance sheets for each for the year 19x5 are presented below:

Profit and loss accounts	Morris Tools	Green Machinery
	£	£
Turnover	4,000,000	2,000,000
Cost of goods sold	3,200,000	1,600,000
Gross profit	800,000	400,000
Operating expenses	250,000	130,000
Interest charges	65,000	40,000
Profit before taxation	485,000	230,000
Taxation (@ 50%)	242,500	115,000
Profit after taxation	£242,500	£115,000

Balance sheets	Morris Tools £	Green Machinery £
Fixed Assets (net of depreciation)	1,000,000	500,000
Current Assets		
Stock and work in progress	800,000	600,000
Debtors	552,500	376,000
Cash and bank balances	80,000	40,000
	1,432,500	1,016,000
Current Liabilities		
Creditors	450,000	300,000
Accrued expenses	282,500	116,000
	732,500	416,000
Net Current Assets	700,000	600,000
NET TOTAL ASSETS	£1,700,000	£1,100,000
Financed by		
Share capital (£1 shares)	800,000	400,000
Revenue reserves	400,000	350,000
Shareholders' funds	1,200,000	750,000
Long term loan	500,000	350,000
	£1,700,000	£1,100,000

(a) Calculate the gross profit ratio, the net profit ratio, the return on investment for each of the above companies and comment on the information revealed.

(b) Using the answer to problem 3 in Chapter 5 (pp. 89–90) and (a) above, extend your analysis of Morris Ltd and Green Ltd to write a more comprehensive report on the performance of both companies.

6.8 Further Reading

Anthony, R.N., J. Dearden, & N.M. Bedford (1984), *Management Control Systems*, Homewood; Illinois: Richard D. Irwin (5th edition)
A classic text on management control in business enterprises.

Dudick, T.S. (1972), *Profile for Profitability*, New York: John Wiley and Sons.
This is a very helpful managerial text which focuses on the sources of and analysis of profitability in business enterprises.

Matz, A., & M. Usry (1984), *Cost Accounting Planning and Control*, Cincinnati, Ohio: South Western Publishing Company. (8th edition)
This is a comprehensive textbook incorporating a good, detailed section on profitability control and analysis.

Chapter 7
───────Capital Structure Evaluation───────

7.1 Introduction

In Chapter 4, when discussing the management of liquidity, we commented on the differences between the management of short term and long term financial funds. The management of long term funding in an enterprise is commonly referred to as *capital structure management*. In this chapter we examine the sources and management of these funds.

7.2 Nature of Long Term Finance

An enterprise's long term financial funds usually comprise debt (e.g. debentures and bank loans) as well as share capital (i.e. equity or preference capital). The proper balance of share capital and debt capital will tend to be determined by:
- the enterprise's growth rate;
- the stability of sales;
- the competitive structure of the industry;
- the enterprise's asset structure;
- lenders' attitudes towards the enterprise and its industry;
- the control position of owners and management;
- the enterprise's attitude towards risk.

Commonly, cautious enterprises tend to have little debt and large current liquid resources. In contrast, aggressive enterprises often employ large amounts of debt, and also make extensive use of overdraft facilities in an effort to grow quickly. As we shall see later, this is because the debt is a cheaper form of finance than share capital. Thus, as a general rule, the higher an enterprise's earnings and the faster its growth rate, the greater is the financial incentive to finance by debt rather than shares.

All enterprises need long term permanent financial funding which can be used to purchase long term assets (such as plant and machinery) and to provide the working capital needed to trade. The relationship between long term permanent finance and short term finance is illustrated in Fig. 7.1.

Figure 7.1 helps to draw out two important points concerning financing in business enterprises. Firstly, the area indicating the level of permanent capital rises steadily over time, indicating that as an enterprise grows its capital base needs to expand to finance the larger activity base. Secondly, it shows that at certain intervals the long manent capital may need to be supplemented by short term funds to cover changes in the demand for funds. We have already examined this second hapter 5.

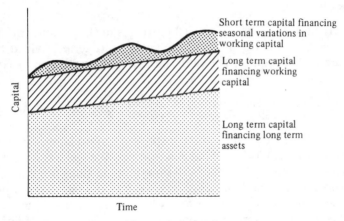

Figure 7.1 *Relationship between short and long term capital*

The reason why finance should be long term rests on the need for an enterprise to have a degree of stability: in order to grow, an enterprise needs to plan a number of years ahead and the more parameters that are known, the better will be the planning. A balanced mix of share capital and long term debt is one source of this stability (a skilled work force is another). It is difficult to conceive of an enterprise planning its growth effectively where the quantity, availability and timing of its funding in future years has not also been planned.

A second, and related, reason for using long term funds is that it may take some time before an enterprise begins to earn a return on the assets it purchases with those funds; therefore, it will wish to ensure that finance provided will not be repayable until the company is firmly established. Whether or not interest has to be paid in the short term depends on the type of borrowing. Shareholders, for example, may not expect to receive a dividend on their capital until the enterprise is earning satisfactory returns. However, the providers of interest-bearing capital, such as financial institutions, will usually require that interest payments are made even where repayment of the capital sum is not due for some years.

There are four topics which we wish to address in this chapter. These are:
- the ratio measures that can be used for examining capital structure
- the sources of long term funding
- the costs associated with different forms of funding
- the evaluation of capital structure in CKD Ltd

7.3 Ratio Measures

As already mentioned, the mix of debt and equity finance used in capital structure differs between companies for a variety of reasons. Measures of the relationship between debt and equity usage are called measures of *gearing*; or, alternatively, measures of *leverage*. Three ratios of financial gearing deserve close attention: the debt-equity ratio; the debt ratio; and the times interest earned ratio.

Debt-equity Ratio

The most widely-used measure of financial gearing is the debt-equity ratio. This ratio is simply the value of total debt (long term and short term) divided by the total amount of shareholders' equity. The ratio shown below is based on the 19x1 balance sheet for CKD Ltd:

$$\frac{\text{Long and short term debt}}{\text{Shareholders' capital and reserves}} = \frac{£1,200,000 + £602,500}{£1,000,000 + £965,830} \times 100 = 91.7\%$$

Some texts show the debt-equity ratio as expressing the relationship between long term debt only and shareholders' capital and reserves. We feel it is important that the ratio includes all the company's debt—both short term and long term. Short term debt is inherently more risky than long term debt because the interest and principal are both usually due and payable within one year. In addition, for many small and medium-sized companies, short term debt is often a major source of finance.

The debt-equity ratio is an important indicator of an enterprise's financial risk: as the debt-equity ratio rises, financial risk increases. The increase in risk arises from the fact that the interest payments on debt have to be repaid regardless of the profit levels: interest is a fixed cost. So, if trading profitability is decreasing, the existence of fixed interest costs may result in a greater than proportionate decrease in the profits available to shareholders. Thus, the greater is the debt-equity ratio, the greater will be the chance that if the enterprise encounters financial difficulty the shareholders will lose their investment.

Debt Ratio

The debt ratio indicates the percentage of an enterprise's assets that is financed by outsiders to the enterprise. The ratio is given by dividing the total debt by the total assets. For CKD Ltd in 19x1, the ratio will be calculated as follows:

$$\frac{\text{Total debt}}{\text{Total assets}} = \frac{£1,802,500}{£4,419,360} \times 100 = 41\%$$

This ratio simply informs us that 41 per cent of the enterprise's total assets are financed by both short and long term debt and that 59 per cent are financed by shareholders' funds. Again, it is a measure of financial risk and is very closely related to the previous ratio. It is interpreted in the same way: as the debt ratio increases, debt is financing an increasing proportion of the assets and thus increasing the business risk.

Times Interest Earned Ratio

This ratio indicates the margin of safety with which interest costs are being earned. It is very important for both existing and potential suppliers of debt capital. The ratio is calculated by taking the enterprise's total profit, before interest and taxation, divided by the annual interest charge. Again, for CKD Ltd the ratio in 19x1 is as follows:

$$\frac{\text{Profit before interest and taxation}}{\text{Interest cost}} = \frac{£396,500}{£146,500} = 3.71 \text{ times}$$

Another way of looking at this ratio is to appreciate that CKD Ltd's profit before interest and taxation can fall to 1/3.71 (27 per cent) of its present level before interest charges would not be covered by earnings. An interest cover of this size would generally be considered acceptable.

This review of capital structure ratios has been necessarily brief. In section 7.5 we will have an opportunity to examine these issues in more detail when evaluating the capital structure of CKD Ltd over the past five years.

7.4 Sources of Finance

There is a range of sources of long term finance, from owners' funds (provided by the shareholders of an enterprise either directly in cash or via retention of profits in the business) to long term debt provided by individuals or financial institutions. In this section we examine some of these sources and follow this with an analysis of the costs associated with each of these categories of finance.

Ownership Capital

Ordinary (Equity) Share Capital

Ordinary share capital (equity) refers to the finance injected into an enterprise by the owners. Ordinary capital is the risk capital of a business; if a business fails it is the ordinary shareholders who will be first to lose. Of course, the opposite is also true. *Ordinary* capital is so called to distinguish it from the *preference* capital (see below) which does not have the same risk attaching to it.

Most managers will be familiar with the procedure whereby the large industrial and commercial public companies raise ordinary share capital by asking the public to subscribe for their shares through the main market of the Stock Exchange. These companies are not the concern of this book and we do not deal with their financial arrangements here.

It is important to note, however, that in November 1980 a second tier market was added to the Stock Exchange with the formation of the Unlisted Securities Market (USM). This market is for successful small and medium-sized companies wishing to become public but which are not in a position, for whatever reason, to comply with the onerous and costly requirements of obtaining a listing in the main market.

Here we are more concerned with raising share capital in the small to medium-sized private company. Private companies are forbidden by the Companies Act 1985 from offering their shares to the public. For those private companies that do not wish to become public or to join the Unlisted Securities Market, risk capital must be raised privately. If the company is in the formation stage those involved in setting it up will often provide all of the risk capital. At later stages they may increase their investment by injecting additional capital into the business. There are no administrative or other problems involved; the company simply issues the owner with share certificates to the value of the investment in the business. (Note that the maximum number of shareholders permitted in a private company is fifty.)

It is also possible for companies to interest financial institutions (such as banks and insurance companies) and private individuals to invest risk capital in a business. In Chapter 2, section 2.2, we were informed that various financial institutions have acquired an interest in CKD Ltd through this route. These arrangements are made privately by agreement between the institution or individual and the company. It is a method of financing which is becoming increasingly popular. In recent years many financial institutions have begun to offer what is called a venture capital service, aimed at providing such finance themselves or locating other organizations and individuals interested in doing so. We are witnessing the emergence and rapid development of a venture capital industry.

Where finance is provided in this way there is no question of creating a market in the company's shares: the financial institution or individual simply becomes a shareholder in the company, accepting all the risks and benefits associated with ownership. Of course, one of the drawbacks of this arrangement is that a ready market in the company's shares does not exist and in addition the shareholders in private companies usually reserve some control over those to whom shares can be sold. This veto typically requires that a shareholder wishing to dispose of shares must first offer them to existing shareholders.

Preference Share Capital

Preference share capital, like ordinary share capital, represents ownership in a company. The difference between the two forms of finance lies in their respective claims on the company's earnings and its assets. Preference shares are issued with a stated dividend rate attaching to them. Thus, preference shares combine some of the characteristics of both debt and equity; the preference shareholders participate in the profits ahead of the ordinary shareholders, and the shares are backed up by preferential claims on the assets in the event of liquidation.

In the legal sense, preference shares represent an equity interest in a company. However, there are a number of reasons why it is more expedient to think of preference shares as debt rather than equity. Firstly, preference shares are usually non-voting unless the company fails to pay the dividend for some period. For that reason it is a useful method of raising the equity base of a company without losing control. Secondly, because the dividend rate is fixed, preference shareholders cannot benefit from growth in profitability as do ordinary shareholders. Note that another consequence of a fixed dividend rate is a reduction in the *real* return in times of inflation.

Retained Earnings

Retained earnings comprise those profits not distributed by a company as dividends. That is, the profits are retained in the business to finance its growth and expansion (e.g. by expanding productive capacity, by financing research and development, or whatever). In theory, the reason for retaining funds in this way is that the return expected from retaining them in the business is higher than the return which shareholders could expect to get by investing those funds elsewhere if they were distributed as dividends.

In practice, and on the basis of a somewhat modified version of the above criterion, an enterprise will decide each year what proportion of profit to retain in the business and what proportion to pay out as dividend. There are administrative benefits to be had from retaining profit as a source of finance, mainly because there are no costs associated with raising the finance in this way as compared with raising the finance through the market.

Debt Capital

In the last section we discussed the provision of risk capital. One might be forgiven for asking if there is such a thing as *non-risk* capital. As far as commercial enterprises are concerned, the answer is no; there is no such thing as finance without risk. (Note that the term 'risk capital' does have a colloquial usage meaning the capital with most risk attaching i.e. ordinary share capital.)

The second source of long term company capital is *debt capital*, and there are a number of ways in which this may be raised.

Long Term Loan

The definition of the time periods of long term loans varies: by 'long term', banks usually mean finance with a repayment date of seven to fifteen years hence. Accountants tend to view as long term any loans with a repayment date in excess of four years. It is the latter meaning which we shall use in this chapter.

Long term loans are used by companies to buy assets such as plant and machinery and to provide a proportion of permanent working capital. The rates of interest are higher than for bank overdrafts (to allow for the increased risk) but the benefit to the company is that it has a guaranteed form of finance for a fixed (known) period of time.

It is unusual for high street commercial banks and financial institutions to provide loan finance for periods in excess of seven years. However, some of the more specialized financial institutions (such as Investors in Industry) do provide loan finance up to a maximum period of between 15 and 20 years.

One way of arranging such finance is to issue what is called a *debenture*. A debenture contract usually requires that, in return for a fixed sum of money for a fixed time period, the borrower agrees to pay interest at a fixed rate half-yearly or annually. Alternatively, the loan may be arranged in accordance with the bank's normal contractual documentation. In either event the lender will usually secure the loan by registering a *charge* on certain of the company's assets (i.e. preventing the company disposing of the assets without prior consultation with the lender). This is analogous to a mortgage loan that an individual may take out, secured on his house.

Long term loans and debenture loans are usually arranged with financial institutions (such as merchant banks) or institutional investors (such as pension funds); in the case of public companies, they may even be arranged via the Stock Exchange.

Leasing

Leasing is a means of obtaining the use of assets without having to incur long term capital liabilities. Strictly, leasing is an alternative to borrowing rather than a form of borrowing. The idea is very simple; the leasing company (the lessor) purchases an asset for use by its customer (the lessee) over a pre-agreed term in return for regular rental payments. This has the advantage of enabling an enterprise to acquire the use of assets without a large initial outlay. The disadvantage is that the lessee may not able to benefit from appreciation in the value of the assets (because they are owned by the lessor).

There are two types of leasing: finance leasing and operating leasing. In its most common form, finance leasing, rentals are set at a level sufficient to repay the capital cost plus interest incurred by the leasing company together with a margin of profit. This effectively means that an enterprise pays for the asset over the period of its use. Operating leasing, on the other hand, involves leasing goods for a specified period and the return of those goods at the end of that period: company cars are often leased on this basis. The lessee, in that case, can opt to renew the lease, or take out another lease, or opt for a completely different form of financing. The lessor does not recover the full capital cost during the first period of the lease. Leasing is becoming an increasingly popular form of finance and in 1984 some 15 per cent of all investment in new plant and machinery in the UK was financed by leasing.

7.5 Costs Associated With Different Forms of Finance

All funds have a cost associated with their use. Calculating these costs can be quite complex. In this section we avoid making the issues too technical and instead try to give the manager some feel for the general issues involved in assessing the cost of funding in the small to medium sized business. We consider the costs in the same order as we addressed the sources of finance in the last section.

Ordinary share capital

At a simple level (i.e. ignoring such difficulties as the costs of raising finance in the market, the underlying risk associated with the investments of the company) the cost of equity finance is equal to the return which shareholders require on the funds provided. The return which they require is directly related to factors such as the risk involved, market and economic conditions, and the range of alternatives available. More formally, the cost can be defined as the minimum that must be earned on the equity financed investments in order to keep unchanged the value of the existing equity.

Let us look at the cases of public and private companies separately. In the case of a public company where a Stock Market valuation of the share is available, it is possible to measure the cost of equity by calculating the shareholders' return on a share (comprising the annual dividend and the increase in share price or capital gain) and expressing this return as a percentage of the share price. An example will help to illustrate this. Suppose a company is paying an annual dividend of £0.20 on each of its £1.00 ordinary shares. Its share price is currently listed at £2.00 and it is expected to grow in the coming years at an annual rate of 20 per cent. Under these circumstances the shareholders' expected rate of return (Ke) would be given by the following formula:

$$Ke = \frac{\text{Dividend 1}}{\text{Price 0}} \div \text{expected growth rate}$$

giving

$$Ke = \frac{£0.20}{£2.00} \div 0.20 = 50\%$$

This simple method is generally considered to be a plausible and reliable method of assessing the cost of a company's ordinary capital.

Unfortunately, no such procedure exists for unlisted companies. Where a company does not have a Stock Exchange listing a number of alternatives exist for trying to approximate to market type measures. We do not intend to examine these in any detail here, but offer one intuitively easy and practical approach. The procedure is to estimate the company's cost of equity by adding a premium for risk of some 2–4 per cent to the interest rate on the company's long term debt. Taking the case of CKD Ltd for 19x5, this estimate of cost of equity might be calculated in the following manner: at 31 December 19x5 CKD Ltd had long term debt outstanding of £2.2m; £1.8m at an interest rate of 12 per cent and £0.4m at 15 per cent. The resulting weighted average interest rate in this case is 12.5 per cent. Thus, allowing a premium for risk of 4 per cent, we have an estimate for the cost of equity of 16.5 per cent (12.5% + 4%).

In most small to medium-sized companies this will be an acceptable approach to estimating the cost of equity. The important element of the calculation is selecting the appropriate risk premium which will be decided by factors internal to the company (such as profitability, liquidity, and growth rate) as well as by external factors in the industry and the general economy.

Retained earnings

It is sometimes believed, mistakenly, that retained earnings constitute a source of funding that has no cost. However, if a company paid out all its earnings in the form of dividends, its shareholders could reinvest these funds in other securities. The return from this alternative use of the funds (the *opportunity cost*) is the cost of retained earnings, and if a company cannot earn a return equal to its shareholders' after-tax opportunities, it should pay out all retained earnings as dividends. From the foregoing it should be clear that the cost of retained earnings will be the same as the cost of ordinary capital discussed in the last section; shareholders will expect the same return from earnings retained on their behalf as they will from a cash investment made by them. Thus the approximation we will use for CKD Ltd will be 16.5 per cent.

Preference share capital

As a first approximation, the cost of preference share capital is simply the rate of dividend that a company must pay on its preference shares. Therefore, where a company issues preference shares at, say, 8 per cent that becomes the cost of the finance. However, because of issue costs, discounts, etc., the issuing company may not receive the full market price of the share and an adjustment is required to calculate the cost more precisely. The cost of preference shares (Kps) is given by the following formula:

$$\text{Kps} = \frac{\text{Annual dividend in pounds}}{\text{Net proceeds from share issue}}$$

CKD Ltd does not have any preference share capital in issue, but the following example helps to illustrate the calculation. Assume a company can issue 8 per cent preference shares at a nominal value of £100 each, but that flotation or selling costs will be £4 for each share. Using the above formula, the cost of new preference shares is calculated as follows:

$$\text{Kps} = \frac{£8}{£100 - £4} \times 100 = 8.33\%$$

Debt

If we assume that there are no corporate taxes, the cost of debt can be taken to be the rate of interest on the debt. If the company earns a return on the debt-financed investments just equal to the interest rate, then the profit available to the ordinary shareholders will remain unchanged. However, existing taxation law allows for the deduction of interest as an expense in calculating profits subject to taxation and, consequently, the effective cost of debt will be lower than the stated interest rate. For example, we have already established that the interest rate on the long term debt in CKD Ltd is 12.5 per cent. In 19x5 the rate of taxation (as evidenced by the charge in CKD Ltd Profit and Loss account) is 50 per cent. As a result the cost of debt is really only 6.25 per cent because the company's taxation bill will be reduced by 50 per cent of the interest charge (50% × 12.5%). Of course, when inflation is rising the real cost may be even less.

Weighted Average Cost of Capital

Now that we have examined each component cost in the capital structure of CKD Ltd, we can pull all the costs together and calculate an average cost for the entire capital mix. An alternative way of looking at this is to see it as the average return to the providers of capital as a whole. In calculating this average, the cost of each kind of capital is weighted according to its percentage share in the company's capital structure. Fig. 7.2 illustrates this for CKD Ltd for 19x5.

Type of capital	Weight (1)	Cost (2)	Weighted cost (1) × (2) = (3)
Equity shares	41.8%	16.5%	6.89%
Capital and revenue reserves	27.53%	16.5%	4.54%
Long term loans	30.67%	6.25%	1.92%
Weighted average			13.35% (say 14%)

Figure 7.2 *Weighted average cost of capital*

One of the main tasks of the financial manager is to keep this cost at a minimum. This is done by choosing the financing mix best suited to the risk profile of the company. Choosing the best is is not a precise activity; there are many external factors that can affect the availability and desirability of particular forms of finance at different times. For example, the financial controller of a property company may decide that the capital structure of the company would be strengthened by issuing new equity share capital. If, however, the market in property company shares has been poor for some time, it is unlikely that the present is the best time to attempt such an issue. Usually, financial managers have an optimal range for finance structure and they will work within that range, issuing debt one year, equity the next, in order to take advantage of market conditions at the time.

A second use for the weighted average cost of capital has traditionally been as the financial standard of return required on investment projects made by the company. It is still widely used for this purpose but we leave the discussion of this until Chapters 13 and 14.

In our review of the different sources and costs of finance we have restricted ourselves to providing a fairly general overview of the issues. The manager should be aware of these. However, managers should also bear in mind that capital structure management is a very specialized area of financial management and there are no simple strategies or rules of thumb which can be followed to produce perfect results.

7.6 Evaluation of CKD's Capital Structure

In this section we examine the capital structure of CKD Ltd following the model used in Chapters 5 and 6 when examining liquidity and profitability.

Stage 1 - Overview

In each of the years 19x1 to 19x5 the total asset value of CKD Ltd has increased. The finance for this growth in assets has been obtained from a number of sources. In 19x1,

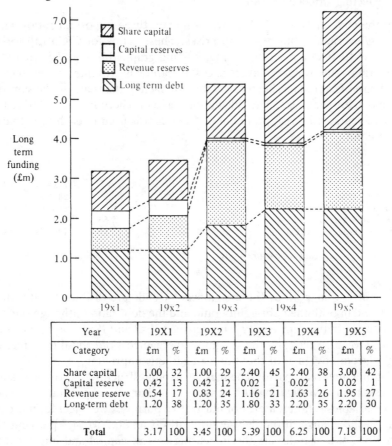

Year	19X1		19X2		19X3		19X4		19X5	
Category	£m	%	£m	%	£m	%	£m	%	£m	%
Share capital	1.00	32	1.00	29	2.40	45	2.40	38	3.00	42
Capital reserve	0.42	13	0.42	12	0.02	1	0.02	1	0.02	1
Revenue reserve	0.54	17	0.83	24	1.16	21	1.63	26	1.95	27
Long-term debt	1.20	38	1.20	35	1.80	33	2.20	35	2.20	30
Total	3.17	100	3.45	100	5.39	100	6.25	100	7.18	100

Figure 7.3 *CKD's long term funding, 19x1–19x5*

for example, CKD Ltd used funds from shareholders (Capital and retentions—see Table 1, pp. 38–9) amounting to £1,965,000; a long term bank loan of £1,200,000; and bank overdraft finance amounting to £602,500. The capital structure for each of the years 19x1 to 19x5 is graphed in Fig. 7.3.

As a consequence of the continued growth in the company, the mix of financing changes in subsequent years: the graph in Fig. 7.3 clearly shows that shareholders are financing an increasing proportion of the company's assets. This should not be surprising. We observed in Chapter 6 that CKD Ltd is a successful and profitable firm and hence we would expect to find the shareholders' funds growing. In addition, it is evident from the balance sheets in Table 1 that CKD Ltd issued new share capital during 19x3 and 19x5.

Again, as we observed when examining liquidity in Chapter 4, the analysis of the capital structure of CKD Ltd should be set in the context of an expanding company. It is particularly important that we do this here, because during a period of rapid expansion, selecting the most beneficial mix of finance is a crucial part of the financial manager's task.

Stage 2 - Selecting Important Ratios

Earlier in the chapter (pp. 111–113) we examined three important ratios concerned with gearing/leverage in business enterprises. These ratios for CKD Ltd for each of the years 19x1 to 19x5 are set out in Fig. 7.4 and graphed in Fig. 7.5. In addition to these three ratios, the weighted average cost of capital is presented for each of the five years. The cost of capital has been calculated for each of the years on the same basis as outlined above for year 19x5. The calculations take into account the differing tax rates over the five years and a risk premium of 4 per cent is used in each year to calculate the cost of equity.)

	19x1	*19x2*	*19x3*	*19x4*	*19x5*
Debt-equity ratio	91.7%	55.5%	50.2%	54.3%	44.2%
Debt ratio	40.8%	25.6%	26.3%	26.8%	23.5%
Times interest earned ratio	3.71	5.36	5.53	5.79	6.35
Weighted average cost of capital	10.96%	11.22%	12.86%	13.11%	13.35%

Figure 7.4 *Some important capital structure ratios*

Over this five year period, three significant trends are visible. Firstly, there is a declining trend in both the debt-equity ratio and the debt ratio (although there is a 4.1 per cent increase in the debt-equity ratio between 19x3 and 19x4, this reverses again in the following year). Secondly, the weighted average cost of capital is increasing; and thirdly, the profit coverage of the interest charge is improving.

Investigating the reasons for changes in capital structure ratios is a somewhat simpler task than investigating the reasons for changes in profitability where the number of variables is far greater. For illustrative purposes we select for more detailed investigation the change in the debt-equity ratio from 50.2 to 54.3 per cent between 19x3 and 19x4. We also discuss the increasing cost of capital and improved interest cover.

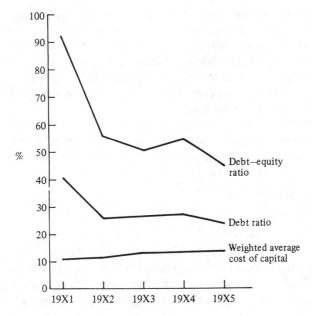

Figure 7.5 *Capital structure measures of CKD, 19x1–19x5*

Stage 3 - Detailed Investigation

Change in Debt-equity Ratio

In general, the source document for investigating changes in capital structure is the balance sheet and its supporting schedules. The immediate reason for the change in the debt-equity ratio in 19x4 is that in that year CKD Ltd increased its long term borrowing by £400,000. What is more important from the point of view of our analysis is to understand why the additional borrowing was sought. To discover this we can refer to the funds flow statement for the year ended 31 December 19x4 (see Table 3, p. 41). This statement tells us that £880,000 was expended on long term assets (land and buildings and office equipment). The funds for this investment were raised from two sources: £400,000 was raised by borrowing long term, while the remainder was provided by retaining profits in the business.

Increasing Weighted Average Cost of Capital

There has been a small rise in the weighted average cost of capital (WACC) from 19x1 to 19x5. Given our discussion on the costs of alternative sources of finance, this should not be surprising. In all years (except 19x4) the percentage of debt (the cheapest form of finance) in the capital structure is decreasing, and therefore we would expect the weighted average cost to rise. However, this should not be seen as a bad sign. Neither does it mean that CKD Ltd should have maintained the capital structure as in 19x1, where the lowest WACC of the five years is experienced. The high debt ratio of 91.7 per cent in 19x1 was short term and mainly the result of borrowing £602,500 on overdraft. This was presumably realized by shareholders and lenders and in estimating the cost of equity, we did not incorporate any revision for risk to take account of the high gearing (as one might do in practice). It is unlikely that a debt-equity ratio of this magnitude would be allowed to continue for long without a major revision in the returns required by both shareholders and lenders. The reason for such revision would be to adjust returns relative to the risks being taken by the two providers of capital. Thus, it is likely that the cost of capital in 19x1 particularly is understated because of the unscientific nature of our estimate.

This is the very way the cost of capital problem will arise in practice. For unlisted companies it is a very difficult concept to quantify accurately. The best the manager can do is to estimate the cost along the lines we have outlined and use this as one input for the decision problem in hand.

Increasing interest coverage

The times interest earned ratio has increased from 3.71 times to 6.35 times. The reason for this is clearly a function of profitability, discussed in detail in the previous chapter. From CKD Ltd's viewpoint, we can be reasonably confident in that there is a significant margin of safety covering the existing interest charges and also the capacity to take on extra debt.

Stage 4 - General Summary and Advice to CKD Ltd

The evidence available in the financial statements of CKD Ltd suggests that management has given serious consideration to selecting the most appropriate mix of finance to suit its needs. Given the extent of change in the company's business during the past five years (the expansion into the design business, the doubling of sales, the 300 per cent increase in profit after tax), it is not surprising that quite dramatic changes in financial structure are taking place. Happily, it seems that no difficulties have been encountered in doing this; it is particularly encouraging that the company's bankers have been willing to lend such large sums without (as yet) requesting repayments of capital.

The general advice for the management of CKD Ltd is that they should develop a policy for financing and capital structure. In the light of this policy management should review, on a continuing basis, the mix of capital funds and the weighted average cost of capital. The weighted cost of capital should be kept at a minimum. One way that the management of CKD Ltd can do this is by monitoring the company's capital for alternative types of finance (e.g. the company may have unused debt capacity) and ensuring that the cheapest form of finance appropriate to the circumstances is used.

Lastly, it is important to remember that arranging to raise long term finance (either equity or debt) usually involves some time-consuming negotiations and, consequently, there may be a time lag between the decision to raise the finance and actually obtaining the finance. With very large sums the time interval could be anything up to one year. Thus, effective management of capital structure has a long term planning horizon and management must prepare financing plans between one and five years in advance.

7.7 Summary

This chapter has examined the evaluation and management of capital structure in the small to medium-sized enterprise. We have considered the sources of long term finance. We have also seen how to apply the relevant analytical techniques by examining the capital structure in CKD Ltd.

Taken together with Chapter 5 on liquidity, consideration has been given to the major sources of short term and long term finance available to small and medium-sized companies. The use of the short term funds was discussed in Chapter 4 and is referred to again throughout the book. Although we have briefly referred here to the uses of the long term funds, it is not until Chapters 13 and 14 that we examine in detail the process by which long term funds are allocated to particular investment projects; hence, this chapter should not be considered in isolation.

7.8 Exercises

Review Questions

1. Discuss the role of the financial manager in a medium-sized manufacturing enterprise.

2. What are the most important financial decisions facing the financial manager today?

3. A basic rule of borrowing is that it should be carefully chosen to suit the uses made of the funds. Discuss.

4. What is meant by optimal capital structure? At the start-up stage, how might the financial manager go about deciding upon such a structure in practice?

5. Differentiate between the rights of shareholders and the rights of lenders.

6. Discuss the advantages of the corporate form of organization.

7. Consider the ways in which CKD Ltd's financing will differ between its two business divisions.

8. In what ways can poor financial planning contribute to business failure? Use examples of cases you are familiar with to explore the problems.

9. Why do enterprises retain a sizeable percentage of earnings in the business as a source of finance? How do retained earnings differ from other sources of finance?

10. Consider, with examples, how the seasonality of an enterprise's sales might influence its choice of capital structure.

Problems

1. The following figures relate to three companies:

	Alpha £	Beta £	Gamma £
Fixed assets	2,000,000	1,000,000	2,300,000
Current assets	2,700,000	2,400,000	3,200,000
Net total assets	1,800,000	1,600,000	2,500,000
	£	£	£
Book values of:			
Ordinary shares of £1	500,000	1,000,000	800,000
10% Preference shares of £1	100,000	—	—
Revenue reserves	500,000	400,000	600,000
Loan Stock	750,000	250,000	1,100,000
Trade creditors	2,000,000	950,000	1,500,000
Bank overdraft	150,000	400,000	1,000,000
	4,000,000	3,000,000	5,000,000
	£	£	£
Market values of:			
Ordinary shares	3.00	1.00	4.00
Preference shares	1.00	—	—
Loan stock (per £100 nominal value)	80.00	100.00	60.00

(a) Calculate the gearing ratio of each company, explaining fully the nature of the ratio which you use and the reasons why you feel that it is an adequate indicator of gearing.

(b) Consider the effect which the level of gearing of a company might have upon the value of its ordinary shares.

2. The following extracts are taken from the financial statements of Javelin Limited:

	19x8 £	19x7 £
Current liabilities	420,000	550,000
Long term liabilities	1,000,000	900,000
Ordinary shares	500,000	500,000
Retained earnings	2,080,000	1,550,000
Total	4,000,000	3,500,000

Javelin's interest charge for 19x8 was £100,000 and corporation tax amounted to £250,000. No dividends were paid during the year.

Calculate the following ratios for 19x8:
(a) The debt ratio (debt to total assets).
(b) The debt-equity ratio.
(c) The times interest earned ratio.

3. Rothwell Electronics plc is financed by the following range of securities:
   (i)   Ordinary shares   400,000 of £1 each
   (ii) 8% Preference shares   £100,000
   (iii) 10% Loan stock   £200,000

The current market price of the ordinary shares is 120p. The expected dividend for next year is 10% and this is expected to grow at a rate of 10% per annum. The preference dividend was paid last week and the current price of the shares is 80p. The loan stock is priced at £85 per £100 nominal value and it is irredeemable.

Calculate the weighted average cost of capital for Rothwell Electronics plc.

4. Morris Tools Ltd and Green Machinery Ltd are both manufacturers operating in the machine tool industry. The profit and loss accounts and balance sheets for each for the year 19x7 are presented below:

Profit and loss accounts	*Morris Tools*	*Green Machinery*
	£	£
Turnover	4,000,000	2,000,000
Cost of goods sold	3,200,000	1,600,000
Gross profit	800,000	400,000
Operating expenses	250,000	130,000
. Interest charges	65,000	40,000
Profit before taxation	485,000	230,000
Taxation (@ 50%)	242,500	115,000
Profit after taxation	£242,500	£115,000

Balance sheets	*Morris Tools*	*Green Machinery*
	£	£
Fixed assets (net of depreciation)	1,000,000	500,000
Current assets		
Stock and work in progress	800,000	600,000
Debtors	552,500	376,000
Cash and bank balances	80,000	40,000
	1,432,500	1,016,000
Current liabilities		
Creditors	450,000	300,000
Accrued expenses	282,500	116,000
	732,500	416,000
Net current assets	700,000	600,000
NET TOTAL ASSETS	£1,700,000	£1,100,000
Financed by		
Share capital (£1 shares)	800,000	400,000
Revenue reserves	400,000	350,000
Shareholders' funds	1,200,000	750,000
Long term loan	500,000	350,000
	£1,700,000	£1,100,000

(a) Calculate the debt ratio, the debt-equity ratio, and the times interest earned ratio for each enterprise.

(b) Assuming both enterprises plan to raise £500,000 for a new investment project, advise each on the best way to raise the additional finance.

5. You are forming a new company to export electrical domestic appliances. You estimate an initial capital requirement of £1,000,000. Your investment advisers explain to you that the costs of debt and equity capital will differ depending on the proportions of each used in the following manner:

Debt ratio	*Below 20%*	*21%–50%*	*51%–70%*
Pre tax cost of debt	8%	10%	14%
Cost of equity capital	12%	16%	22%

Assuming a 50 per cent tax rate, calculate the after-tax weighted cost of capital of each of the following financial structures:

	(a)	(b)	(c)	(d)	(e)
Debt (£)	0	200,000	250,000	450,000	580,000
Equity (£)	1,000,000	800,000	750,000	550,000	420,000

Which structure will you adopt, and why?

7.9 Further Reading

Bank of England (1983), *Money for Business*, London: Bank of England/City Communications Centre. (4th Edition)
   A first-rate guide to the range of sources and types of finance for businesses of all sizes.
Dewhurst, J., & P. Burns (1983), *Small Business: Finance and Control*, London: Macmillan Press.
   A comprehensive guide to problems of finance and control in the smaller business.
The Institute of Directors (1984), *The Director's Guide to Sources of Business Finance*, London: The Director Publications Ltd. for The Institute of Directors. (6th edition)
   This book provides an excellent and practical summary of the various sources of business finance.

Chapter 8

——————————Inflationary Impacts——————————

8.1 Introduction

The cumulative change in the value of the pound since World War II has been so great that many people are now completely disoriented when attempting to compare prices over any period of time.

Even over shorter time spans, changes in the value of money are often significant. During 1985, for example, price inflation was sufficiently evident to ensure that £1.05 had to be spent to buy consumer goods at the end of the period that could be bought for £1.00 at the beginning of the period. Within industry, the cost of essential products, components, and services has advanced just as strongly. Even at an inflation rate of 5 per cent per annum, it takes less than 15 years for the purchasing power of money to halve, and at 15 per cent it takes less than 5 years.

We are all familiar with some of the more obvious political, economic and social consequences of inflation which have manifested themselves in the UK: industrial profitability has fallen, new investment in industry has stagnated, unemployment has risen, and the opportunities for employment have been greatly reduced.

Understandably, the individual business manager may feel helpless in dealing with problems of such proportions. However, these problems are also evident at the level of the individual business enterprise, and it is at this level that the manager *can* effect change. One part of this task will be to improve the quality of financial management and in today's environment that involves assessing the implications of inflation for an enterprise's activities.

In this chapter we address some of the issues involved in taking account of inflation in financial analysis. We do not go too deeply into the technical accounting procedures involved; rather, we consider the problems from a financial control viewpoint.

8.2 The Problem Defined

We have observed throughout this book that in the vast majority of cases, accountants use the convention of historical cost in preparing and presenting accounting information: that is, they ignore changes in the price level. To the extent that accounting information does not take account of price level changes, its measurements of performance (profitability) and of financial position (value and wealth) will be misleading.

When price levels are rising the tendency is for the historical cost basis of accounting to overstate profit. The consequences of such overstatement can be very serious. For example, if one recalls that historical cost profit is used as a basis for calculating a company's liability to taxation, and also as a basis for deciding on the level of annual dividend to be paid, one can appreciate that these appropriations of profit (taxation and dividend) may well be overstated. The most serious consequence of this for the company is that it can lead to erosion of the company's capital base. Accountants describe this problem as *failure to maintain real capital*.

We can gain some appreciation of the problem by examining those aspects of an enterprise's transactions where inflation has greatest effect but for which no account is taken under the historical cost method. The problem is particularly acute in connection with the valuation of inventories, the depreciation of fixed assets, the value of working capital, and the value of long term liabilities. In the next section we examine each of these in turn and comment on the implications for the manager.

8.3 Problems Associated with Capital Maintenance

Valuation of Inventory

Changes in the price level have a major impact on the valuation of inventory and the computation of the cost of goods sold during an accounting period. The effect can be understood by considering the normal trading pattern for purchases and sales. In most businesses, inventories are purchased continually during the year and are subsequently sold. Inevitably, there is a time lag between the date of purchase and the date of sale of the goods, and in a time of inflation the price of goods may rise during this interval. When profit is calculated on transactions it is taken to be the difference between the revenue received from the sale of goods (which is at current prices) and the (historical) cost of the goods sold. However, when the company wishes to replace the goods sold, the cost of replacing them is likely to be higher, and thus the profit calculated on the historical cost basis is not an accurate indicator of the funds remaining to the owners of the business after replacement. (An example of this problem is given in Chapter 6, pp. 92–93.) The historical cost calculation of profit therefore does not provide for the maintenance of capital in the business. In a period of high inflation, the difference between the historical cost of goods sold and the current cost of goods sold can be quite considerable, giving rise to grossly inflated—but unreal—profits.

The valuation of inventory thus has a most important significance in profit determination. In analysing financial information prepared under the historical cost convention, the manager should attempt to assess the effect of increasing prices on the cost of sales. There are two things to consider: firstly, the extent of price changes in the range of goods purchased by the company; and secondly, the length of time inventory is held in the business (inventory turnover ratio). The lower the inventory turn (i.e. the longer inventory is held), the greater will be the effect of inflation on the cost of sales. Conversely, the effect of inflation on the cost of sales in, say, a retail grocery store will not be great because inventory turns over very rapidly.

Clearly, it would be a difficult and wasteful task to try to calculate the replacement or current cost of goods sold each time a sale is made. However, a simple way of estimating the effect of inflation on the historical cost of sales is to use an averaging method. This method proceeds by restating opening inventory, purchases, and closing inventory in terms of the same unit of value, a mid-year (average) index. We illustrate the adjustment below using the 19x5 figures for CKD Ltd. Let us assume that the rate of inflation during 19x5 was 20 per cent so that the index on 1 January 19x5 was 100, the mid-year index 110, and the closing index on 31 December 19x5 was 120.

The adjustment of the historical cost of manufactured sales (taken from Table 8, p. 46) might be calculated as follows:

	Historic cost (£)		Inflation adjusted (£)
Opening inventory	1,894,280	$\times$ 110/100	2,083,708
Inputs during year	5,586,630		5,586,630
	7,480,910		7,670,338
Closing inventory	1,952,810	$\times$ 110/120	1,790,075
Cost of goods sold	£5,528,100		£5,880,263
Effect of inflation on cost of sales:			
Inflation adjusted cost of goods sold			£5,880,263
Historic cost of goods sold			£5,528,100
Increase due to price level change			£352,163

The figure of £352,163 is a close approximation of the amount by which historical cost profit is overstated as a result of failing to recognize the changes in price through the period 19x5. In the assessment and evaluation of the level of profit for the period, therefore, the manager should allow for this overstatement before establishing the amount of profit available to the shareholders in the company. On that basis CKD Ltd's profit and loss account for 19x5 (Table 2, p. 40) might be redrafted as in Fig. 8.1.

CKD Ltd. Redrafted profit and loss account
for the year ended 31 December 19x5

		£
Net operating profit per historic cost accounts		1,492,340
Less: Adjustment for the effect of price changes on the cost of sales (COSA)		352,163
Net operating profit after COSA		1,140,177
Gain on disposal	10,000	
Interest earned	40,000	
		50,000
Net profit before taxation		1,190,000
Taxation at 50% per historic cost accounts		771,170
Net profit after taxation		416,830
Dividends proposed (15%)		450,000
Deficit against revenue reserves		£(31,170)

Figure 8.1 *Redrafted profit and loss account showing the effect of price level changes on cost of sales and profit for the year 19x5*

This redrafted profit and loss account illustrates vividly the effect on capital where an enterprise does not recognize the effects of inflation on its cost of sales. In declaring a dividend of £450,000 CKD Ltd is eating into accumulated revenue reserves to the tune of £31,170 because the amount declared is in excess of the net after tax profit for the year. Clearly, the amount of £321,170 described as 'retained' in the historical cost profit and loss account is inaccurate.

Having examined the impact of inflation on the cost of goods sold, and hence on profits, we must also remember that inflation affects the values at which inventory is maintained in the records of the company (i.e. historical cost) and thus the value at which it is stated in the balance sheet. This difficulty is easily overcome. From the viewpoint of decision-making, historical inventory figures are irrelevant; managers should use an estimate of the current market prices of inventory.

Fixed Assets

The fixed assets of most companies will have been acquired at various times over many years. Again, because of price fluctuations, the historical cost of these assets is a questionable base for either the computation of depreciation for profit measurement or their valuation for balance sheet purposes. It is desirable that depreciation charges measure the economic cost of operations, and this can only be the case if depreciation is expressed in units of the same purchasing power as the revenues earned during the period to which it relates.

If depreciation is not charged on this basis, the capital of the company will not be maintained intact. Consider the following example: a company purchases an asset costing £1,000 with an estimated useful life of ten years and the depreciation rate is set at 10 per cent (£100) per annum. Assume that inflation is running at an average rate of 10 per cent per annum. At the end of ten years the total depreciation on the asset charged against revenues will amount to £1,000 (i.e. the historical cost of the asset). However, this seriously undercosts the benefit of the asset to the business because it matches a cost stated in historical terms with income stated in current terms. Thus, the capital of the company will not be maintained and the profits for the ten years will be overstated. In fact, what is occurring is that each year a portion of the company's capital is being treated as profit.

The manager should take account of both the overstatement of profit and undervaluation of fixed assets when analysing the financial performance and position of an enterprise. For example, in calculating the return on investment (ROI) which is given as:

$$\frac{\text{Net profit after taxation}}{\text{Net asset investment}}$$

the numerator (profit) will be overstated and the denominator (assets) understated, resulting in ROI being grossly overstated.

The net asset investment can be adjusted by revising upwards the valuation of the fixed assets by a specific index of the cost increases for each type of asset, or by applying a general index of the price level. The cost, benefit and degree of accuracy required will help to decide which approach to use. This conversion process will give a measure of the real economic sacrifice of utilizing the assets in question and will form the basis for a more realistic estimate of depreciation, and hence of profit performance.

Monetary Current Assets and Current Liabilities

Monetary assets and liabilities (such as debtors, bank balances, and creditors) are also affected by inflation. For example, when sales are made on credit the business ties up funds in debtors. To the extent that prices increase during the period the debt is outstanding, there is a cost to the company allowing the credit due to the falling value of money. Conversely, if the suppliers of goods and services to the business allow a period of credit the real burden of repayment is reduced and there is a monetary gain to the company receiving the credit. (The same argument applies to all debt financing.)

The following example helps to illustrate the point. If a grocer allows ten people to take one week's credit before paying the weekly grocery bill, and the price of the average 'shopping bag' rises from £10 to £11, then it is the grocer who has to finance the £10 change in input price (£1 × 10) until payments by the debtors result in the receipt of cash. On the other hand, a benefit accrues to the grocer where prices increase during the period of trade credit offered by a supplier. Historical cost accounting does not recognize the effect of inflation on these monetary assets and liabilities. Where the monetary working capital increases during a reporting period the historical cost profit will generally be overstated, and vice versa.

The task for the manager when analysing financial statements is thus to try to estimate the extent of the mis-statement. This means isolating that element of the increase in the net monetary working capital during the period that results from changes in the price level. The following example helps to illustrate this: assume the net monetary working capital of a company (comprising debtors less creditors and assuming zero bank balances, for simplicity) at the beginning and end of a year are as follows:

	Opening £	Mid-year	Closing £
Debtors	1,000		1,500
Creditors	500		660
Monetary working capital	500		840
Price level index	100	110	120

By restating the opening and closing monetary capital in terms of the average index we can isolate the element of the increase of £340 (£840–£500) that is solely due to price level changes.

	£
Increase in MWC on historical cost basis	340
Opening MWC £500 × $^{110}/_{100}$ = £550	
Closing MWC £840 × $^{110}/_{120}$ = £770	
Increase in MWC on inflation-adjusted basis	220
Increase due to price level changes	£120

This amount of £120 should be charged against profit to take account of the decline in the real value of monetary working capital due to inflation.

Long Term Liabilities

In order to appreciate the effects of inflation in their entirety, we must also consider the situation where the company has long term monetary liabilities. Take, for example, a company with a ten year term loan of £10,000. The company repays £1,000 each year and inflation is running at 10 per cent per annum. The £1,000 repaid each year is, in effect, worth less in purchasing power than the £10,000 originally borrowed because money is reducing in value. Therefore, the loan is repaid in pounds worth less than the pounds borrowed. This gives rise to a gain which is not recognized in historical cost accounts.

Financial analysts can adjust for this when analysing company accounts. The adjustment should calculate the beneficial effect of using long term liabilities to finance the company's assets (i.e. the fixed assets, the inventory, and the net monetary assets). The benefit is given by the extent to which the inflation adjustments already made to the cost of sales, the depreciation charge and the increased investment in monetary funds can be offset by the gains due to the underlying assets having been financed by borrowing.

8.4 The Accounting Profession's Response to the Inflation Problem

Most managers will be familiar with the controversy over inflation accounting which has raged both within and outside the accounting profession during the past fifteen years. To say the very least, the problem of how best to account for the effects of inflation has been a thorn in the profession's side. Numerous attempts have been made to formulate a standard practice for the treatment of inflation in external financial reports, beginning with the first provisional standard (PSSAP No. 7) published in 1974 and culminating in SSAP 16 *Current Cost Accounting* published in 1980. In June 1985 the Accounting Standards Committee (ASC) suspended the mandatory status of SSAP 16 though it still remains the authoritative reference on accounting under the current cost convention. The ASC is continuing to work on the development of a new standard to replace SSAP 16 which will allow more choice of method than the original standard. (The Appendix gives some background to the setting of accounting standards: see pp. 291–295.)

8.5 Conclusion

It would be unreasonable to expect that after this brief introduction to the shortcomings of traditional accounting information the manager could be in a position to prepare inflation-adjusted financial statements. What we hope to have shown is that in times of even moderate inflation, the usual measure of performance (profit) and of financial position (balance sheet items) based on historical cost can be very misleading. Thus, in times of inflation, the limitations of historic cost financial information should be kept to the forefront of any analysis.

8.6 Further Reading

Baxter, W.T. (1984), *Inflation Accounting*, Deddington: Philip Allen.
    A masterly overview of the problems of accounting for inflation combined with an assessment of progress to date in their resolution.

Part 3

Sources of Profitability

Chapter 9

——————Analysis of Costs——————

9.1 Introduction

Everything that a manager does, as well as many things he or she fails to do, has an associated cost. This is not to suggest that the costs of taking (or not taking) a particular course of action are all identifiable or measurable. However, it does beg the question of what is meant by 'cost'.

Cost is characterized by the word *sacrifice* and, as such, it is very much in management's interests to control and reduce where possible the sacrifices involved in achieving desired results. In this broad sense cost is equivalent to sacrifices of various types, although they are not all reflected in a company's cash flow. Let us briefly consider some of the concepts of cost that we are certainly all familiar with intuitively, if not formally.

Non-financial costs are those costs that are not directly traceable through a company's cash flow. (While such costs certainly involve sacrifices and may lead eventually, in complex ways, to a reduced cash flow in the future, they do not represent immediate cash outlays.) Psychic costs are a good example: these are the costs of mental dissatisfaction such as one might find in the lowering of the workforce's morale following a 5 per cent (rather than 10 per cent) pay rise, or on the part of manager B when C is promoted on the retirement of A. Another non-financial cost is that associated with a diminution of a company's public image if it is guilty of acts of pollution, unfair trading, etc. (This cost would be reflected in a fall in the value of a company's goodwill—if only we had a satisfactory way of measuring this.)

Non-cash costs are financial sacrifices that do not involve cash outlays at the time when the cost is recognized. Two important examples of this concept are to be found in charges for depreciation and in the idea of opportunity cost.

When a long-lived asset, such as a major item of plant, is acquired for cash this transaction clearly entails a cash outlay, but since the purchase price is almost certainly deemed to be at least equivalent to the value of the asset to the business at the time of purchase there is no diminution of value, hence no sacrifice (other than in terms of financial flexibility), and hence no cost. However, as the plant is used it will physically wear out, or otherwise lose value (e.g. due to its reducing market value, or due to reasons of technological obsolescence), and this is seen as being the depreciation cost to be charged against the revenue of the business on a periodic basis. Thus depreciation charges are costs, but these costs do not represent an outflow of cash at the time the costs are recognized.

Every manager, and consumer, is accustomed to the problem of trying to cope with limited resources, which means that one is invariably unable to do all the things that one would like to do. This is the setting within which opportunity cost is most apparent: if you allocate your scarce resources to one purpose you cannot also allocate the same resources simultaneously to another purpose. One forgoes the potential benefits of strategy X if the resources are applied to strategy Y and these *forgone benefits* constitute the *opportunity cost* of strategy Y (i.e. the sacrifice involved in pursuing Y is given by the benefits that one has to forgo by not pursuing X). It will be apparent that there is not a cash outlay corresponding to the opportunity cost of a given situation.

Cash costs are those sacrifices that are reflected in actual cash outflows. Thus when one pays a fare for an immediate journey by some form of public transport the cost (i.e. that which one gives up) is incurred at the same time as the cash expenditure. In a corporate setting it is a reasonable approximation to equate operating expenses (excluding depreciation) with cash outlays, provided stock levels are not fluctuating in anything other than a minor way.

Business transactions usually involve both reward (or revenue) and sacrifice (or cost), with the difference between the two being gain (or profit). Thus:

$$\text{Reward} \quad - \quad \text{Sacrifice} \quad = \quad \text{Gain}$$
$$\text{Revenue} \quad - \quad \text{Cost} \quad = \quad \text{Profit.}$$

In measuring the outcome from business activity this general concept of sacrifice must be simplified by being expressed in numerical terms, in order that it can be manipulated in a company's accounting system. The common denominator in business is money, and it follows that cost is best represented in financial terms, despite the inherent limitations of this.

It is important to recognize that the term 'cost' only has meaning in a given context and always requires an adjective accompanying it to avoid confusion. There are different cost concepts that are appropriate for different purposes, and no single cost concept is relevant to all situations.

9.2 The Role of Cost Accounting

Cost accounting has been conventionally associated with *product costing*. This is concerned with the determination of the amount of cost to be assigned to each unit of manufactured output as a basis for valuing stocks of goods (as shown in a balance sheet) and as a basis for computing the cost of goods sold (which is deducted from sales revenue to show profit). Apart from aiding in these ways in inventory valuation and income determination, product costing is employed in the cost-plus approach to product pricing (e.g. in the contracting and printing industries).

The approach to product costing is generally to assign to each unit of output a 'fair share' of the total cost of operations. This is quite straightforward in a single product (or single service) company, but complexity tends to increase in proportion to the number of product lines manufactured and/or marketed. In a single product company *all* costs can be seen to be incurred to support that product (e.g. an output of 1,000,000 units at a cost of £5,000,000 gives a unit cost of £5.00). If there are two product lines—or 2,000 product lines—the problem is much more difficult and it is impossible to measure accurately the cost of any one item from a multi-product line.

In addition to product costing, cost accounting is also concerned with deriving costs for other units of activity. The products produced by a company are not the only cost units: one can be interested in the cost of operating particular departments; in the cost of operating in certain sales territories; in the cost of serving various industries and customer groups; in the cost of using different channels of distribution; in the cost of servicing orders below a given value; in the cost of hiring a new salesman; and so forth. Many of these topics will be dealt with more fully in Chapters 10 and 11.

The analysis of *segments* is usually concerned with measuring the profit from each defined segment of a business firm's market. This usually involves a prior consideration of product-market segmentation: the customers that a company is serving can be classified into various categories ('market segments') according to such criteria as age, occupation, number of children and income in the case of individual consumers; or size, location and SIC code in the case of organizational consumers. In order to ascertain the profit consequences of supplying specified products to identifiable market segments, it is necessary to match the revenues from the sales made to each segment with the costs of supplying these segments. The revenue aspect is not too difficult, but the cost determination aspect is fraught with problems. For example, to attempt to allocate a proportion of total marketing and distribution costs to each segment in accordance with the percentage of the total revenue attributable to each segment is too simplistic, while to attempt to fully apportion each elemental category of cost is likely to be potentially misleading. (This is so because, as we shall see later in this chapter, fixed costs are a function of time and variable costs are a function of activity, so to apportion these different categories of costs to segments could be misleading if the object of the exercise is to make decisions relating to which segments to continue to serve. For example, if on the basis of a 'full cost' calculation it was decided to withdraw from segment X, it would not follow that the fixed cost element of servicing segment X would be avoided, even though the variable costs are likely to be.) It is important, therefore, to consider the purpose for which costs are being computed and the implications of employing different concepts of cost and alternative techniques of analysis.

In comparison with the attention that has been given over the years to the costing of physical products there has been relatively little given to the costing of services (such as those supplied to the final marketplace by accounting firms, advertising agencies, management consultants, architects, engineering consultants, or solicitors). In part this is due to the difficulty of being able to define and measure that which is to be costed. For example, is it the audit certificate in the case of an accounting firm, or the television commercial in the case of the advertising agency? By far the largest category of expenditure in service firms is on payroll items, but individuals have different rates of pay, work varying numbers of hours, are capable of different qualities of output, etc., so to cost a service on the basis of, say, staff input hours, is not appropriate. The increasing size of the service sector of the British economy, in both its commercial and non-profit sectors, makes this a problem area of increasing significance, and we should bear it in mind throughout the following discussion. (There is, of course, a number of internal departments within manufacturing and service organizations that provide services as inputs to the final market offer, and the costing of some of these is considered below.)

In broad terms we can identify the main purposes of cost accounting as being:

- to show the cost structure of each activity carried out by the enterprise in order to facilitate planning;
- to facilitate product costing for inventory valuation and income determination purposes;
- to show not only whether a profit has been made on the working of the business as a whole, but whether a profit has been made in each division, or on each job or product, thus aiding in the determination of that combination of outputs that optimizes profit;
- to aid in the pricing decision by distinguishing between fixed and variable costs, with the latter forming the lowest price level that should be set;
- to prevent wastage by the use of an efficient system of stores and wages control;
- to provide cost data on which to base tenders for government and other contracts;
- to secure more efficient operations, and more effective use of resources, by the comparison of results with predetermined standards (variance analysis);
- to permit the establishing of uniform cost accounting systems for interfirm comparison purposes;
- to achieve control by the assigning of costs to responsibility centres (this point will be developed in Chapter 12);
- to help in decision-making by giving a basis for identifying the cost implications of alternative courses of action, such as:
  - What would be the effect on the company's net profit of discontinuing product A and re-allocating the resources to product B?
  - If an order/contract is accepted at a given price, will that price be sufficient to enable the company to earn a profit on the job?
  - What will be the effect of a given wage increase on product costs and hence on profits?
  - What effect will replacing specified equipment have on costs?

These purposes essentially relate to the managerial tasks of planning, decision-making and control, so it is appropriate to consider the categories of costs that are applicable to each of these tasks.

9.3 Cost Analysis for Planning

While plans are primarily concerned with the future, the *process* of planning usually starts from the present or the recent past by examining the pattern of resource allocation and its effectiveness. This can be illustrated by thinking of available resources as *effort*, and then seeking to know how that effort was applied in the recent past, and with what results.

For example, an enterprise might operate in five sales territories, which prompts the question: how much effort was applied to each sales territory last year, and how much revenue—and profit—did each generate? Similarly, the enterprise will serve different categories of customers, and the same questions about effort and payoff can be raised in order to identify the pattern of resource allocation and its effectiveness.

Two issues are especially important in this context:

1. The focus of attention can be on *any* activity (or 'cost object') that is of managerial interest. The origins of cost accounting—and the subsequent preoccupation of most costing systems—are to be found in product costing (which seeks to value

inventory as a basis for measuring periodic profit), and this explains the traditionally introspective focus of costing on manufacturing processes. However, manufacturing does not produce profits or generate sales: it is transactions in the marketplace that bring in revenue, and this highlights the relevance of sales territories, product lines, customer groups, channels of distribution, and size of order as legitimate alternatives to the unit of manufacture when considering costs.

2. In seeking to establish the pattern of resource allocation it is necessary to make use of simplifying assumptions and techniques that inevitably involve approximations of an unknown (and unknowable) 'full' cost for selected activities. As a result one can only sensibly use full cost data as a basis for asking questions (e.g. Which product lines are earning their keep in overseas markets? How well are salesmen performing relative to one another?). It is inappropriate to use full cost data as a basis for making decisions (such as adding or dropping product lines, eliminating particular channels of distribution, and so on).

Whatever cost object (or activity) is selected as the focus of attention, some costs will be *direct* (in the sense of being traceable to the activity; such as direct labour and direct material inputs into a unit of manufactured output, or a salesman's salary and expenses in relation to his sales territory), while others will be *indirect*. By definition, indirect costs cannot be traced directly to cost units, so any procedure whereby these costs are assigned to cost units will mean that the resulting full (or 'absorbed') cost is inaccurate to an unknown extent. The assigning of a 'fair share' of indirect costs, along with direct costs, to cost units is at the heart of *absorption costing*.

A particular cost item can only be termed direct or indirect once the cost object has been specified. Thus a salesman's salary will be indirect in relation to the individual product lines he sells (assuming he carries a range of products), but it will be a direct cost of the territory in which he is operating. In the same way the costs of distributing various products to wholesalers may be indirect with regard to the goods themselves but direct if one is interested in costing the channel of distribution of which the wholesalers are part.

If we consider the way in which the full cost of units of production might be determined we will be able to show how this procedure can be adapted for use in other settings. Data inputs will come from several sources examined below.

Labour

The initial point to observe in relation to payroll data is that the cost of employing a man is not just his gross wage or salary. In addition to gross earnings the company must pay its contribution for national insurance, superannuation, and so on.

In a manufacturing or distribution environment, time sheets can be used to record, in summary form, the time that each operative spends on different jobs. The onus will often be on an operative to record the time he spends on each job that he works on during a week. This highlights a major danger: unless there is some incentive towards the accurate booking of time, the validity of labour costings will be highly suspect. An operative may attach little importance to tediously recording the time he spends on different tasks if he fails to understand the importance of this function. Further, he may be reluctant to record accurately because lost time, idle time and waiting time can reflect partly on himself, partly on his supervisor, and partly on his colleagues.

An analysis of indirect labour hours—especially where reasons can be clearly given—is of great value in pinpointing areas of weakness. Account codes can be drawn up to facilitate the analysis, and each source of indirect labour expense can be recorded against its particular code as it is incurred. For idle time, for example, we may have the following codes:

X123   waiting for orders
X124   waiting for stock
X125   waiting for materials from previous operation
X126   waiting for fitter
X127   waiting for power
X128   waiting for supervisor
X129   waiting for drawings
X130   waiting for maintenance
X131   waiting for jigs
X132   waiting for instructions

If idle time booked to X126 (waiting for a fitter) amounted to, say, £7,500 during the course of a year, a good argument could be put forward for hiring another fitter. A weekly report can be compiled to show how lost time is made up and the proportion it bears to direct labour time.

Materials

All issues of materials should be authorized by a requisition, but note should be taken that the requisitioned quantity may not always be available, so either a lesser amount will be withdrawn from stores (in which event the requisition must be amended) or the full amount will be issued when available. A material requisition should bear the cost allocation/job number in every instance.

A difficulty that arises over material issues is the cost to associate with each issue. It might appear simple to charge against production *actual* material cost (i.e. the price paid). However, a problem usually arises because the same type of material has been purchased at a variety of prices. 'Actual cost', then, has several different meanings and some systematic method of pricing material issues must be selected. It is usual to use the same method for the valuation of material stocks – perhaps adjusted according to the 'lower of cost or market value' convention.

Suppose the following information is available for Material A (given in chronological order):

(a)	Opening stock	100 units	Cost £1.00 per unit = £100.00
(1)	Issue	75 units	
(b)	Purchase	400 units	Cost £1.10 per unit = £440.00
(2)	Issue	100 units	
(3)	Issue	50 units	
(c)	Purchase	80 units	Cost £1.20 per unit = £96.00
(4)	Issue	150 units	
(5)	Closing stock	205 units	(assuming no wastage) £636.00

A price per unit is required for issues (1)–(4) and a valuation for closing stock (5).

First In, First Out (FIFO) Method

This assumes that the various units of material are used in the order in which they are received. Closing stock will consist of the last items purchased. Whenever stores are issued, the issue price will be calculated by working forwards from the oldest batch in stock.

	Stock (a)	Purchase (b)	Purchase (c)	
Issue (1)	$75 \times £1.00$			$= £75.00$
Issue (2)	$25 \times £1.00 \ +$	$75 \times £1.10$		$= £107.50$
Issue (3)		$50 \times £1.10$		$= £55.00$
Issue (4)		$150 \times £1.10$		$= £165.00$
Stock (5)		$125 \times £1.10 \ +$	$80 \times £1.20$	$= £233.50$
	100 units	400 units	80 units	£636.00

This method is easy to operate unless many small purchases at different prices occur. Stock balances approximate current costs, and costs are recognized in a manner which should correspond to the physical use of the stock. However, the system is inequitable if a sudden change in price results in similar jobs being charged with different material costs, and where stock turnover is slow and there are substantial price changes, current material costs will not be apparent in the account.

Weighted-average Cost Method

This assumes that all material of a given kind is so intermingled that an issue cannot be made from a particular lot and the cost should therefore represent an average of the entire supply. A new issue price is calculated every time a purchase is made by dividing (the cost of material received plus the cost of material on hand) by (number of units received plus the number of units on hand).

Issue	(1).	$75 \times £1.000 = £75$	
Issue	(2)	$100 \times £1.094 = £109$	$\dfrac{(25 \times £1) + (400 \times £1.10)}{25 + 400} = 1.094$
Issue	(3)	$50 \times £1.094 = £55$	
Issue	(4)	$150 \times £1.118 = £168$	$\dfrac{(275 \times £1.094) + (80 \times £1.20)}{275 + 80} = 1.118$
Stock	(5)	$205 \times £1.118 = £229$	
		$£636$	

Note that the calculation may be done on a periodic basis instead of on the occasion of every purchase. Issue and stock pricing would then be recalculated as follows and no entries would be made until the end of the period.

$$\frac{£100 + £440 + £96}{100 + 400 + 80} = £1.093 \text{ per unit}$$

This method is easy to operate, smooths out the sudden jumps likely to occur in pricing under other methods, and gives stock balances that represent relatively current costs. However, the influence of a large purchase on favourable terms may influence stock pricing for many periods if usage is slow.

Last In First Out (LIFO) Method

This assumes artificially that the last items purchased are the first used. Closing stock will be valued at the price of the first goods purchased. Whenever stores are issued the issue price will be calculated by working back from the most recent batch received.

		Stock (a)		Purchase (b)	Purchase (c)		
Issue	(1)	75 × £1.00				=	£75.00
Issue	(2)			100 × £1.10		=	£110.00
Issue	(3)			50 × £1.10		=	£55.00
Issue	(4)			70 × £1.10	+ 80 × £1.20	=	£173.00
Stock	(5)	25 × £1.00	+	180 × £1.10		=	£223.00
		100 units		400 units	80 units		£636.00

The only advantage of this method is that it matches recent material cost with current revenue—hence cost of goods manufactured will fluctuate with the market price of material used (unless stock levels are sharply reduced). However, stocks are valued at prices paid for the earliest purchases (including previous periods) which may deviate considerably from current market values.

Conclusion If prices are reasonably stable it matters little which of the above methods is employed. Average cost would probably be best but any of the three applied consistently should be satisfactory.

If prices are not stable the fact that all the above methods (and others) are 'generally acceptable', and therefore are used not only by management internally but for reporting externally, is alarming.

Some means of isolating the effect of price changes is essential both from a control point of view and an income reporting point of view. One suggestion is to use LIFO for pricing issues and FIFO for pricing stocks and transfer the ensuing 'difference' to a 'price gains' or 'price losses' account. A far better solution is to employ standard costing whereby all material pricing is based on attainable standards as calculated at the beginning of the period. The effect of unforeseen price changes is then automatically segregated and can be both examined for control purposes and reported separately in income statements.

Once purchased, some materials are difficult to control as a result of their physical nature. For example, temperature changes may affect the apparent volume of an issue of a liquid chemical; wastage may arise due to inevitable evaporation or because issues do not correspond with purchases (e.g. galvanized wire may be purchased by the ton but be issued in coils or lengths). These are all examples of *unavoidable* causes and allowances can (and should) be made for such losses and gains. If experience shows that only 19 issues of 10lbs can be made from a purchase of 200lbs of material X at a cost of £20, it will be necessary to use the following formula to compute the cost per *usable* pound of material X: $^{20}/_{190}$ (i.e. £0.105 per lb as opposed to $^{20}/_{200}$ or £0.100 per lb).

Avoidable losses are, however, quite a different matter. Such losses may result from causes that include:
• Pilferage.
• Careless handling.

- Careless measurement of issues.
- Incorrect allowances for variations due to evaporation, absorption of moisture, changes in temperature, etc.
- Unsuitable storage.

Care should be taken in deciding which issues to value on an individual basis and which to value on a collective basis. Items of small value (e.g. nails, nuts, etc.) are of the latter type and although they are strictly in the nature of direct materials (i.e. their cost can be specifically identified with particular products), it will usually be unnecessarily expensive in terms of clerical labour to do this. The usual procedure, therefore, is to issue such items in bulk and classify them in the overheads as consumable stores, rather than issue them at a specially computed price to specific jobs.

Indirect Cost Items

Indirect (or overhead) labour costs will be obtained from work sheets and labour summaries, and indirect material costs (such as the nails referred to above) will be obtained from requisitions. Further indirect cost details covering electricity and other utilities, bought-out services, supervisory and managerial salaries, depreciation, and so on will be obtained from expense summaries compiled from either invoices or internal work sheets. The next step is to develop overhead rates by which the indirect costs may be absorbed into the manufactured output. A basic procedure for doing this involves the following steps:

1. Analyse and classify all costs into their direct and indirect categories. (This can be done as a retrospective exercise using actual costs, or as a predictive exercise using estimated costs.)
2. Relate direct costs to the particular jobs, processes, etc., for which they were/are to be specifically incurred.
3. Of the indirect costs, some will relate to particular production departments through which products pass in the course of the manufacturing cycle, and others will relate (on a responsibility basis) to service or ancillary departments (i.e. non-production departments such as maintenance, production control, stores, costing, etc.). The cost of these service departments is then apportioned to the production departments on some 'fair' basis relating to the benefits enjoyed by different production departments.

   The most important criterion in selecting a base is to relate the overhead cost to its most causal factor: machines require maintenance, space involves paying rates, outputs require inputs. Nevertheless, the whole methodology of apportioning service department costs is plagued by the necessity of having to rely on some arbitrary rules (i.e. relating to 'benefit' or 'fair share') that have been developed in order that service department costs may be rationally spread over production departments. Such apportionments are carried out solely for product costing purposes: the control of individual overhead costs will not be achieved by cost apportionments, and nor will the method of cost apportionment influence cost control.
4. An overhead rate can be established for each production department or cost centre, determined by the formula:

$$\frac{\text{departmental overheads} + \text{apportioned service overheads}}{\text{level of activity}}$$

and applied to each job, process, or whatever. This is termed the *recovery of overheads*. (A simpler alternative of obvious applicability in a single product company, but also applicable in other circumstances, is to have a single, company-wide overhead rate. However, even in the single product company it will often be desirable to know the cost of each operation through which the work passes, and also to know the cumulative cost of the product as it passes through the various stages of manufacture.)

Overhead rates in practice are generally determined once a year, and preferably in advance rather than retrospectively, but in changing circumstances it will be advisable to revise them as necessary. The level of activity at which a department is expected to operate during a given period is of crucial importance and whenever overhead rates are determined in advance, very careful attention must be paid to estimating this dimension.

There should be some cause-and-effect link between an overhead cost and the basis of absorption (e.g. if supervisory labour is apportioned to productive cost centres on the basis of direct labour cost, then it should be absorbed into product costs in accordance with direct labour costs).

It is not always necessary to distribute each overhead cost separately: some fixed costs—such as depreciation, rates, insurance premiums, and rent—can be spread collectively on the basis of, say, machine hours (since this factor represents the time during which a product 'rents' the machinery and premises).

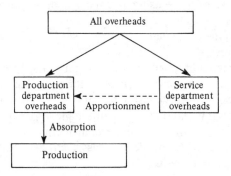

Figure 9.1 *Overhead apportionment and absorption*

Other costs—such as maintenance, certain utilities, operating supplies, and so forth—may be distributed on the basis of units of output. However, those costs that are proportional to direct labour (such as indirect labour, supervision, holiday accruals, overtime premiums, welfare services, personnel department, etc.) can be distributed on the basis of labour cost, manhours, or the number of people employed, whichever seems most appropriate.

Diagrammatically, Fig. 9.1 summarizes the apportionment/absorption routine. The first step is to separate service centre costs from production department overheads. The service department overheads are then apportioned over the production departments. Finally, the resulting departmentalized overheads are absorbed into units of production.

It should again be emphasized that when a company produces a heterogeneous range of jobs/products, with each receiving an unequal amount of attention as it moves from one cost centre to another, it is essential to develop and apply departmental overhead rates (rather than one total company-wide overhead rate) to each job if the resulting product cost is to bear any relation to the true (but unknown) full product cost.

The actual overhead costs of a particular period will only be equal to the applied overheads of that period (i.e. predetermined overhead rate × number of units produced) by chance (unless, of course, the period's costs and activities were all rigidly determined in advance, or the forecaster was in the improbable position of having a perfect view of the future).

If more overheads are applied to units of output than are actually incurred, then overheads are said to be *over-absorbed* (or over-applied or over-recovered). Conversely, if too little overhead is applied to units of output, then overheads are said to be *under-absorbed* (under-applied, under-recovered). The degree to which overhead costs are over- or under-absorbed is a useful piece of management information. A record should be kept of the extent to which the overheads of each cost centre are over- or under-absorbed, and this can be a guide that indicates when overhead recovery rates require adjustment. (Because over- and under-absorbed overhead costs are charged directly to the profit and loss account, they are not reflected at all in any product cost. Clearly this is unsatisfactory in an absorption costing system that exists purely for product costing reasons.)

An over- or under-absorption of overheads may arise because the actual level of overhead costs has varied from the amount anticipated, or because the level of activity actually experienced during a period has differed from the level predicted. Either of these causes—or the two of them acting together—can render the predetermined overhead recovery rate inappropriate. (It is also possible for these two causes to act together in such a way that the overhead rate remains appropriate: thus an expected level of activity of 10,000 direct labour hours in conjunction with a predicted level of overhead costs of £20,000 gives an overhead rate per direct labour hour of £2.00. If costs actually amount to £25,000 and the level of activity was 12,500 direct labour hours, the effective overhead recovery rate remains £2.00 per direct labour hour.)

The explanations behind the major causes of over- and under-recovery are price rises, an expanding level of general economic activity, poor marketing, and so on. If plant capacity along with materials are available but sales volume is so low as to create an under-recovery of overheads, then this may be considered to be a marketing responsibility. However, if there is a backlog of orders and under-absorbed overhead costs result from the ineffective use of manufacturing facilities, then it becomes a manufacturing responsibility.

So far the discussion has focused exclusively on deriving overhead rates that do not distinguish fixed from variable costs, but an important refinement of absorption costing is to derive different rates for both variable overheads and for fixed overheads.

Consider, for instance, a labour-intensive cost centre having estimated fixed overheads of £40,000 for a period, and estimated variable overheads of £30,000 for the same period, with an expectation of working 20,000 direct labour hours. A fixed overhead recovery rate of $^{£40,000}/_{20,000}$ = £2.00 per direct labour hour, and a variable overhead recovery rate of $£30,000/20,000 = £1.50$ per direct labour hour can be readily derived. If the actual figures for the period in question are:

Fixed overheads	£41,500
Variable overheads	£31,500
Direct labour hours	19,500

then the fixed overhead will be under-applied by £1,000 [.e. £40,000 − (19,500 × £2.00)], while fixed overhead prices have risen by £2,500 [i.e. £41,500 − (19,500 × £2.00)]. Variable overheads to the extent of £29,250 (i.e. 19,500 × £1.50) will have been absorbed, but the actual variable overheads incurred (£31,500) are made up of price changes and inefficiencies of £2,250 (i.e. £31,500 − £29,250). (Chapter 12 will deal at greater length with this topic.)

Let us now attempt to put all the pieces together in order to show how the full cost of a job/batch/process/activity can be ascertained by combining the direct and indirect cost elements.

Fig. 9.2 shows a job cost sheet for a job passing through two departments. Direct material costs are obtained from coded requisitions, the direct labour costs from labour analyses, and the overheads on the basis of whichever costing method is employed.

In the job costing example shown in Fig. 9.2 no attempt is made to compute the cost of running a department, but process costing is based on knowing the cost of operating each processing department. Fig. 9.3 gives an example of a cost sheet for a process costing exercise in a company having two processes—X and Y. The cost per unit (ton) can be built up as production progresses from raw materials to the finished product through, initially, process X and then through process Y.

Process costing is associated with flow production in industries such as chemicals, oil, textiles, plastics, paints, glass, and so on. All costs of each process (i.e. direct material costs, direct labour costs, any direct expenses and overheads) are accumulated and related to the units produced. During any period for which costs are accumulated it is probable that there will be some incomplete units of product on hand at the beginning of the period and, similarly, some partly processed units will be present at the close of the period. In order to work out a unit cost for the process it is necessary to convert all partly processed units into the equivalent of fully processed units. Thus 100 units that were complete in terms of material inputs but only half finished in terms of the labour and overhead input would be converted into *equivalent units* in the following way:

	£
Material input (total)	600
Labour input (50%)	200
Overhead allocation (50%)	100
	900

The completed units would cost:

	£
Material input	600
Labour input	400
Overhead allocation	200
	1200

Equivalent units are thus $900/1200 \times 100 = 75$ units.

JOB COST SHEET								

Product _____ Date started _____ Order number _____

Stock _____ Date completed _____ Quantity _____

Customer _____

DEPARTMENT A

Direct material			Direct labour			Overhead		
Date	Code	Cost	Date	Code	Cost	Date	Code	Cost

DEPARTMENT B

Direct material			Direct labour			Overhead		
Date	Code	Cost	Date	Code	Cost	Date	Code	Cost

SUMMARY

Selling price

                                  Dept A   Dept B   TOTAL

Costs: Direct material
        Direct labour
        Overhead
Gross profit

Figure 9.2 *Job cost sheet*

Details	This month actual		This month budget		Year to date		Budget to date		Remarks
	£	per ton	£	per ton	£	per ton	£	per ton	
Process X									
Materials									
Wages									
Expenses (detail)									
Overhead allocation									
Process Y									
Materials									
Wages									
Expenses (detail)									
Overhead allocation									
Office and establishment overheads									
Selling overheads									
Cost of Sales (A)									
Sales									
Deduct: outward freight containers									
Net sales (B)									
Profit (B-A)									
Quantity of sales	Tons		Tons		Tons		Tons		

Title of table: PROCESS COST SHEET — Month _____

Figure 9.3 *Process cost sheet*

9.4 Cost analysis for decision-making

In making decisions managers must pay a great deal of attention to the profit opportunities of alternative courses of action. This requires that the cost implications of those alternatives be assessed.

An important distinction in cost analysis for decision-making (but, as we shall see, not the most important one) is often made between fixed and variable costs. A cost can be classified as being either fixed or variable in relation to changes in the level of activity within a given period of time. (In the long run, of course, *all* costs are variable).

Fixed Costs

A cost is fixed if, within a specified time period, it does not change in response to changes in the level of activity. For example, a managing director's salary will not vary with the volume of goods produced during any year; interest payable at 10 per cent per annum on a loan of £500,000 will not vary with changes in level of activity of a business; and the road tax payable for a motor vehicle will not vary with the vehicle's annual mileage.

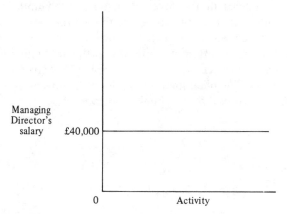

Figure 9.4 *Fixed cost curve*

Fig. 9.4 illustrates a typical fixed cost curve. (If one looks beyond the current time period, however, the managing director's salary may change to £50,000—but not purely in response to changes in output).

If we relate fixed costs to the level of activity (e.g. road tax to miles travelled) we will find that the fixed cost *per unit* of activity is variable: as activity increases, so the fixed cost per unit decreases, and vice versa.

We can categorize an enterprise's fixed costs in the following way:

Committed costs Costs that are primarily associated with maintaining the company's legal and physical existence, and over which management has little (if any) discretion. Insurance premiums, rates and rent charges are typical examples.

Managed costs Such costs are management and staff salaries that are related to current operations but which must continue to be paid to ensure the continued operating existence of the company.

Programmed costs Costs that are subject both to management discretion and management control, but which are unrelated to current activities. R & D is a good example, and it will be apparent that these costs result from special policy decisions.

Variable Costs

A variable cost is one that changes in response to changes in the level of activity. Sales commissions in relation to sales levels, petrol costs in relation to miles travelled, and labour costs in relation to hours worked are obvious examples. Fig. 9.5 shows a variable cost curve for direct materials. It will be apparent that, with certain exceptions, variable costs tend to be fixed per unit of output but are variable in total in relation to the level of output. The exceptions result from costs that do not vary in direct proportion to changes in the level of activity. One underlying reason for this—in so far as labour costs are concerned—is the *learning curve*. It is a generally valid element of experience which suggests that our ability to carry out a particular task will be better at the second attempt than it was at the first, and better again, up to a certain optimum point, on each successive attempt. (This gives rise to the adage, 'practice makes perfect'.) This phenomenon applies to groups working together on a common task in the same way that it applies to individuals.

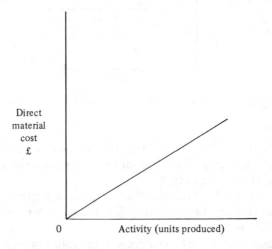

Figure 9.5 *Variable cost curve*

The explanation behind this phenomenon is given in the *learning curve theory*. This was initially developed in the US aircraft industry when it was observed that the man-hours spent in building planes declined at a regular rate over a wide range of production, which contradicts the widespread tendency to compile budgets and standards on the assumptions of level performance and constant costs.

Human beings have the capacity to learn, and this enables them to avoid earlier errors in subsequent attempts at a task and, as a result, to become more efficient in the execution of their jobs. In general, the greater the frequency of repetition of tasks the greater will be the efficiency of performance. In diagrammatic terms this is shown in Fig. 9.6: the more units produced, the lower is the man-hours input per unit.

Evidence suggests that a predictable decrease in man-hours will be found. For example, within the aircraft industry the pattern that has been observed is that each subsequent production run only required 80 per cent of the previous run, on a recurring basis. It also seems to be the case that, in connection with more complex tasks, there is greater scope for learning and that a larger reduction in inputs in successive attempts at a given task will be found than is the case with simpler tasks.

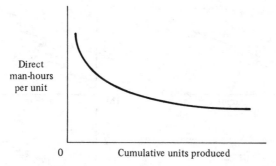

Figure 9.6 *The learning curve*

On the other hand, when a factory is operating at, or near, full capacity it may be necessary for overtime to be worked and this will increase the labour cost per unit of output.

The combination of fixed and variable costs gives us Fig. 9.7.

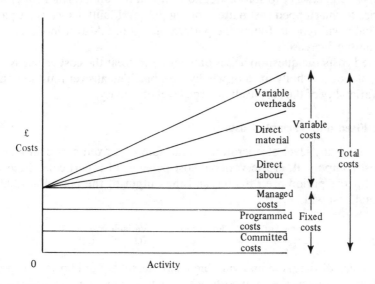

Figure 9.7 *Classified cost pattern*

Mixed Costs

Certain costs are of a hybrid nature, being partly fixed and partly variable. An example is found in telephone charges: the rental element is a fixed cost, whereas charges for calls made are a variable cost. Fig. 9.8(a) illustrates this behaviour pattern, and Fig. 9.8(b) shows the semi-variable cost behaviour that will be found if new telephones are installed as the level of business changes.

Some mixed costs are characteristically semi-fixed. Up to a given level of output it may only be necessary for a factory to work one shift and it may only need one foreman; a simple instance of a fixed supervisory cost. However, beyond that level of

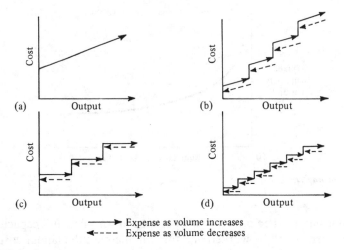

Expense as volume increases
Expense as volume decreases

Figure 9.8 *Cost behaviour patterns*

output is may be necessary to start a second shift and recruit a further supervisor, and this gives rise to the stepped cost pattern of Fig. 9.8(c). Maintenance costs payable on a contract basis will tend to follow the pattern of Figure 9.8(d) if more machines are bought as output increases.

With mixed costs the question arises of whether to treat the cost as partly fixed and partly variable, or as wholly fixed or wholly variable. The answer must depend on the degree of variability of the cost itself and the level of activity.

Separating Fixed and Variable Costs

The total cost at any level of operations is the sum of a fixed cost component and a variable cost component. If the variable cost per unit of a particular item is £1.25, fixed costs for the period are £10,000, and the output of the period is 12,000 units, then the total cost will be:

$$\text{Total cost} = \text{Fixed cost} + \text{Variable cost}$$
$$\text{£25,000} = \text{£10,000} + \text{£(12,000} \times 1.25)$$

When the values of the fixed and variable components are unknown it is possible to estimate them so long as the total costs are known for any two levels of activity. The procedure is as follows:
1. Deduct total cost at the lower of the two levels from total cost at the higher level. Since fixed costs do not vary with volume, the difference must be entirely composed of variable costs.
2. Divide the difference in cost by the difference in volume (i.e. units produced) to give the unit variable cost.
3. Multiply one observed level of activity by the unit variable cost and deduct this from the total cost of that level to give the fixed cost component.
The following example will clarify the method fully:

Total cost at output of 15,000 units per period:		£25,000
Total cost at output of 10,000 units per period:		£20,000
Difference	5,000 units	£5,000

The unit variable cost is therefore £5,000/5,000 = £1. At the higher level of activity the variable cost must be 15,000 × £1 = £15,000. Since total cost is £25,000 it follows that fixed costs must be £10,000. (This answer can be checked by applying the same reasoning to the lower level of activity.)

This method is simple and rather crude. More refined statistical techniques can be applied to obtain more precise results.

Usefulness of the Fixed-Variable Split

The importance of separating variable from fixed costs stems from the different behaviour patterns of each, which have a significant bearing on their control: variable costs must be controlled in relation to the level of activity, while fixed costs must be controlled in relation to time. From a decision-making point of view, it is also important to know whether or not a particular cost will vary as a result of a given decision.

By plotting a company's (or division's) total fixed cost curve and then adding the variable cost curve for the expected possible levels of activity in a forthcoming period, the total cost curve shown in Fig. 9.9(a) is obtained. Alternatively, if the variable costs are plotted and the fixed costs added, as in Fig. 9.9(b), the same total cost curve is obtained but by another means.

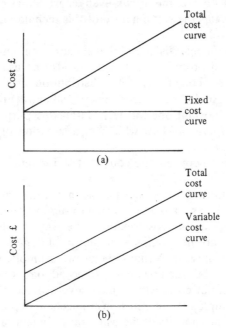

Figure 9.9 *Total cost curves*

Because fixed costs must be incurred even when there is no activity, the fixed cost curve (and hence the total cost curve) cuts the vertical axis above the origin, and this results in the total cost curve being proportional—but not strictly proportional—to the level of activity.

If a revenue curve is superimposed on the same graph as the cost curves, the result is the break-even chart (see Fig. 9.10) which depicts the profit/loss picture for several

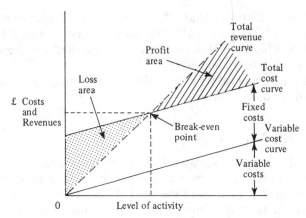

Figure 9.10 *Break-even chart*

possible cost-revenue situations at different levels of activity. Various assumptions underlying break-even analysis—such as constant prices, a constant sales mix, and a greater degree of independence among costs, revenue and profits than can be found in most real-life situations—make the break-even chart a basic tool. Nevertheless, provided its user appreciates the static nature of this technique, he or she should be able to employ it effectively.

In particular, break-even analysis is useful as a background information device for reviewing overall cost and profit levels, but it can also be used in connection with special decisions such as selecting a channel of distribution or make-or-buy decisions.

It was stated at the beginning of this section (p. 148 above) that the fixed/variable split was not the most important one for decision-making purposes. That distinction goes to the notion of *differential cost* which, in a situation of choice, exhibits the following characteristics:
• it is the cost that differs between one course of action and another;
• it is a future cost.
We should note that a differential cost may be one that varies with changes in the level of activity, or it may not. Thus it would be wrong to suppose that differential costs are exclusively composed of variable costs in the same way that it would be wrong to suppose that direct costs are necessarily variable: it all depends upon the particular situation and the question at issue. Perhaps one or two examples will clarify this point.

If a choice is being made between owning as opposed to renting warehouse space as it is needed, the differential costs will include several fixed elements. Among the ownership costs, for example, will be rates, insurance and depreciation, which are all fixed costs in relation to the capacity of the warehouse. In contrast, the cost of renting space varies with the space rented. Differential costs are future costs that differ between one course of action and another, whether fixed or variable.

When the choice is between an existing way of doing something and a new alternative it is helpful to think in terms of *avoidable* versus *unavoidable* costs: thus the costs of adopting an alternative are avoidable if one persists with the present way of doing things, but not all of the present costs will necessarily be avoidable if one changes to an alternative. (For example, if one manufactures gas appliances, and plans are being made to bring out a new range and cease offering the existing range, it will continue to be necessary—according to British Gas Corporation rules—to maintain an inventory of spares for the existing range for 15 years after it ceases to be offered. There are unavoidable costs involved in maintaining stocks of spares.)

A direct cost is one that is traceable to a given cost object. If we are interested in establishing the cost of operating in a particular region, the annual rent of the regional office, the salaries of regional personnel, and the depreciation charges on fixed assets located in the region are all examples of direct costs of the region that are of a fixed character.

Once funds have been committed to a particular purpose—especially in the case of capital expenditure—the chances of recovering them depend upon how much can be obtained from either disposing of the asset, or selling the output from the asset. The funds so committed are termed *sunk costs*, and are irrelevant in deciding whether to abandon or continue operations, or to replace an old asset with a new one. This is so because no present or future action can undo the decision to spend the money. The money has been spent regardless of what happens next.

Finally in this section, we might note the problem over terminology concerning costs for decision-making. Differential costs are also known as relevant costs, incremental costs, and marginal costs. Strictly, *marginal* cost refers to the change in total cost resulting from the production of one more (or one less) unit of output. Almost certainly, therefore, marginal cost is a variable cost concept, whereas the other versions may be treated as synonyms and are not restricted to variable costs.

9.5 Cost Analysis for Control

The most important categories of cost for control purposes are *controllable* and *uncontrollable* costs. Costs can only be controlled if they are related to the organizational framework: in other words, costs should be controlled in accordance with the concept of responsibility; a cost should be controlled at whatever level it is originated and initially approved, by the individual who did the initiating and approving. In this way it will be clear that certain costs are the responsibility of, and can only be controlled by, the chief executive of a company (such as corporate public relations expenditure) whereas others are controllable by responsible individuals at lower levels of the organizational hierarchy (e.g. a departmental manager will be responsible for the salary expense of those who work within the department, and a foreman will be responsible for the cost of consumable materials used in his productive department: strictly, a foreman should only be held responsible for usage rather than prices, due to his lack of control over the latter). Cost control can only be effective if individuals are held responsible for the costs over which they have authority. This is the essence of responsibility accounting, and it will be covered at length in Chapter 12.

At this stage, however, it is important to distinguish between costs that are controllable at a given level of managerial authority within a given period of time, and those that are not. This distinction is not the same as the one between variable costs and fixed costs. For example, rates are a fixed cost that are uncontrollable, for a given time period, by any managerial level, whereas the annual road licence fee for a particular vehicle is a fixed cost that is controllable by the fleet manager who has the power to dispense with the vehicle. In the same way the insurance premium payable on inventories is a variable cost (fluctuating with the value of the inventory from month to month) that is not controllable at the storekeeper level, but it is controllable at the level of the executive who determines inventory policy (subject, of course, to the environmental vagaries of such factors as consumer demand which can never be removed).

Controllability is affected by both managerial authority and the element of time: a short-run fixed cost can become a long-run variable cost. (Thus the managing director's salary is fixed for 12 months, but can be varied thereafter.) All costs are controllable to some extent over the longer term, even if this involves a change in the scale of operations or a relocation of the company.

The problem of distinguishing between controllable and uncontrollable costs is more difficult in relation to overheads as opposed to direct costs. It is vitally important that costs be regulated at source, and this means that for many overhead items the beneficiary of cost incurrence is very often not the person to be charged with the cost. Obvious examples are overhead services—maintenance, the personnel department, post room/switchboard facilities—from which all members of the company derive benefits, but for which cost responsibility is accorded to the respective supervisors and managers of these service functions.

In a control sense, overhead absorption rates and full product costs (made up of direct labour cost, direct material cost and applied overhead) are not helpful. These rates and product costs must be broken down into their constituent parts and these parts must be controlled at source. It is impossible for one manager to control an overhead *rate*, but it is possible for him or her to control those specific costs over which he or she has authority.

To sum up so far, the approach to cost control that is based on the concept of responsibility accounting involves designing the cost control system to match the organizational structure, in order that it reflects realistically the responsibilities of departmental managers, supervisors, etc.

In devising an accounting system for securing cost control that accords with the organizational structure, it will usually be found necessary to define more closely the duties of responsible individuals, and various responsibilities will have to be re-assigned in order to give a logical structure to an organization that may have grown in a haphazard manner. All subsequent organizational changes that lead to changes in individual responsibilities should be accompanied by suitable modifications to the cost control system.

Once the organizational structure, and associated responsibilities, have been established it may prove helpful to the control exercise to employ a *standard costing* system.

Standard costs are costs that should be obtained under efficient operations. They are predetermined costs and represent targets that are an essential feature of cost control. An important measure of performance is derived from a comparison of actual performance and standard performance. For example, if the standard material input for a unit of production is 50p and the actual cost is 48p, then the variance of −2p is the appropriate measure of performance and, assuming a satisfactory quality level, the actual performance is an improvement on the standard. It is better to compare actual costs with a cost standard than with, say, comparative figures from the company's previous financial results. The main reason for this is that a comparison between current results and previous results presupposes that the previous results were at a level of efficiency sufficiently suitable to be emulated: this will rarely be the case. The future is a much better perspective, and future circumstances will almost certainly differ from past circumstances. If this year's profit is £3m and last year's was £2m, this may be seen as a remarkable improvement and a highly desirable state of affairs—but perhaps this year's profit should have been £5m.

The establishing of standards as a basis for setting standard costs is an important part of the work of the industrial engineer. Without standards, a company's management has no way of knowing if the company's overall performance, or the performance of one of its divisions, etc., was average, below average, exceptional or whatever.

While standards are closely related to budgets, the two are not identical. A budget is a prediction of probable future results that has been formalized into a plan (see Chapter 10) whereas a standard is a cost level that should be achieved by efficient working under prevailing conditions. (Budgets are also authorities to spend, or to limit spending, and are prepared for all departments and operations of a company, but standards are simply benchmarks that tend to be used mainly for manufacturing activities.)

The general nature of a standard costing system is shown in Fig. 9.11, which is self-explanatory. The major difficulty lies in setting realistic standards, accompanied in many instances by the educational problem of introducing such a system into a company for the first time.

Among the benefits of standard costing are the following:
- It results in simpler systems.
- It produces the same costs for physically identical products, whereas a batch or process costing system would probably not.
- The whole costing system need not be based on standards, but selected parts only (e.g. material costing) may be 'standardized' and the remainder based on actual costs.
- Control information is specific, and produced for each appropriate level of management, thereby permitting delegation to be effective.

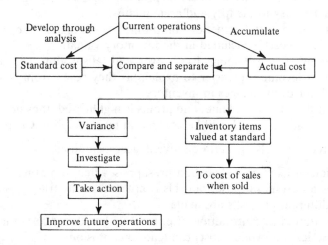

Figure 9.11 *A standard costing system*

- Management by exception is permitted by setting both standards and tolerance limits.
- A forward-looking attitude is encouraged throughout the firm.
- It segregates the effect on costs of temporary variations in the level of output and sales.

9.6 Alternative Costing Systems

In section 9.3 above we looked in some detail at absorption costing. The most controversial issue concerning this technique is the treatment given to fixed overheads: at best it can be little more than arbitrary, and at worst it can be positively misleading.

An alternative approach is to adopt variable, marginal, or direct costing (these terms are used interchangeably). This differs from absorption costing in that no attempt is made to absorb fixed overheads, with the result that only costs of a variable nature are applied to the chosen cost object.

The assumption behind direct costing is that fixed manufacturing costs (i.e. overheads) are of the same nature as administrative expenses: they are incurred to support the productive activities of the firm. As a result, they are not considered to be product costs to be assigned to the units produced, but are treated instead as 'period costs' and charged wholly against profits in the period in which they arise.

The question to be answered is not whether direct costing is better than absorption costing, but whether direct costing is better *in a particular situation*. The disadvantages and advantages of direct costing in each specific case must be considered and if the former do not outweigh the latter, then direct costing should be adopted. (These advantages and disadvantages should relate to the information that management will receive, and not to the theory of cost accounting.)

Direct costing has the following advantages:

1. It is simple to operate, since there are no problems of fixed cost allocations, and the direct costs are easy to identify and accumulate.
2. The effects of inventory fluctuations on profits are eliminated because no varying element of fixed costs is included in the inventory valuation.
3. The difficulties of explaining fixed overhead absorption are avoided, and fluctuations in income are easier to explain as they result from changes in sales volume and not from changes in inventory.
4. The relationship of cost, volume, and profits is highlighted, thus helping to decide between alternatives (which will be covered in more detail in Chapter 11).

Inevitably, there are also general disadvantages, including:

1. The omission of fixed cost allocation presupposes that allocating these overhead costs serves no useful purpose, but this is not necessarily true, especially when a variety of different products are made.
2. The substitution of a 'contribution' (i.e. revenue less direct cost) for 'gross profit' (i.e. revenue less absorption cost) can lead to confusion.
3. The exclusion of fixed overheads from product costs can give a feeling of false

security over performance, with the possible result that fixed overheads are ignored for control as well as product costing purposes.

4. The absence of an approximation to 'full' cost may discourage cost reduction efforts.

The choice between using absorption costing or direct costing will be determined by such factors as:

1. The system of financial control in use (e.g. responsibility accounting is inconsistent with absorption costing).
2. The production methods in use (e.g. marginal costing is favoured in simple processing situations in which all products receive similar attention; but when different products receive widely differing amounts of attention, absorption costing may be more realistic).
3. The significance of the prevailing level of fixed overhead costs.

Distribution Cost Analysis

This chapter has so far concentrated on production costs, but the rising level of marketing expenditures in the last 10 to 15 years has increased the need for means of controlling these outlays.

Distribution cost analysis fulfils this need by its use in:

- analysing marketing costs so that they can be combined with production cost data to determine overall profitability;
- analysing the marketing costs of individual products to determine their profitability;
- analysing the costs required to serve different classes of customer and different territories or areas;
- computing such figures as cost per call, cost per order, cost to put a new customer on the books, or cost to hold £1 worth of inventory for a year;
- evaluating alternative strategies by indicating their cost and profit implications; and
- evaluating managers according to their actual controllable cost responsibilities.

Contract Costing

This is adopted for large jobs undertaken by civil engineering or building concerns, and often lasting through several accounting periods. Essentially, it is a large-scale application of the job costing system described earlier in this chapter.

When, as is usually the case, most of the work is done on site, it is very simple to collect the direct costs for each job, and the only overheads to assign are head office and central stores with, perhaps, central fabrication expenses.

Uniform Costing

This is not a separate system of accounting, but indicates the adoption of common definitions and practices within an industry, or among the member firms of a trade association.

The major benefit of uniform costing is in inter-firm comparisons (see Chapter 10), but it also means that new or small firms are able to use an adequate accounting system that has been developed by experts for their type of business and which would otherwise be beyond their means; that is, it does not necessarily require a high-salaried expert to operate a uniform costing system (but it takes such a specialist to develop one).

9.7 Summary

The main message of this chapter has been different costs for different purposes.

'Cost' is equivalent to sacrifice, and it needs to be qualified by an adjective before it can be sensibly measured. For planning purpose it is helpful to know how the available resources (or effort) have been allocated among the enterprise's various activities, and with what degree of effectiveness. This can be achieved with the use of absorption costing, which can be applied to any activity that is of managerial interest (and not purely manufacturing activities). In arriving at fully absorbed costs there is little alternative to using essentially arbitrary overhead rates.

Whereas absorption costing reflects the distinction between direct and indirect costs, costing for decision-making needs to focus on differential costs (that differ between alternative courses of action). The analysis of fixed and variable costs is useful background to costing for decision-making, but differential costs may consist of fixed *and* variable elements.

Finally, cost analysis for control requires the identification of organizational responsibilities and the personalizing of responsibility for cost-incurring activities. Standard costing can be a valuable aid in the control effort.

9.8 Exercises

Review Questions

1. What do you understand by the term 'cost'? Is it desirable in a managerial context to use the term without a qualifying adjective?

2. Are financial costs more important to managers than non-financial costs?

3. Outline the role of cost accounting in so far as this is relevant to non-accountants.

4. Define a 'segment', and give examples from CKD Ltd as well as from any other organization with which you are familiar. Why is it considered helpful to analyse costs by segments rather than in total?

5. Distinguish between 'direct' and 'indirect' costs. Do you consider this distinction to be useful? Justify, and illustrate, your answer.

6. Describe three methods of valuing issues of raw materials from stock, and indicate their relative suitability in times of changing price levels.

7. Contrast the behaviour patterns of fixed and variable costs. In what circumstances are fixed costs variable and variable costs fixed?

8. What relevance does the learning curve have to cost analysis?

9. Specify the concept of cost that is most useful in a decision-making context. What are its key characteristics?

10. How does time influence the controllability of costs? Is this a more potent influence than the organizational level of a manager?

Problems

1. Gilligan & Co. Ltd manufactures gazebos and currently operates an absorption costing system for valuing inventory, but the company's financial controller, Leslie Axelby, has suggested that it consider switching to variable costing. To help him understand the impact of the change, the managing director of the company has asked Mr Axelby to produce statements that show last month's results using both approaches.

Details relating to last month's operations are:

Opening inventory (units)	Nil
Units produced	500
Closing inventory (units)	100
Manufacturing costs:	
Direct materials	£37,500
Direct labour	£25,000
Overheads	£40,000
Sales revenue	£120,000

Manufacturing overheads have not hitherto been split between fixed and variable categories, but it is estimated that a fixed overhead rate would approximate to £3.00 per direct labour hour. The direct labour rate paid during the month was £4.00.

(a) Value the inventory at the month's end using (i) absorption and (ii) variable costing approaches. (Show workings.)

(b) Produce statements that show the trading results for last month under: (i) absorption costing; (ii) variable costing.

2. Sullivan Company does custom information retrieval and report preparation for a variety of clients. There are two production cost centres: Information Retrieval and Report Writing. Supporting service cost centres are Data Processing and Library Services. Sullivan Company does not attempt to charge costs for Data Processing and Library Services to projects according to actual use of these services, but rather at month-end allocates these costs to Information Retrieval and Report Writing according to the number of direct labour hours spent on projects in those two production centres. Then each project is charged an amount per direct labour hour for each production cost centre's overhead.

Indirect costs are primarily rent, utilities and labour. Rent and utilities are allocated to the four cost centres according to square footage of office space; indirect labour is assigned to each department as incurred. Information Retrieval and Report Writing each occupy 5,000 square feet. Data Processing occupies 1,250 square feet and Library Services occupies 10,000 square feet.

The following transactions took place in November:

(i)   £560 (80 hours) of direct information retrieval labour were incurred for Project A.

(ii)   £175 (25 hours) of direct information retrieval labour were incurred for Project B.

(iii)   £1,120 (160 hours) of direct information retrieval labour were incurred for Project C.

(iv)   £140 (20 hours) of direct report preparation labour were incurred for Project A.

(v)   £70 (10 hours) of direct report preparation labour were incurred for Project B.

(vi)   £350 (50 hours) of direct report preparation labour were incurred for Project C.

(vii)   £2,000 rent expense.

(viii) £3,200 indirect Data Processing labour expense.

(ix)   £1,380 indirect Library labour expense.

(x)   £350 indirect Information Retrieval labour expense.

(xi)   £400 utilities expense.

(xii)   £1,000 other Data Processing expense.

(xiii) £100 other Library expense.

(a) Determine the amount of direct costs for each project during November.

(b) Calculate indirect costs for each of the production and service departments for November.

(c) Calculate the rates at which indirect costs should be allocated to each project for each of the two production departments.

(d) Determine the full costs of each of the three projects carried out in November.

3. Baldwin Enterprises Ltd is a small manufacturing company providing a standard product that is widely available from other sources, and other products to customer specification. The company's management accountant, John Ellis, prepared the following income statement for last year:

	Standard product	Customer specified products	Total
Sales revenue	£250,000	£500,000	£750,000
Material	80,000	100,000	180,000
Labour	90,000	200,000	290,000
Depreciation	36,000	63,000	99,000
Power	4,000	7,000	11,000
Rent	10,000	60,000	70,000
Heat & Light	1,000	6,000	7,000
Other	9,000	4,000	13,000
Total expenses	230,000	440,000	670,000
Net Profit	£ 20,000	£ 60,000	£ 80,000

The depreciation charges relate to equipment used currently only for standard products or customer specified products in separate departments.

Power costs are apportioned in accordance with estimates of power consumed. Rent, heat and light costs are apportioned according to floor space occupied by the departments manufacturing standard products on the one hand, and customer specified products on the other. The building has been leased for 10 years at an annual rental charge of £70,000. All other costs are direct costs of the product line to which they have been charged.

Stephen Cook, who is a regular customer of the company, has asked if 5000 units of a special item can be produced for him with some urgency. Baldwin Enterprises is currently operating at full capacity, and it is clear that some other business would have to be given up to meet Mr Cook's request. However, the company's sales director is unwilling to renege on other orders for customer specified products that have already been accepted.

One way of accommodating Mr Cook's order would be to cut back on the production of the company's standard product by about 50 per cent for a year and devote the capacity thus freed to Mr Cook's order. The unit costs are estimated to be:

Direct material	£20.00
Direct labour	£36.00

A special piece of plant will be needed to help make the product, and this will cost £20,000 with no likely value at the end of the year. Mr Cook is willing to pay £70.00 per unit.

(a) Calculate the following figures:

(i)   the incremental cost of Mr Cook's order;

(ii)   the full cost of the order;

(iii) the opportunity cost to Baldwin Enterprises of accepting the order;

(iv) the sunk costs relating to the order.

(b) If you were John Ellis would you recommend that the order be accepted? Justify your answer.

4. Omicron Ltd consists of three departments, grinding, turning, and milling, all of which have the same productive capacity. The overheads budget for the next cost period of 1000 machine-hours' capacity for each department is as follows:

	Fixed costs	Directly variable costs (per machine-hour)
	£	£
Grinding	2,000	0.25
Turning	1,000	0.20
Milling	750	0.375

A tender by the company is invited in respect of each of three contracts, X, Y, and Z, and it appears to the management that no other work is likely to become available during the cost period in question.

The Works Manager has studied the specifications relating to these three contracts and makes the following calculations with regard to costs and production times:

	Contract X	*Contract Y*	*Contract Z*
	£	£	£
Direct materials costs	1,800	1,610	1,240
Direct labour costs (rate per hour) which differ due to the varying skills involved:			
Grinding	0.30	0.25	0.45
Turning	0.20	0.25	0.40
Milling	0.15	0.20	0.225
Use of capacity (in machine-hours):			
Grinding	660	400	400
Turning	760	500	420
Milling	864	400	320

It will be necessary to employ three men in each department for the number of hours during which machine facilities are used on the work in respect of each of the three contracts.

(a) Compile a comparative statement showing the minimum amount at which the firm could afford to accept each of these contracts.

(b) Would it make any difference to your calculations if you were informed that it was necessary to employ at least one man (included under direct labour) in each department regardless of the level of activity? If so, indicate the necessary amendments to your computations under (a) above.

(c) Assuming that each of the three tenders would be accepted by the customer concerned if the manufacturer quoted the following prices: contract X £4,100, Y £3,200, Z £2,650, advise the manufacturer what he should do concerning contracts to be accepted, if any, if the circumstances are (i) as in (a) above, and (ii) as in (b) above.

5. Nuts
A Tragedy in One Act

The Scene:	A small store deep in the jungle of accounting logic.
The Time:	Today—and tomorrow, if you are not careful.
The Cast:	Joe, owner and operator of a small store-restaurant in the jungle. An accounting efficiency expert.

As the curtain rises we find Joe dusting his counter and casting admiring glances at a shiny new rack holding brightly coloured bags of peanuts. The rack is at the end of the counter. The store itself is like all small store-restaurants in the jungle of accounting logic. As Joe dusts and admires his new peanut rack, he listens almost uncomprehendingly to the earnest speeches of the accounting efficiency expert.

Eff. Ex.:	Joe, you said you put in these peanuts because some people ask for them, but do you realize what this rack of peanuts is costing you?

Joe:	It isn't going to cost anything. Indeed it will make a profit. Sure, I had to pay £20 for a fancy rack to hold the bags, but the peanuts cost only 6 pence a bag and I sell them for 10 pence. I reckon I will sell 50 bags a week at first. It will take 10 weeks to cover the cost of the rack. After that I've got a clear profit of 4 pence a bag. The more I sell, the more I make.
Eff. Ex.:	That is an anticipated and completely unrealistic approach, Joe. Fortunately, modern accounting procedures permit a more accurate picture which reveals the complexities involved.
Joe:	Huh?
Eff. Ex.:	To be precise, those peanuts must be integrated into your entire operation and be allocated their appropriate share of business overhead. They must share a proportionate part of your expenditures for rent, heat, light, equipment, depreciation, decorating, salaries for waitresses, cook . . .
Joe:	The cook? What has he to do with peanuts? He doesn't even know I've got them.
Eff. Ex.:	Look, Joe, the cook is in the kitchen, the kitchen prepares the food, the food brings people in, and while they're in, they ask to buy peanuts. That is why you must charge a portion of the cook's wages, as well as a part of your own salary to peanut sales. This sheet contains a carefully calculated cost analysis which indicates the peanut operation should pay exactly £1,278 per year towards these general overhead costs.
Joe:	The peanuts? £1,278 a year for overhead? That's NUTS!
Eff. Ex.:	It's really a little more than that. You also spend money each week to have the windows washed, to have the place swept in the mornings, and keep soap in the washroom. That raises the total to £1,313 per year.
Joe:	But the peanut salesman said I'd make money. Put them at the end of the counter, he said, and get 4 pence a bag profit.
Eff. Ex.:	(*With a sniff*) He's not an accountant. Do you actually know what the portion of the counter occupied by the peanut rack is worth to you?
Joe:	It is not worth anything. There is no stool there. It is just a dead spot at the end.
Eff. Ex.:	The modern cost picture permits no dead spots. Your counter contains 60 square feet and your counter business grosses £15,000 a year. Consequently, the square foot of space occupied by the peanut rack is worth £250 per year. Since you have taken that area away from the general counter use, you must charge the value of the space to the occupant.
Joe:	You mean I've got to add £250 a year more to the peanuts?

Eff. Ex.:	Right. That raises their share of the general operating costs to a grand total of £1,563 per year. Now then, if you sell 50 bags of peanuts per week, these allocated costs will amount to 60 pence per bag.
Joe:	(*Incredulously*) What?
Eff. Ex.:	Obviously, to that must be added your purchase price of 6 pence per bag, which brings the total to 66 pence. So you see, by selling peanuts at 10 pence a bag, you are losing 56 pence on every sale.
Joe:	Something's crazy!
Eff. Ex.:	Not at all! Here are the figures. They prove your peanut operation cannot stand on its own feet.
Joe:	(*Brightening*). Suppose I sell a lot of peanuts—a thousand bags a week instead of 50?
Eff. Ex.:	(*Tolerantly*) Joe, you don't understand the problem. If the volume of peanut sales increased, your operating costs will go up—you will have to handle more bags, with more time, more general overhead, more everything. The basic principle of accounting is firm on that subject: The bigger the operation the more general overhead costs must be allocated. No, increasing the volume of sales won't help.
Joe:	Okay. You are so smart. You tell me what I have to do.
Eff. Ex.:	(*Condescendingly*) Well—you could first reduce operating expenses.
Joe:	How?
Eff. Ex.:	Take smaller space in an older building with cheaper rent. Cut salaries. Wash the windows fortnightly. Have the floor swept only on Thursday. Remove the soap from the washrooms. This will also help you decrease the square foot value of your counter. For example, if you can cut your expenses by 50 per cent, that will reduce the amount allocated to peanuts from £1,563 down to £781.50 per year, reducing the cost to 36 pence per bag.
Joe:	(*Slowly*) That's better?
Eff. Ex.:	Much, much better. However, even then you would lose 16 pence per bag if you charge only 10 pence. Therefore, you must also raise your selling price. If you want a net profit of 4 pence per bag, you would have to charge 40 pence.
Joe:	(*Flabbergasted*) You mean even after I cut operating costs 50 per cent I still have to charge 40 pence for a 10 pence bag of peanuts? Nobody's that nuts about nuts! Who'd buy them?

Eff. Ex.:	That's a secondary consideration. The point is at 40 pence you'd be selling at a price based upon a true and proper evaluation of your then reduced costs.
Joe:	(*Eagerly*) Look! I've got a better idea. Why don't I just throw the nuts out—put them in the ash can?
Eff. Ex.:	Can you afford it?
Joe:	Sure, all I've got is about 50 bags of peanuts. I am going to lose £20 on the rack, but I will be better off out of this nutty business, and no more grief.
Eff. Ex.:	(*Shaking head*) Joe, it isn't quite that simple. You are IN THE PEANUT BUSINESS. The minute you throw those peanuts out, you are adding £1,563 of annual overhead to the rest of your operation. Joe—be realistic—can you afford to do that?
Joe:	(*Completely crushed*) It's unbelievable! Last week I was making money. Now I'm in trouble—just because I thought peanuts on my counter would bring me some extra profit—just because I thought it would be easy to sell 50 bags of peanuts a week.
Eff. Ex.:	(*With raised eyebrows*) That is the reason for modern cost studies, Joe—to dispel those false illusions.

Discuss this case.

[This case is included in Volume 1 (pp. 240–2) of: Wilson, R.M.S. (1981) *Financial Dimensions of Marketing*, London: Macmillan.]

9.9 Further Reading

Belkaoui, A. (1983), *Cost Accounting: A Multidimensional Emphasis*, Chicago: Dryden Press.
  A technically comprehensive text that draws on a range of disciplines to show how to analyse costs.
Cowe, R. (ed.) (1987), *Handbook of Management Accounting*, Aldershot: Gower (2nd edition).
  A comprehensive array of commissioned contributions from experts across the domain of management accounting (covering planning, control, and much more).
Drury, J.C. (1985), *Management & Cost Accounting*, Wokingham: Van Nostrand Reinhold.
  This book gives a very thorough treatment of the approaches that have been referred to in this chapter.
Hart, H. (1973), *Overhead Costs: Analysis & Control*, London: Heinemann.
  In this text the author deals more thoroughly than is usual with overhead costs and the alternative ways of apportioning them.
Horngren, C.T. and G. Foster (1987), *Cost Accounting: A Managerial Emphasis*, Englewood Cliffs, N.J.: Prentice-Hall (6th edition).

The leading international text in the field, offering lucid and comprehensive coverage.

Solomons, D. (editor) (1968) *Studies in Cost Analysis*, London: Sweet & Maxwell (2nd edition).

An excellent collection of articles looking in an authoritative way at a range of relevant issues concerning the aims and methods of cost analysis.

Chapter 10

———————————— Planning ————————————

10.1 Introduction

Our concern in this chapter is to consider how direction might be given to the
enterprise's future activities. This requires that thought be given to some fairly basic
questions, such as:

What products is it proposed to produce and market?

What machinery and factory facilities are required?

What type of materials are required, and where can they be obtained?

What rate of expansion is aimed for?

What future development is intended?

What level of staffing is required in the field, the factory, the laboratory, the
offices?

What level of overhead expenditure is to be incurred?

To a significant extent managers can be guided in answering these types of question by
a careful analysis of recent activities. For example, it is important to know how much
of the available resources (or effort) were devoted to particular activities in the recent
past, and with what results. We can attempt to answer this by means of techniques
such as segmental (or productivity) analysis and ratio analysis. However, these
techniques will only give a baseline from which managers must then develop plans
(preferably in the form of integrated budgets) indicating the desired future course for
the enterprise. This chapter will also deal with budgetary planning.

10.2 The Nature of Planning

The typical manager, although theoretically concerned with both day-to-day
operations and planning, pays more attention to operations. This emphasis inevitably
leads to sub-optimization, since any company can only have limited resources and
should take as few unnecessary risks as possible. This is only feasible if the utilization
and allocation of its resources are planned.

In view of increasing competitive effort (especially due to mergers) and the
ever-increasing advances of technology, complacency is an evil that no firm can really
afford. Indeed, any firm that does not look ahead and make plans for the future is
clearly courting disaster, and any manager who does not plan ahead is not performing
one of his or her major functions.

Planning is the continuous process of making current decisions systematically, with
the best possible knowledge of the future, and organizing the efforts necessary to
carrying out these decisions. Although planning as an integral part of management is

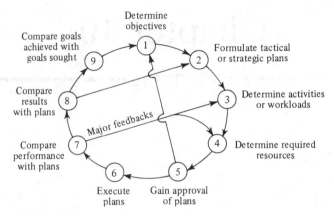

Figure 10.1 *The cycle of control*

not new, it is vitally important in that it forms the basis for subsequent control. Without planning, control cannot be effective in any meaningful sense.

The link between planning and control can be seen in Fig. 10.1. This framework incorporates the following features:

- means of establishing and communicating the objectives that the system is to serve (step 1);
- means of adding the additional detail to complete the planning phases (steps 2, 3, 4, and 5);
- means of communicating with the performance group (step 7);
- methods of reporting on accomplishments (step 8);
- methods of comparing performance with plan and identifying significant variations (step 8); and
- identification of the variety of corrective actions that may be taken, and the means of taking them (steps 8 and 9).

In considering how an enterprise's activities might be fitted into a cycle of control it is clear that assumptions must be made about the abilities and efforts of a company's managers. Additional demands are placed on all executives in the planning process, and this burden becomes heavier the smaller is the company and the fewer are the specialists. Planning involves the exercising of analytical abilities to the utmost and the making of decisions about many indeterminate variables. It is much easier to ignore the need for planning, but to do so is to turn away from reality—and also from future profitability.

Can we specify some of the conditions that are necessary for effective planning? Perhaps the most fundamental prerequisite for planning is a sound understanding at top level of the benefits of planning and the need for its adoption. Expectations must be realistic since it is clear that no plan can guarantee the attainment of objectives if it is based upon unrealistic premises. By adopting planning it becomes possible to view the future implications of current decisions in a way that is not possible without a planning framework. It should be possible for future decisions to be made more rapidly and with less disruption to routine activities when a planning perspective exists.

There are various implicit aspects of planning that must always be considered.

Perhaps the most important is that of deferred benefits due to the fact that time, money and energy must be expended at one point in time to realize benefits at another (rather distant) point in time. The assurance of benefits is probabilistic rather than deterministic, and short-run benefits should usually be forgone in favour of long term returns stemming from the execution of a long term plan. An investment in planning should ensure that future returns are greater than the sacrifices necessary to attain these returns, and since business is an on-going activity the future should not be mortgaged in favour of short-run gains.

Another implicit assumption relates to the availability of adequate resources (in terms of time and effort principally) to facilitate planning. The need for the manager to be involved both in day-to-day matters and in the formulation of plans has already been mentioned, but it will usually be necessary to supplement this latter effort with specialist staff who devote their full attention to planning.

A further implicit assumption involves risk-taking and may not be immediately recognized as such, but the further one strays from the present, the greater the risk. This requires, on the part of top management, a willingness to face up to risk—this being more a mental characteristic of individuals than a feature of the organization itself. Planning should be seen to exist in order to identify the risks of the future which must be faced sooner or later with or without planning.

Planning should be distinguished from the integral aspects of the planning process. This applies in particular to *forecasting*. A forecast is *not* a plan; it is a projection from which plans are developed. For example, a cash forecast might indicate how much cash the company will have on various dates in a future period, and this may show that excess cash is idle at certain times, and that there is insufficient cash at others. A *plan* would specify what is to be done when there is excess cash on hand, or a cash shortage.

However, the financial plan should allow for the maximum flexibility consistent with the attainment of objectives. If this condition is not observed, changing parameters may render a rigid plan invalid. Consequently, planning must cater for the dynamics of the real world. For example, should conditions change when the original plan has only partly run its course, the necessary information must be fed back to the decision-makers so that the remainder of the programme can be adjusted. The more rapidly the firm can react to a dynamic environment, the greater will be its competitive advantage.

Single-figure estimates are not the best elements of plans, even if they do make specific allowance for the contingencies of an uncertain future. Cognizance should be taken of uncertainty by developing plans for the *range* of possible outcomes. Thus, the most likely level of activity (e.g. sales) may be 1,000 units during the forthcoming period, but it could happen that only 800, 900, or as many as 1,200 may be sold, depending on competitive activity. Whatever the outcome, the firm should be prepared by planning ahead for a variety of eventualities. (Chapter 11 covers various ways in which planners may cater for uncertainty.)

If these matters are borne in mind by the planners they can expect:
• a clearer understanding of the likely future impacts of present decisions;
• to be able to anticipate areas requiring future decisions; and
• faster and less disruptive implementation of future decisions.
Efficient management should not be satisfied with anything less.

The creation of a plan is expensive and must therefore be done correctly. The only

justification for the expense involved is the use of the plan as an effective instrument of company policy. To achieve this end three conditions must be fulfilled:
1. The plan must be flexible in the face of changing conditions.
2. The plan must be subject to specific review on at least a semi-annual basis to permit the inclusion of up-to-date information.
3. The plan should be communicated to all concerned if company-wide motivation is to be encouraged.

Before planning can become effective the various elemental parts of the master plan (e.g. product development plan, long term market development plan, and so forth) must be prepared along a common time dimension, and integrated. Until the plan is fully integrated it will be impossible for the board to see the full picture and thereby determine whether or not it is desirable. It is at the integration stage that errors, omissions, and inconsistencies should be noted and amended. Conformity with objectives should also be ensured at this stage. All is wasted unless the blueprint is actually implemented with each manager being committed to its attainment. At all times, of course, successful planning will be associated with the thinking and aspirations of top management.

In planning efforts, the financial analyst must be aware of all the company's activities and policies. Total financial planning can then follow, involving the developing of financial plans and their integration with operating plans. More specifically, the steps in financial planning are:
- to determine the financial resources needed to meet the company's operating programme;
- to forecast how much of the required resources can be met by the internal generation of funds, and how much must be raised externally;
- to determine the best means of obtaining the required funds;
- to establish and maintain systems of control over the allocation and use of funds;
- to formulate programmes to provide the most effective cost-volume-profit relationships; and
- to analyse the financial results of all operations, report them, and make recommendations concerning future operations.

The analyst, in essence, is thus responsible for ensuring the financial viability and stability of the company, and for monitoring the company's progress in following established plans.

10.3 Information for Planning

A great deal of information, while useful for planning and control, is primarily raised for some other purpose that is only tangentially related to planning and control.

The accounting routine provides the bulk of data in many companies, derived from:
- payroll procedures;
- the order-processing cycle, beginning with the receipt of an order and ending with the collection of accounts receivable; and
- the procurement and accounts payable cycle.

The inadequacy of these information flows as a basis for decision systems is highlighted by the omission of:
- information about the future;

- data expressed in non-financial terms (such as share of market, productivity, quality levels, adequacy of customer service); and
- information dealing with external conditions as they might bear on a particular company's operations.

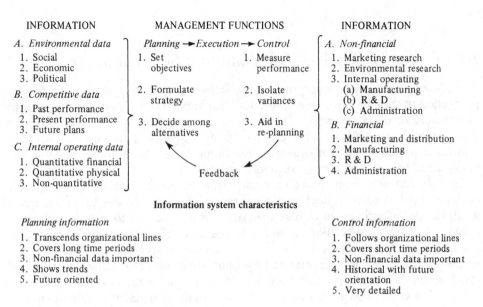

INFORMATION	MANAGEMENT FUNCTIONS	INFORMATION
A. Environmental data	Planning → Execution → Control	A. Non-financial
1. Social	1. Set objectives	1. Marketing research
2. Economic		2. Environmental research
3. Political		3. Internal operating
	2. Formulate strategy	(a) Manufacturing
B. Competitive data		(b) R & D
1. Past performance		(c) Administration
2. Present performance	3. Decide among alternatives	B. Financial
3. Future plans		1. Marketing and distribution
	1. Measure performance	2. Manufacturing
C. Internal operating data	2. Isolate variances	3. R & D
1. Quantitative financial	3. Aid in re-planning	4. Administration
2. Quantitative physical	Feedback	
3. Non-quantitative		

Information system characteristics

Planning information
1. Transcends organizational lines
2. Covers long time periods
3. Non-financial data important
4. Shows trends
5. Future oriented

Control information
1. Follows organizational lines
2. Covers short time periods
3. Non-financial data important
4. Historical with future orientation
5. Very detailed

Figure 10.2 *The anatomy of management information*

Fig. 10.2 indicates the information flows that are necessary to facilitate effective planning and control. For planning purposes these flows include:
- environmental information, relating to social, political, economic, and general business conditions;
- competitive information, provided by marketing research and intelligence; and
- internal operating information, consisting of all the measurable information arising from the operational divisions of the firm.

However, the information flows necessary for control purposes are not the same as those required for planning: the former revolve around communication, motivation, and performance measurement, whereas the latter reflect forecasting, choosing among alternatives, and setting objectives.

The role of financial analysis (as opposed to the accounting routines referred to above) is of considerable value in generating information for planning that includes:
- the profitability (expressed as either contribution or gross margin) of products and markets;
- the relationship of volume and profitability of products over their life-cycles (i.e. product history as a basis for projection);
- the impact of competitive activities and products on volume and profitability;
- the impact of environmental factors, such as technology, on potential demand and profitability (bearing in mind the elasticity of demand at varying prices, and the variability of market share); and

- the general effectiveness of the marketing (e.g. promotion) and organizational (e.g. administration) backing in optimizing market share, capacity utilization, and profitability.

We will now turn to consider the ways in which financial analysis can be undertaken to help managers in their planning endeavours.

10.4 Financial Analysis for Planning: Segmental Analysis

It is usually found that enterprises—especially smaller ones—do not know what proportion of their resources are devoted to their various activities or segments, or the profitability of these allocations. Useful computation of segmental costs and profit contributions can readily be achieved by adopting analytical methods which, while not difficult in principle, are not widely adopted (due largely to the preoccupation with manufacturing cost accounting mentioned in Chapter 9).

The fact that most companies do not know what proportion of their total marketing outlay is spent on each product, area or customer group may be due to the absence of a sufficiently refined system of cost analysis, or it may be due to vagueness over the nature of certain costs. For instance, is the cost of packaging a promotional, production or distribution expense? Some important marketing costs are hidden in manufacturing costs or in general and administrative costs (including finished goods inventory costs in the former and order-processing costs in the latter).

Since few companies are aware of costs and profits by segment in relation to sales levels, and since even fewer are able to predict changes in sales volume and profit contribution as a result of changes in marketing effort, the following errors arise:

1. Marketing budgets for individual products are too large, with the result that diminishing returns become evident and benefits would accrue from a reduction in expenditure.
2. Marketing budgets for individual products are too small and increasing returns would result from an increase in expenditure.
3. The marketing mix is inefficient, with an incorrect balance and incorrect amounts being spent on the constituent elements—such as too much on advertising and insufficient on direct selling activities.
4. Marketing efforts are misallocated among products and changes in these cost allocations (even with a constant level of overall expenditure) could bring improvements.

Similar arguments apply in relation to sales territories or customer groups as well as to products. The need exists, therefore, for control techniques to indicate the level of performance required and achieved as well as the outcome of shifting marketing efforts from one segment to another. As is to be expected, there exists great diversity in the methods by which manufacturers attempt to obtain costs (and profits) for segments of their business, but much of the cost data is inaccurate for such reasons as:

1. Marketing costs may be allocated to individual products, sales areas, customer groups, etc., on the basis of sales value or sales volume, but this involves circular reasoning. Costs should be allocated in relation to causal factors, and *it is marketing expenditures that cause sales to be made* rather than the other way round: managerial decisions determine marketing costs. Furthermore, despite the fact

that success is so often measured in terms of sales value achievements by product line, this basis fails to evaluate the efficiency of the effort needed to produce the realized sales value (or turnover). Even a seemingly high level of turnover for a specific product may really be a case of misallocated sales effort. (An example should make this clear: if a salesman concentrates on selling product A which contributes £20 per hour of effort instead of selling product B which would contribute £50 per hour of effort, then it 'costs' the company £30 per hour he spends on selling product A. This is the *opportunity cost* of doing one rather than another and is a measure of the sacrifice involved in selecting only one of several alternative courses of action.)

2. General overheads and administrative costs are arbitrarily (and erroneously) allocated to segments on the basis of sales volume.
3. Many marketing costs are not allocated at all as marketing costs since they are not identified as such but are classified as manufacturing, general, or administrative costs instead.

Distribution cost accounting (or analysis) has been developed to help overcome these problems and aims to:

- analyse the costs incurred in distributing and promoting products so that when they are combined with production cost data overall profitability can be determined;
- analyse the costs of marketing individual products to determine their profitability;
- analyse the costs involved in serving different classes of customers and different areas to determine their profitability;
- compute such figures as cost per sales call, cost per order, cost to put a new customer on the books, cost to hold £1's worth of inventory for a year, etc.;
- evaluate managers according to their actual controllable cost responsibilities;
- evaluate alternative strategies or plans with full costs.

These analyses and evaluations provide senior management with the necessary information to enable them to decide which classes of customer to cultivate, which products to delete, which products to encourage, and so forth. Such analyses also provide a basis from which estimates can be made of the likely increases in product profitability that a specified increase in marketing effort should create. In the normal course of events it is far more difficult to predict the outcome of decisions that involve changes in marketing outlays in comparison with changes in production expenditure. It is easier, for instance, to estimate the effect of a new machine in the factory than it is to predict the impact of higher advertising outlays. Similarly, the effect on productive output of dropping a production worker is easier to estimate than is the effect on the level of sales caused by a reduction in the sales force.

The methodology of distribution cost analysis is similar to the methodology of product costing. Two stages are involved:

1. Marketing costs are initially reclassified from their *natural* expense headings (e.g. salaries) into *functional* cost groups (e.g. sales expenses) in such a way that each cost group brings together all the costs associated with a particular element of the marketing mix.
2. These functional cost groups are then apportioned to control units (i.e. products, customer groups, channels of distribution, etc.) on the basis of measurable criteria that bear a causal relationship to the total amounts of the functional cost groups.

While costs can be broken down in a microscopic manner, there are dangers and limitations which should not be overlooked since they can hinder the control of marketing costs. If the outcome of functionalizing all marketing costs is to compute a unit cost for every activity, then this can be misleading. At the least a distinction should be made between fixed and variable costs, and the focus should be on the *purpose* for which a particular cost is to be derived and not simply on the *means* by which a figure is computed. Thus costs and units can be looked at separately, thereby avoiding myopic confusion.

An important distinction to make in distribution costs analysis—beyond the basic fixed-variable split—is that between *separable* fixed costs and *non-separable* fixed costs. A sales manager's salary is a fixed cost in conventional accounting, but in so far as his or her time can be linked to different products, sales territories, customers, etc., the salary (or at least portions of the salary) can be treated as being a separable fixed cost attributable to the segments in question, in accordance with time devoted to each. In contrast, corporate advertising expenditure that is concerned with the company's image is not specific to any segment, hence it is non-separable and should not be allocated. Any non-specific, non-separable cost allocations would inevitably be very arbitrary, and such costs should therefore be excluded from all detailed cost and profit computations.

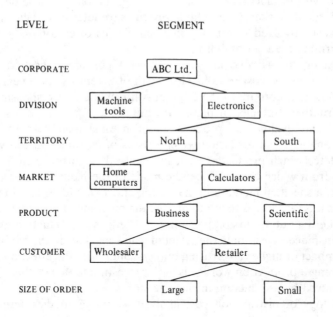

Figure 10.3 *Segmental levels*

An Illustration of Segmental Analysis

In Fig. 10.3 a number of segments are illustrated for a hypothetical engineering company, ABC Ltd. It is possible to measure the costs and revenues at each level in order to highlight the profit performance of each segment. Thus, for example, the profit performance for the calculator market may be measured along the lines shown in Fig. 10.4.

Product: Calculators	North territory £	South territory £	Total £
Net sales	xxx	xxx	xxxx
Variable manufacturing costs	xx	xx	xxx
Manufacturing contribution	xx	xx	xxx
Marketing costs			
Variable:			
Sales commissions	x	x	x
Selling expenses	x	x	x
Variable contribution	xx	xx	xxx
Assignable:			
Salesmen's salaries	x	x	x
Manager's salary	x	x	x
Product advertising	x	x	x
Product contribution	xx	xx	xx
Non-assignable:			
Corporate advertising			x
Marketing contribution			xx
Fixed common costs:			
Manufacturing			x
Administration			x
Net profit			xx

Figure 10.4 *Segmental contribution statement*

The approach adopted in Fig. 10.4 is a *contribution approach*, with costs and revenues being assigned to segments on bases that are essentially direct. Common costs have not been assigned to segments at all.

While the contribution approach avoids the controversies surrounding the apportionment of indirect costs to segments, there can be benefits in carrying out apportionments—provided the bases are clearly thought out and have a causal connection with cost levels. This approach gives the foundation of *marketing productivity analysis*.

The steps to be followed in carrying out productivity analyses were hinted at above. They are:
1. determine the analysis to be made;
2. classify costs into appropriate categories (as discussed above);
3. select bases for apportioning indirect costs to functional activities;
4. allocate revenue and direct costs to the chosen segment;
5. apply indirect costs to the segment;
6. summarize (4) and (5) into a statement showing the net profit of the segment.

It is vital to recognize that this net profit approach to segmental analysis can only raise questions: it cannot provide any answers. (The reason for this, of course, is that the apportionment of indirect costs clouds the distinction between avoidable and unavoidable costs, and even direct costs may not be avoidable in the short-run.) The application of the above steps to a company's product range may produce the picture portrayed in Fig. 10.5.

Product	% Contribution to total profits
Total for all products	100.0
Profitable products:	
A	43.7
B	35.5
C	16.4
D	9.6
E	6.8
F	4.2
Sub-total	116.2
Unprofitable products:	
G	−7.5
H	−8.7
Sub-total	−16.2

Figure 10.5 *Segmental profit statement*

The segment could equally be sales territory, customer group, etc., and after the basic profit computation has been carried out it can be supplemented (as in Fig. 10.6) by linking it to an analysis of the effort required to produce the profit result. (Clearly this is a multi-variate situation in which profit depends upon a variety of input factors, but developing valid and reliable multi-variate models is both complex and expensive. As a step in the direction of more rigorous analysis, one can derive benefits from linking profit outcomes to individual inputs—such as selling time in the case of Fig. 10.6.)

Product	% Contribution to total profits	% Total selling time
Total for all products	100.0	
Profitable products:		
A	43.7	16.9
B	35.5	18.3
C	16.4	17.4
D	9.6	5.3
E	6.8	10.2
F	4.2	7.1
Sub-total	116.2	75.2
Unprofitable products:		
G	−7.5	9.5
H	−8.7	15.3
Sub-total	−16.2	24.8

Figure 10.6 *Segmental productivity statement*

From Fig. 10.6 one can see that product A generates 43.7 per cent of total profits, requiring only 16.9 per cent of available selling time. This is highly productive. By contrast, product E produces only 6.8 per cent of total profits but required 10.2 per cent of selling effort. Even worse, however, is the 24.8 per cent of selling effort devoted to products G and H which are unprofitable.

A number of obvious questions arise from this type of analysis. Can the productivity of marketing activities be increased by:

- increasing net profits proportionately more than the corresponding increase in marketing outlays?
- increasing net profits with no change in marketing outlays?
- increasing net profits with a decrease in marketing costs?
- maintaining net profits at a given level but decreasing marketing costs?
- decreasing net profits but with a proportionately greater decrease in marketing costs?

How can these ideas be applied to the circumstances of CKD Ltd? In the first place we need to identify the segments, and this is done in Fig. 10.7. Taking the company as a

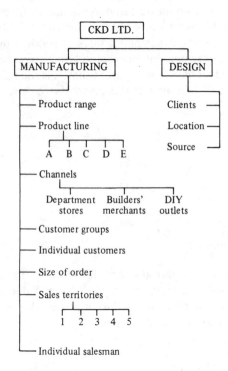

Figure 10.7 *CKD by segments*

whole (as in Table 2, p. 40) is not very helpful if one is concerned to identify the sources of profit with a view to improving future profit performance, so (as a minimum) we need to identify the manufacturing and design segments. Their respective gross profit figures are shown in Table 17 (p. 54). From this we see, for example, that the manufacture and marketing of kitchen units has produced a gross profit in 19x5 of £3,603,650 from the full product range but we do not know how much was made by individual product lines. This can be determined by reference to Tables 12 and 14 (pp. 50 and 52) as shown in Fig. 10.8.

Product line	Units sold	Unit selling price	Total sales revenue	Unit cost	Total cost of sales	Gross profit
		£	£	£	£	£
A	18,500	105	1,942,500	89.25	1,651,125	291,375
B	27,500	75	2,062,500	33.64	925,100	1,137,400
C	13,500	140	1,890,000	97.99	1,322,865	567,135
D	13,800	110	1,518,000	52.72	727,536	790,464
E	13,750	125	1,718,750	65.57	901,474	817,276
TOTAL			9,131,750		5,528,100	3,603,650

Figure 10.8 *Product line profit, 19x5*

A similar analysis can be made for years 19x1–19x4 in order to show trends, but even on the basis of one year's data we can make some useful analyses. For instance, sales of product line A in 19x5 constituted 21 per cent of total sales revenue, but only 8 per cent of gross profit. On the other hand, sales of product line B constituted only slightly more of total sales revenue but generated four times as much gross profit (see Fig. 10.9). Of all the product lines it is apparent that A is the least profitable: this may be for good reasons, but the simple analysis given above raises the question of what these reasons might be.

Product line	% Sales revenue	% Gross profit
A	21	8
B	23	32
C	20	16
D	17	22
E	19	22
	100	100

Figure 10.9 *Sales and profit analysis - 1*

However, this analysis is only partial since it fails to take into account the allocation of effort from functions *other than manufacturing*. From Tables 2, 18, and 19 (pp. 40, 55 and 56) we can see that the effort needed to produce sales of the full product range amounting to £9,131,750 consisted of:

	£
Manufacturing	5,528,100
Marketing	896,170
Distribution	636,830
*Administration	1,072,500
*Financial	305,160
	8,438,760

(*Some of the administrative and financial outlays will have benefited the design side of the business.)

Using appropriate bases of apportionment and absorption (in a way that was suggested in the previous section, and which is analogous to the procedures detailed in section 9.3 of Chapter 9) it might emerge that the full cost (including manufacturing, marketing, distribution, administrative, and financial elements—where appropriate) by product line for 19x5 was as shown in Fig. 10.10.

Product line	Full cost (£)
A	2,086,125
B	1,675,100
C	1,782,865
D	1,137,536
E	1,236,474
Attributable to design	142,350
Unallocable costs	378,310
TOTAL	8,438,760

Figure 10.10 *Full cost analysis*

A revised product line profit tabulation (as in Fig. 10.11) can then be prepared.

Product line	Sales revenue £	Full cost £	Profit
A	1,942,500	2,086,125	(143,625)
B	2,062,500	1,675,100	387,400
C	1,890,000	1,782,865	107,135
D	1,518,000	1,137,536	380,464
E	1,718,750	1,236,474	482,276
Unallocable		378,310	(378,310)
	9,131,750	8,296,410	835,340

Figure 10.11 *Revised product line profit, 19x5*

From Fig. 10.11 we can now produce a revised comparison of sales profit percentages, as in Fig. 10.12. (The profit figure used in calculating the profit breakdown in Fig. 10.12 is £835,340 + £378,310 = £1,213,650.) It now appears that product line A is making a loss; product line C is earning a low return; and product lines B, D, E are the high earners. Some obvious questions arise from this analysis, and Chapter 10 will deal with ways of answering them.

Product line	% Sales revenue	% Profit
A	21	(11.83)
B	23	31.92
C	20	8.83
D	17	31.35
E	19	39.73
	100	100.00

Figure 10.12 *Sales and profit analysis -2*

Referring again to Fig. 10.7, the next segments after product lines are channels and customer groups. In the case of CKD these happen to coincide and consist of department stores, builders' merchants, and DIY outlets. It is a straightforward matter to ascertain the sales revenue arising from each channel/customer group. If the associated costs of operating in each of those segments can then be sensibly estimated it will be possible to show the effort and reward attributable to each. Let us suppose that the pattern is that of Fig. 10.13.

Customer group	% Sales revenue	% Profit
Department stores	30	40
Builders' merchants	45	40
DIY Outlets	25	20
	100	100

Figure 10.13 *Sales and profit analysis - 3*

This raises obvious questions—such as why do department stores generate a higher proportion of profits than other outlets? Should sales via DIY outlets be diverted (if possible) to more profitable channels?

A refinement of customer analysis is to examine individual customer accounts and the size of orders received. It may be the case, for example, that the effort expended in servicing small accounts, or in fulfilling orders of small value, is much too high relative to their profit potential. This can raise further questions that require policy decisions to be made if they are to be answered, such as the specification of a minimum order size.

As yet another basis for segmental analysis we have sales territories followed by individual salesmen. The breakdown for CKD's five sales areas in 19x5 may be as shown in Fig. 10.14.

Sales area	% Sales revenue	% Profit
1	20	17
2	25	27
3	16	13
4	16	19
5	23	24
	100	100

Figure 10.14 *Sales and profit analysis - 4*

Areas 2, 4 and 5 are earning proportionately more than their respective share of sales revenue, while areas 1 and 3 are earning proportionately less. Why is this? Can anything be done in 19x6 to improve the performance of area 3 in particular?

This approach to segmental analysis is appealing due to its apparent simplicity and ease of application, but two warnings are in order. Firstly, the way in which costs are apportioned will inevitably influence the profit outcomes, so the figures need to be viewed as being *suggestive* rather than *definitive*. Secondly, a sale actually arises from a combination of the issues that we have been dealing with one by one: it is a particular product (or mix of products) amounting to a specific sum that is the subject of a sales order given by a particular customer within a specific channel and sales territory, taken by a particular salesman. Handling all these aspects via one analysis is beyond the capability of almost any enterprise's financial analysts, but the implementation of the approach suggested above will raise a variety of questions which should lead to improvements in the enterprise's effectiveness even if the approach is a simple one.

Let us now turn our attention to the design side of the business. There are fewer bases for segmentation here, with the only sensible analysis focusing on clients.

Analyses could be made of the clients by location, but the effort expended on clients by CKD is not influenced in any material way by their location, so this would be of no real value. Similarly the source of clients (e.g. by response to advertisements, PR efforts or personal recommendation) does not provide a meaningful basis for segmental analysis, although it will be of importance in determining the promotional plans for design services in the future. What we have, then, is a key segment that is similar to the individual customer segment discussed in the context of manufacturing above. However, there is a significant difference present due to the labour-intensive and personalized nature of the design service.

Apart from advertising expenditure, Table 16 (p. 53) shows payroll is by far the largest element of the cost of providing design services, so it will be helpful to have:
1. An hourly or daily charge-out rate for design personnel. This rate will include the back-up costs (e.g. consumables, services such as telephone, secretarial/clerical support, depreciation of equipment/furniture, space costs; also rent, rates, insurance, heating, etc.) since the 'sharp-end' is the attention that the designer (with back-up) gives to the client's needs. It will be desirable in a design department of any size to devise charge-out rates for personnel in different grades.
2. Carefully completed time sheets compiled by each designer to show how much time has been given to serving each client.
3. A system whereby additional costs relating to particular clients' requirements can be identified and charged out accordingly.

Via a simple client-by-client analysis it will be possible to build up the total cost and to compare this with the revenue that is being generated. Not only should each client be contributing to CKD's profits but, collectively, all the costs of operating the design service should be covered by the total revenue.

Over time Alice Gunton will develop a capacity for making accurate predictions of the time that is likely to be required by a member of her design team to fulfil a client's requirements, and her ability to quote suitable prices will follow from this. (Since it is unlikely that every available hour will be spent on clients' projects, the charge-out rates should represent a target percentage utilization of available hours—such as devising rates based on an 80 per cent utilization factor).

10.5 Financial Analysis for Planning: Ratio Analysis

The use of ratio analysis as a diagnostic device was introduced in Chapter 4, where it was emphasized that *relative* figures are more valuable to managers than are *absolute* figures.

A great many ratios can be computed—as earlier chapters have shown—pertaining to liquidity and capital structure, but our main concern in this chapter is to look at the role of operating ratios in a planning context. In the main this boils down to the constituents of profit.

Diagnosis proceeds by working through a ratio pyramid. An overall ratio pyramid is given in Fig. 10.15, and a pyramid developed specially for marketing activities is shown in Fig. 10.16. As one works down through the pyramid it is vital to recognize that any ratio is only meaningful when compared with some benchmark from which one might be able to interpret its significance. Suitable benchmarks might come from:
• budgeted performance levels;
• previous figures for the company; or

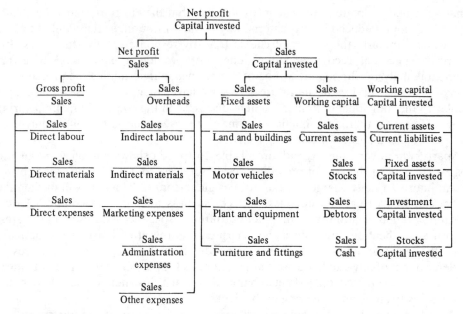

Figure 10.15 *Ratio pyramid*

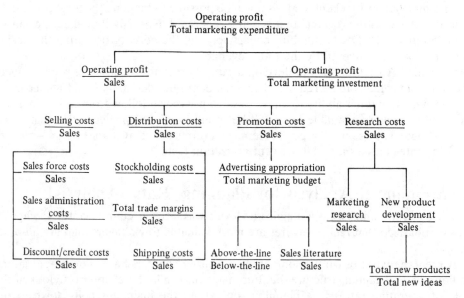

Figure 10.16 *Marketing ratio pyramid*

● external standards, relating to other companies (in the same industry especially). The advantage of comparison is that it suggests important questions that need to be investigated. However, it rarely indicates answers to the questions.

Comparison with purely historical figures is of no significance, but the indications of performance given by ratios can *cumulatively* assist management in appraising the firm's financial position and operations. For example, ratio trends over a period of

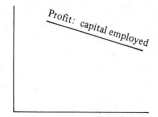

Figure 10.17 *Primary trend*

time may show that there has been continuing pressure on profit margins, and this may be found to be due to an inability to pass on increases in material or wage costs by increasing selling prices.

It may be necessary to work right through the pyramid of ratios to isolate areas creating problems in higher layers of the pyramid. The trend in Fig. 10.17 is downward, and Fig. 10.18 indicates that the fall is in the profit rate rather than in the rate of capital turnover. (It is possible that the upward-sloping capital turnover trend may be concealing negative trends in the tertiary stage of course, but for reasons of simplicity this will be ignored.)

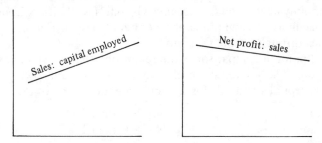

Figure 10.18 *Secondary trends*

Taking the downward-sloping profit rate trend, Fig. 10.19 breaks it down into its tertiary elements, with net profit being equal to gross profit minus overheads.

The process can continue until the cause of upward and downward movements is identified.

Of greater significance, perhaps, is the use of trend data in guiding *future* operations by forecasting the probable and desired relationships in the light of current conditions and expectations. This forms the *internal* basis for establishing budget levels.

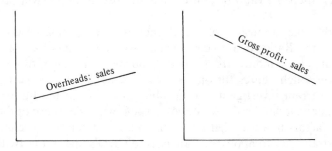

Figure 10.19 *Tertiary trends*

The steps necessary in an *external* comparison exercise are:
1. Ensure that the reports, etc., to be compared are prepared on a comparable basis.
2. Compute the required ratios, percentages, and key totals.
3. Compare internal and external figures.
4. Introduce intangible or qualitative factors that may aid in interpretation.
5. Examine numerator, denominator and lower ratios in cases where a ratio differs significantly from the external standard.
6. Determine the adjustment required (if any) to bring the internal ratio into line with the external standard.

A compromise between comparing internal with external ratios is, in the case of multi-plant firms, the comparison of divisional ratios. These should be automatically prepared along standard lines because of common accounting procedures, but a comparison with overseas divisions raises additional problems.

Inter-*firm* comparisons are published regularly (either publicly or for specific clients) by such organizations as Dun & Bradstreet Ltd, the Centre for Inter-firm Comparison, and various trade associations (e.g. British Prints Industry Federation). The basic dangers in making comparisons with the ratios of other companies include the usual ones of averaging, and more particular ones relating to the peculiar conditions that prevent direct comparison of one firm with other firms. Nevertheless, lessons can certainly be learned from seeing why one's ROI differs from the industry's norm. This is facilitated by the preparation of detailed industrial ratios along uniform accounting lines throughout the pyramid.

The essential point in comparison is the realization that the standard is a band and not a single figure. The situation of each company will have its own peculiarities, but the generally accepted standards for the undermentioned ratios are:

Current ratio	Not less than 2
Acid test ratio	Not less than 1
Inventory turnover ratio	Not less than 3
Average collection period	Usually less than 42 days.

Even these figures will vary from one industry to another, showing that the standards (and tolerances) should be tailor-made for the industry in question.

How can we apply ratio analysis to the performance of CKD Ltd? In the first place we need to specify as clearly as we can which aspects of CKD's performance we wish to investigate: not all the ratios that one can compute are meaningful or useful. For example, the ratio of motor insurance costs to direct labour hours worked is hardly likely to help anyone. On the other hand, if manufacturing overheads consist largely of labour costs, then the ratio of indirect labour cost to output will probably be of value.

Moreover, the analyst must employ both caution and commonsense in using ratios as a diagnostic tool. Ratios tend to cover events with a blanket of averages which can mislead: if figures for a month are given and appear, on average, to be 'normal' this may conceal very high figures for one week and lower than average figures for the others, which warrant investigation. (Our ability to plan for the future depends, in part, on our understanding of the what, how, when, why and where of the past, so we must measure factors in a way that allows us to understand causal relationships.)

We can illustrate how to apply ratio analysis to CKD's operations by the following examples.

Sales Mix, 19x1–19x5

From Table 12 (p. 50) we can identify the trends in the composition (or mix) of sales over the five years 19x1–19x5. Using sales values as the base we can compile Fig. 10.20.

Product line	Sales mix				
	19x1	19x2	19x3	19x4	19x5
A	14	15	18.5	20	21
B	17	18	18.5	20	23
C	25	23	21	23	21
D	19	22	24	19	16
E	25	22	18	18	19
	100%	100%	100%	100%	100%

Figure 10.20 *Sales mix, 19x1–19x5*

The data in Fig. 10.20 can then be plotted to give us Fig. 10.21, which raises questions that can help in formulating future plans. If we relate these trends to the profit analysis of Fig. 10.12 above, it can be seen that the 19x5 profit performance of product line A is very poor despite the upward trend in its proportion of the sales mix. Of the three relatively profitable product lines in 19x5 the presence of D within the

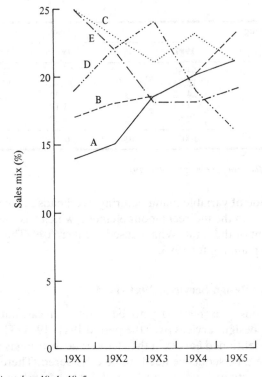

Figure 10.21 *Trends in sales, 19x1–19x5*

sales mix is declining, as is that of E, with only B showing a significant upward trend. Reasons for these trends need to be found and plans developed accordingly.

Variable Manufacturing Overheads, 19x1–19x5

In Table 13(a) (p. 51) we are shown CKD's variable manufacturing overheads, and it is a simple task to express these as a percentage of total manufacturing costs, as in Fig. 10.22.

Year	Variable manufacturing overheads (£) (1)	Total manufacturing costs (£) (2)	(1) ÷ (2) × 100
19x1	221,839	3,548,820	6.25%
19x2	295,816	4,334,630	6.82%
19x3	403,315	5,686,500	7.09%
19x4	399,997	6,010,450	6.65%
19x5	351,187	5,586,630	6.29%

Figure 10.22 *Variable manufacturing costs, 19x1–19x5*

Why is there an upwards variation of almost 12 per cent between 19x1 and 19x3, and then a fall of an almost identical amount between 19x3 and 19x5? Was 19x3 a freak year? Some progress towards answering these questions can be made by analysing the data in Table 15 (p. 53) as shown in Fig. 10.23.

Variable manufacturing overheads	Year				
	19x1	19x2	19x3	19x4	19x5
Indirect labour	64.86	71.02	74.07	71.67	65.43
Sundry materials	15.71	13.04	11.76	12.82	15.59
Power	4.72	3.77	3.42	3.66	4.35
Heating	4.07	3.48	3.18	3.53	4.27
Maintenance	10.64	8.69	7.57	8.32	10.36
	100%	100%	100%	100%	100%

Figure 10.23 *Variable manufacturing overheads, 19x1–19x5*

The overall magnitude of variable manufacturing overheads reached a peak in 19x3 due to the rapid increase in the indirect labour element, which has since returned to its 19x1 level of 65 per cent of the total. What caused the increase? The answer will need to be considered when planning for 19x6.

Advertising to Sales for Design Services, 19x1–19x5

For at least two reasons it is necessary to be careful in calculating the ratio of advertising to sales for design services over the period 19x1–19x5. The first reason is a general one, and was mentioned earlier in the chapter: advertising is a causal factor in generating sales, so the time sequence needs to be considered. There is typically a lag between promotional activity and results, so it may be wrong (especially with consumer durables such as kitchen units) to assume that one can relate all of a given year's advertising expenditure to that year's sales. More specific to CKD is the fact that design services represented a new venture in 19x0, so the trend will not be representative of an established business.

With these warnings in mind the data in Fig. 10.24 have been derived from details in Tables 16 and 17 (pp. 53–4).

Year	Advertising outlays for design services (£) (1)	Design sales revenue (£) (2)	(1) ÷ (2) × 100
19x1	523,264	117,500	445.33%
19x2	544,408	358,500	151.86%
19x3	616,880	954,000	64.66%
19x4	618,634	1,390,000	44.51%
19x5	623,699	1,875,750	33.25%

Figure 10.24 *Advertising and sales revenue, 19x1–19x5*

At face value one can see that the effectiveness of advertising has increased at a remarkable rate, but it is likely that the carryover effects (e.g. 19x2's sales stemming in part from 19x1's advertising) are substantial, and CKD has made a very large investment in advertising to establish its design services.

The examples discussed above are intentionally unrelated to each other, but show how simple analyses can be carried out to ascertain explanations, in part, and to raise questions. A complementary approach is to systematically work down a ratio pyramid—provided it has been designed specially for the enterprise in question.

10.6 Budgetary Planning

A budget is a quantitative plan of action that aids in the co-ordination and control of the acquisition and utilization of resources over a given period of time.

The building of a budget may be looked upon as the integration of the variety of diffuse, and sometimes diverse, interests that constitute the organization into a programme that all have agreed is workable.

Budgeting involves more than just forecasting: it involves the planned manipulation of all the variables that determine the firm's performance in an effort to arrive at some preferred position in the future. Looked at in this way the importance of company-wide participation in the planning phase need hardly be stressed. In the act of participating each department imposes upon itself a commitment, and every such commitment rationalizes the total plan.

Profit-planning and budgetary control are central aspects of the management process, and go directly to the heart of:
- management policies;
- the organizational structure;
- enlightened human relations; and
- the delegation of authority and responsibility.

The overall objective of budgeting should be the optimization of profits over the long term, which can be achieved by:

Planning for Future Needs The budget results from the planned manipulation of the variables within the firm's control in an attempt to achieve the stated objectives. The process of preparing the budget forces managers to become more effective administrators, and puts planning in the forefront, thereby demanding that they think ahead. The outcome is a proposed plan of action.

Co-ordination The inflows and outflows of the corporate system must be regulated by a co-ordinated series of operations and activities. Budgeting enables the efforts of each department to be co-ordinated, integrated, and balanced with the efforts of other departments in the light of overall objectives. Each manager must consider the relationship of his department to all others, and to the company as a whole. This tends to reduce departmental bias and empire-building as well as isolating weaknesses in the organizational structure and highlighting problems of communication. Furthermore, it encourages the delegation of authority and responsibility by reliance upon the principle of management by exception.

Controlling Operations Budgeting facilitates control by providing definite expectations in the planning phase that can be used as the frame of reference for judging subsequent performance. There can be no doubt that *budgeted* performance is a better benchmark than *past* performance, since inefficiencies may be hidden in the latter, and conditions are constantly changing with the result that past performance is usually irrelevant in a managerial control sense.

Assisting Management Planning, co-ordination, and control are all essential dimensions of good management, but budgeting assists even more in helping to achieve the profitability and liquidity objectives of the financial analyst.

Types of Budget

There are essentially two types of budget—the long term and the short term. Obviously time is the factor that distinguishes one from the other, and this raises the point that users of budgets should not be over-influenced by the conventional calendar units (such as months and quarters). The budget period that is most meaningful to the individual firm should be chosen. (For example: the life-cycle of a product from its development, through its market launch, to its eventual deletion from the range is more natural as a budgetary period in many ways than is the calendar year. The product life-cycle links marketing, production, and financial planning on a unified basis; the calendar year does not.)

The actual choice of a time period will depend upon the firm's objectives; the uses and dependability of the budget information (e.g., the period over which forecasts can be made with reasonable accuracy); the type of business in which the firm is engaged; and such related factors as the length of the production cycle.

Different sections of the business may adopt different time periods. Thus, while other departments may plan up to two years ahead, R & D may plan five years ahead; but it is necessary that this be done in such a way that all the budgets can be co-ordinated. It would probably require all departments to plan in periods that were multiples of, say, one year, built up in separate years. In this way, the budgets could be co-ordinated at yearly intervals.

At the minimum, however, the budget period should be sufficiently long to cover at least a seasonal cycle (i.e. including both a 'busy' and a 'slack' season) in order that resource requirements and demands may be balanced.

Budget periods in practice range from one day, at one extreme, to more than 30 years, at the other, but the annual plan is the most common. Nevertheless, more and more firms are adopting long-range budgets in addition. The usual span of these longer budgets is five years, and although the risk of error is greater as one attempts to forecast further and further ahead, the planning process is advantageous even if the figures it produces are somewhat imprecise. This is so because:

- consideration can be given to possible alternative courses of action—such as acquisition, investment in new plant, product diversification, and so forth, all of which have long term, strategic implications;
- the act of setting plans provides a strong incentive to those who carry the responsibility for attaining them, especially since those who plan should be the same people charged with achieving those plans; and
- forward thinking encourages the systematic examination of the variables relevant to corporate growth.

If the planners are able to achieve a high level of accuracy in their long term budgeting, the effort should result in the firm's sights being raised and in strengthened teamwork, because all those involved are confident that the necessary preparatory work has been correctly done. Furthermore, a long term plan gives a long perspective for the preparation of annual budgets in a more purposeful manner than is possible without it.

This is not to say that all firms should adopt detailed long term budgeting: some are involved in areas of business that are too erratic for this to be of any real value; others may believe that their business is too stable to require long term planning; yet others may not be able to afford it; and still others may be geared to particularly large contracts that determine the extent of their planning. However, it is commercial commonsense for some thought to be given to the general direction in which a firm's long term future may develop, with respect to expansion, new products, and the need for new capital. By deciding on the type of future that is desired, and taking positive steps to achieve it, there is a much greater chance of being successful than if the firm is obliged to accept whatever future may come about, due to its preoccupation with day-to-day problems.

From a financial control point of view, the most important part of long term planning is the capital budgeting process (this is the subject of Chapter 14). The capital budget is a list of long term projects expressed in detailed financial terms, and although it should be revised when necessary (usually annually), it has little relation to operating budgets.

Turning to shorter term plans, it has already been stated that the favoured time span is one year, usually broken down into lesser time intervals for reporting, scheduling, and control reasons (i.e. half years, quarters, months, and even weeks in the case of productive and sales activities).

Within this annual framework the *operating budget* will be prepared. Strictly, this is composed of two parts, each of which looks at the same things in a slightly different way, thus arriving at the same net profit and ROI.

On the one hand there is the *programme* (or activity) *budget* that specifies the operations that will be performed during the forthcoming year. The most logical way to present this budget is to show, for each product, the expected revenues and their associated costs. The result is an impersonal portrayal of the expected future—unless, of course, the firm is structured in direct accordance with its product range in which event the portrayal is personal—that is useful in ensuring balance among the various activities, profit margins, volumes, etc.

On the other hand, there is the *responsibility budget* that specifies the annual plan in terms of individual responsibilities. This is primarily a control device that indicates the target level of performance with which the actual level will be compared. The personalized costs in this budget must be controllable at the level at which they are planned and reported, in line with the principles outlined in Chapters 9 and 12 in connection with responsibility accounting.

The significance of these two ways of dealing with the operating budget is of importance as the programme budget is the outcome of the planning phase, whereas the responsibility budget is the starting point for the control phase. The former need not correspond to the organizational structure, but the latter must. Consequently, the *plan* must be translated into the *control* prior to the time of execution, and communicated to those involved in order that no one will be in any doubt about precisely what is expected of him.

Given these two complementary aspects of the operating budget, there are two basic ways in which the budget may be prepared:

Periodic Budgeting This involves the preparation of a plan for the next financial year (the planning period) with a minimum of revision as the year goes by. Generally the total expected annual expenditure will be spread over the year on a monthly basis on the strength of the behaviour of the elemental costs. Thus salaries will be spread over the months simply as one-twelfth of the expected annual total per month; but seasonal variations in sales will require a little more attention to be paid to marketing and production costs and their behaviour over time.

Continuous budgeting (or rolling budgeting) In order to accommodate changing conditions a tentative annual plan may be prepared with, say, the first quarter by month in great detail, the second and third in lesser detail, and the fourth quarter in outline only. Every month (or perhaps every quarter) the budget can then be revised by adding the required detail to the next month (or quarter), filling in some of the vagueness in the other remaining months (or quarters), and adding on a new month (or quarter) in such a way that the plan still extends one year ahead. This type of budget is highly desirable as it forces management constantly to think in concrete terms about the forthcoming *year*, regardless of where one happens to be in the present *financial year*.

Periodic budgeting will often be satisfactory for firms in stable industries that are able to make accurate forecasts covering the budget (or planning) period. Conversely, continuous budgeting is of greater value in the more usual cases of somewhat irregular cyclical activity amid the uncertainties of consumer demand. No matter which method is selected, the principles behind both are the same, with the exception that one comes to an end at the financial year-end and the other does not.

Prerequisites

Whether the concern is with long-range or operational budgeting, there are certain fundamental requirements that must be met if budgeting is to be of maximum value.

Objectives All planning presupposes that objectives have been established since the plan is merely a means to an end, not an end in itself. Objectives are the end.

A Knowledge of Cost Behaviour It is essential that there be an awareness of the firm's particular cost patterns, and the influences thereon. Cost-volume-profit analysis (see Chapter 11) is a useful adjunct to the budgeting exercise as it aids considerably in understanding cost behaviour.

Flexibility True flexibility in budgeting will be discussed in a later chapter (see pp. 242–244), but it should be noted at this point that the budgetary system should be able to recognize and adapt to significant changes in the operating conditions of the firm.

Top Management Sponsorship and Support This type of commitment from the top helps to show that budgeting is a tool of management, rather than just another accounting device. If top management is sceptical, success is unlikely in attempting to exploit the benefits of budgeting.

Education All levels of management must be convinced of the usefulness of budgets, and know the part that each must play in planning and control through budgets. This requires a continuous programme of training in budgeting methods and their value.

Specified Time Period This requirement is obvious, since the whole perspective and framework of the budget will stem from it.

Adequate Systems Support This will come mainly from the accounting sphere where it must be ensured that records and procedures are sufficient for the task in hand. Thus, the budget should be linked to the accounting system in such a way that the same definitions, etc., relate to common elements. (For example, if inventories in the budget system are valued at standard cost, so should be the inventories in the accounting system.)

An Effective Organizational Structure This should be clearly defined, as budgeting is not a substitute for good organization: it is a supplement to effective human relations, and these are at the core of successful budgeting.

If these prerequisites exist, budgeting should enable the company to improve its efficiency by planning for its future and controlling the execution of the plan by comparing actual results with a desired level of performance.

The Master Budget

A comprehensive budget is the formal expression of management's master plan as it specifies the objectives and their means of attainment.

Although it can be applied to a single unit (or department) of a business, budgetary planning is much more effective when it consists of a complete and integrated plan for the entire organization. Planning itself should be seen as the pre-determination of a course of action in such detail that every responsible unit in the firm may be guided thereby. As such, it involves sales forecasting; production scheduling; expense budgeting; the planning of inventory levels; the estimating of manufacturing expenses; the making of decisions ahead of time concerning such matters as new products and purchasing requirements; and a wide range of other factors.

Some cynical managers may argue that a budgetary plan is of little help in guiding the firm towards its objectives. The reason for this would be given as the firm's inability to control its environment and hence to predict its future development.

However, this is a weak argument, since all planners are aware that the future cannot be predicted with complete accuracy or the environment controlled to any major extent by any one firm. But neither is it to be left to chance—the future presents risks and opportunity. By taking the initiative and exploiting the potential opportunities of the future environment the firm should be able to ensure an acceptable ROI. The alternative will be merely to accept what happens.

Changes in the economy (such as varying rates of interest) as well as in competitive behaviour (such as price alterations or the introduction of new products) can be anticipated at least to some extent, and appropriate courses of action can then be determined in an attempt to counter these changes. The alternative to anticipation and adaptation is to be so preoccupied with one crisis after another that no attention is paid to the possible future courses of action available to the company.

By planning ahead the management of a company will have a better basis for understanding the company's operations in relation to its environment, which should lead to faster reactions in the face of developing events, thereby increasing the company's ability to perform effectively. Even though the future actions of, say, competitors cannot be predicted with perfect accuracy, the most probable alternatives can be considered and the company can consider *in advance* how it will respond to whichever comes about. This is known as *contingency planning*.

Furthermore, the budgeting process helps in the attainment of internal co-ordination. Decisions on every aspect of the company's operations affect costs and profits in some way, and the budgeting process provides an overall, integrated view of the cost and profit consequences of the company's activities.

Budgeting, as suggested in Fig. 10.25, has an impact on policies within the company, and the master budget becomes the expression of managerial policies that must be transformed into effective action. This requires, of course, that those who are

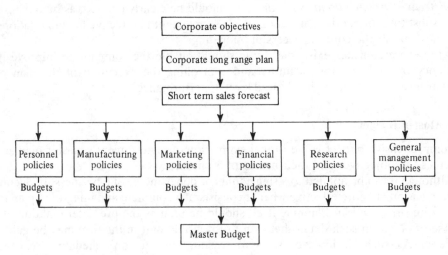

Figure 10.25 *The budgeting process*

to be held responsible for the outcomes of events have been allowed to participate fully in drawing up the budgeted plan of action. (The budgeting process corresponds with the company-wide application of responsibility accounting as discussed in Chapter 12.) Budgets are especially important when a high degree of delegation is found if a company is decentralized into, for example, divisions that are geographically separated.

The other side of planning, as already mentioned, is control, and budgetary control follows the general principles of cost control that are discussed in Chapters 9 and 12.

The actual building up of a budgetary plan requires that those items to be planned be specified, the units of measurement determined, and the desired level of performance established. The budget should reflect *expected* (i.e. reasonably attainable) performance, and not be too tight or too slack. This corresponds with the procedure for setting standards.

Most organizations are too large to permit the detailed planning of all their activities in one budget, so it becomes necessary to use a summary approach that is contained in a *master budget*. Essentially the master budget is a consolidated summary of all the detailed budgets showing their outcomes in terms of their contribution to overall results.

The sales forecast is the starting point for preparing a budget. Sales revenue, stock levels, production requirements and hence most costs and, more especially, profit all follow from a given level of sales activity. If the sales forecast is grossly inaccurate then the entire budget plan will be wrongly balanced. A sensible approach is to acknowledge that more than one level of sales is possible, so consideration should be given to alternatives.

The sum of sales requirements plus changes in stock levels of finished goods gives the production requirements for the period being budgeted. Once it is determined the level of productive activity becomes the starting point for the direct materials, direct labour, and manufacturing overheads budgets. To some extent the purchasing and manpower budgets follow from these production plans: they also depend to some extent on the purchasing and manpower requirements of other functions within the company.

A budgeted cost of sales schedule can be drawn up on the basis of the manufacturing cost of expected sales. The marketing activities necessary to achieve the expected level of sales will be budgeted in accordance with the resources and actions that are necessary to ensure that the sales forecast (in terms of volume, value, and product mix) is achieved. This requires the budgeting of order-getting costs (such as advertising and selling) on the one hand, and order-filling costs (such as transport and warehousing) on the other.

Closely related to both marketing and production operations are the design and R & D functions which must be budgeted in accordance with policy requirements.

An overall administration budget can be compiled so as to include such cost-incurring items as personnel management, training, secretarial activities, general services, and the directorate. And, finally, a financial budget can summarize the whole package in the form of five budgeted statements:
1. Budgeted cash statement
2. Budgeted profit and loss account
3. Budgeted balance sheet
4. Budgeted funds statement

5. Capital budget

It may be useful to itemize more fully the constituent elements of the master budget. These elements are:

Sales Budget This should show volume sales by item, by region, by channel of distribution, and (on a quota basis) by salesman, in a fully reconciled manner. The physical quantities can be extended in accordance with the proposed price list to show revenue by product line, sales territory, and so forth.

Selling Expense Budget Included within this heading will be salesmen's salaries, commissions, expenses, and related administrative costs.

Distribution Budget Transportation, freight charges, stock control, warehousing, wages, expenses, and related administration costs make up this budget. The level of activity and the level of service must both be specified in advance.

Marketing Budget Apart from details of all advertising, promotional activities, public relations, marketing research, customer services, and so forth, the marketing budget can also include a summary of the sales, selling expense, and distribution budgets.

R & D Budget This will cover materials, equipment and supplies, salaries, expenses, and other costs relating to design, development, and technical research projects.

Production Budget The aim of the production function will presumably be to supply finished goods of a specified quality to meet marketing demands. The distribution budget will specify finished goods stock levels, and this can be related to the sales budget to give detailed production requirements. Following from this it is necessary to consider a series of subsidiary budgets:
- Raw materials budget: paying appropriate attention to desired stock levels.
- Labour budget: ensuring that the plan will make the required number of employees of relevant grades and suitable skills available at the right times.
- Maintenance budget: involving a decision between preventative or remedial maintenance.
- Quality control: while not a production responsibility, must be budgeted in accordance with production plans to ensure its adequacy.
- Manufacturing overheads budget: covering items such as consumable materials and waste disposal.

Manpower Budget This must take an overall view of the organization's needs for manpower for all areas of activity—sales, manufacturing, administrative, executive, and so on—for a period of years. It leads to two further budgets:
- Personnel budget: catering for recruitment costs, canteen facilities, first aid, house journals, etc.
- Training budget: covering all aspects of personnel development from apprentices on the shopfloor to management development programmes.

Purchasing Budget Raw materials, consumable items, office supplies and equipment, and the whole range of an organization's requirements, must be considered, along with the questions when, where, at what price, and how often to buy.

Company Secretarial Budget This will include registration expenses, legal fees, pension fund, insurances, reception facilities, etc.

Services Budget Various oddments must not be overlooked, including boilerhouse, gatekeeping, night watchmen, security, gardening, and similar activities.

Administration Budget Apart from the administrative items included in the secretary's budget, others must be covered as well. EDP, executive salaries, typing pool, and any other expenses should be dealt with in this budget.

Financial Budget As we have already seen, this is made up of five individual budgets:
- Cash budget: concerned with liquidity. This must reflect changes between opening and closing debtor balances, and between opening and closing creditor balances, as well as focusing attention on other inflows and outflows of cash (such as those stemming from share issues, or the retirement of debt, or the payment of dividends to shareholders).
- Budgeted profit and loss account: concerned with profitability. This merely reflects the matching of revenues received during a period with costs incurred during that same period. Nevertheless, it is largely on the basis of this budget that a company forecasts its dividend policy, and determines its ability to obtain debt funding.
- Budgeted balance sheet: concerned with the structure of assets and the pattern of liabilities.
- Budgeted funds statement: concerned with the sources of funds and their application in the organization's objective-striving endeavours.
- Capital budget: concerned with questions of capacity and strategic direction. This must deal with the evaluation of alternate dispositions of capital funds as well as with the choice of the best capital structure.

Taken as a whole, these various budgets make up the master budget. Clearly there are very many interrelationships and interdependencies. At the end of the budgeting process, however, every item of cost and revenue (along with the activities that result in these costs and revenues, since the financial dimension is simply a method of expressing underlying transactions of one kind or another in a way that permits addition and mathematical manipulation, evaluation, etc.) should have been planned by whoever is responsible for its incurrence/creation. This should include such items as the sale of scrap, which is easy to overlook, and canteen takings which are so often set off against canteen costs and hence hidden.

Agreement should be reached between each successive superior and subordinate when the budgets are consolidated and summarized as they are communicated upwards in the company's hierarchy. Any fundamental error (such as expected sales demand exceeding productive capacity) will be highlighted as the individual budgets are discussed, analysed, and integrated.

Pressures exist in most companies to grasp opportunities that result in short-term profits. This is not the most desirable situation if it ignores longer term implications, and for this reason the operating budget should be developed in the light of a long-term plan. Profit standards for several years ahead can then be projected, and the whole operation balanced. In addition, increasing specialization means that a long-term dimension should be given to manpower, management, and training needs if necessary expertise is to be available when it is required. (For example, to train a professional manager, and to provide the right tasks for his or her development, may take five years or more. This cannot be accommodated in an annual operating plan.)

Organization for Budgeting

The point has been made before, but is worthy of emphasis, that there is an important distinction between the *staff* function of administering the budget process and the *line* function of making the plans. It is not the job of the staff accountant to decide which figures to put into the budget for areas of responsibility other than his own.

The line organization is responsible for making decisions on what the plans are to be, and the staff organization exists to assist by providing background data, offering technical advice, and overviewing the whole process prior to consolidating the elemental parts of the master budget.

It is beneficial to have a *budget committee* made up of senior executives from all functional areas to perform such functions as:

- ensuring that everyone appreciates that top management supports the budget effort;
- reconciling divergent views;
- offering technical advice;
- co-ordinating budgeting activities;
- reviewing individual budgets;
- suggesting revisions, or approving budget proposals without further revision; and
- scrutinizing control reports in the latter stages of the budgetary process.

The consolidated budgetary plan will pass from the budget committee to the board of directors and should the board find it unsatisfactory, it will be referred to the budget committee for amendment. The unsatisfactory elements can then be discussed with the responsible managers to see if alternative courses of action are available which fit the circumstances a little better. The amended plan will again be sent to the board for approval, and so on.

A major role in this whole planning process is played by the *budget officer*. This individual is usually responsible for the detailed work of drawing up timetables for the preparation of individual budgets and performing all the calculations and adjustments necessary for full consolidation of the master plan. In addition, the budget officer will be responsible for:

- selling budgeting, and educating line managers in the uses and mechanics of budgeting;
- designing the necessary systems and forms;
- reporting on actual performance relative to the plan; and
- carrying out any special studies that may be required.

The various matters relevant to budgeting are best explicitly set out in a *budget manual*. Thus objectives, policies, organizational structures (with a statement of responsibilities and authority), the procedures to adopt when drawing up budgets, the reports that will be produced, and the terms of reference of both the budget committee and the budget officer can be made readily available to those requiring knowledge of such matters.

The outcome of the work of the budget staff and the line organization in this context of planning will be a budget that has been approved by top management and communicated to all as the programme for future action. The next step is to put the plan into operation, which involves a continuous and conscious effort on the part of every responsible individual if budget targets are to be achieved.

10.7 Summary

This chapter has looked at the ways in which an enterprise might go about establishing the amount of effort that has been devoted to its various activities, and the payoff from those allocations of effort, as a basis for understanding which activities are potentially worthy to continue into the future. This diagnostic approach was carried through into a discussion of budgetary planning.

The complementary nature of planning and control was emphasized, and some prerequisites for planning in general, and for budgeting in particular, were specified.

Segmental analysis is a relatively simple approach to the study of the productivity of expenditures: how much output (e.g. profit) was achieved from a given amount of input (e.g. selling effort)? This was illustrated by reference to marketing operations (in contrast to the conventional emphasis placed on manufacturing operations), including several applications to CKD Ltd.

The importance of relative (rather than absolute) figures was highlighted in our coverage of ratio and trend analysis. This diagnostic technique facilitates a systematic investigation into the causes of a business's financial performance. Further examples from CKD were presented, covering sales mix, variable manufacturing overheads, and advertising expenditure.

Finally, the characteristics of budgetary planning were outlined, and the structure of a master budget was explained.

10.8 Exercises

Review Questions

1. Why is planning necessary? What conditions must be fulfilled in setting up a planning function within an organization?

2. Distinguish between plans and forecasts, giving examples of both based on organizations with which you are familiar.

3. In what ways are the outputs from basic financial routines (such as payroll processing) unsuitable as inputs into the planning process? How can the defects you have identified be remedied?

4. Define what is meant by the term 'opportunity cost' and give some illustrations from your own experience.

5. Outline the steps you would follow if you were undertaking a segmental analysis in CKD Ltd with a view to improving productivity. Make explicit any limitations of the approach you specify.

6. Is it best to focus on customer groups, product lines, or sales territories when carrying out productivity analyses? Justify your answer.

7. Is ratio analysis as valuable in practice as it appears to be in principle? (Develop

your answer by discussing what you consider to be the operational weaknesses of ratio analysis.)

8. What benefits are likely to result from the adoption of budgetary planning?

9. What are the respective roles of the manager and the financial analyst in preparing budgets? How might any ambiguities over roles be resolved?

10. Identify the main elements of a master budget.

Problems

1. *Determining charge out rates* Douglas Beaumont recently left the large accounting firm through which he had qualified to set up his own practice. His anticipated monthly costs are:

	£
Secretary's salary	500
Rent of office	250
Other services, etc.	450
Total costs	1,200

In addition, Mr Beaumont aims to earn £2,000 per month for himself through the practice, for which he anticipates having to bill clients for 160 hours of his time each month.

(a) Calculate the hourly charge-out rate that Mr Beaumont must use to bill his clients.

(b) If, in a given month, he is only able to charge clients for 100 hours of his time, what will he earn in that month? (Assume all costs are non-variable.)

2. *Determining full cost* Stevens & Sons manufacture a particular type of picnic table. The costs for a typical month are:

	£
Rent of premises	225
Utilities	150
Insurance	75
Office expenses	450
Depreciation	300
Supervision	600
	1,800

The direct costs per table are:

Materials	25
Labour	15
	£40

Geoff Stevens, the manager of the firm, expects that 200 tables will be made in a normal month, and views the individual table as the most important cost object.

(a) What is the full cost of each table?

(b) If another firm asked Stevens & Sons to supply finished tables at cost, would you expect any difference of opinion to exist over the figure to use?

3. *Determining functional cost* The personnel department of Mansdowne Manufacturing Company has the following costs:

	£
Salaries	17,000
Advertising	1,200
Rent	1,000
Postage and supplies	400
Telephone	200
Depreciation	100
Computer services	300
Total	£20,200

Five personnel functions have been identified:
Personnel records
Recruiting
Management development
Labour relations
Wage and salary administration

You have the following additional information:
(i)   The salaries of the department's ten employees are classified as follows:

	No. of employees	Total salaries
		£
Director	1	2,800
Assistant director	1	2,200
Recruiting	2	3,600
Labour relations	1	2,400
Personnel records	2	2,000
General clerical	3	4,000
Total	10	£17,000

(ii)   The director has made the following estimates for five employees who work on more than one function:

	Director	Assistant	Clerical
	%	%	%
Personnel records	—	10	20
Recruiting	10	40	30
Management development	50	30	20
Labour relations	10	10	10
Wage and salary administration	30	10	20

(iii) All advertising costs relate to the recruiting function.
(iv) The department is charged rent for the space it occupies in the company's headquarters building. The rental charge is based on the average cost of owning and operating the building. Comparable space in the building is now being rented to other tenants at £1,500 a month, but a considerable amount of

rentable space is now vacant. The amount of work space occupied by individual employees varies only slightly from employee to employee.

(v)   The director estimates that half of the postage and supplies and half of the telephone charges relate to recruiting; another 20 per cent relates to management development; the rest is unidentified.

(vi)   Computer services are 90 per cent for personnel records, 10 per cent for wage and salary administration.

(vii) Depreciation is for office furniture and equipment and is approximately equal to average replacement expenditures.

(a) Prepare estimates of the costs of each of the five functions. Explain each of your allocations in a word or a phrase. You should allocate only those costs that seem relevant to managerial decisions relating to individual functions.

(b) What are the most likely uses of this functional cost information?

(c) Which of these functions should be allocated to segments for purposes of product-line analysis?

4. *Determining overhead rate, nonmanufacturing firm* Franklin Associates is a management consulting firm. Each consulting engagement is covered by a contract. The contract price is negotiated in advance, sometimes as a fixed fee, sometimes as professional staff time plus traceable expenses. The billing rates for the various members of the professional staff are always fixed in advance and are expected, in the aggregate, to cover non-traceable (indirect) costs and provide a margin of profit.

The company uses a job costing system to measure the costs of each contract. All costs not directly traceable to specific contracts are recorded as indirect costs; a single predetermined overhead rate is used to assign indirect costs to contracts, based on the number of *professional staff hours*.

Budgeted time and costs for the year and actual time and costs for February were as follows:

	Annual Budget		February	
	Hours	Cost £	Hours	Cost £
Direct costs:				
Professional staff	25,000	300,000	1,800	25,000
Secretarial staff	6,000	36,000	550	3,300
Artwork and printing		7,000		800
Copying		2,000		200
Travel		35,000		2,700
Total		£380,000		£32,000
Indirect costs:				
Professional staff	5,000	£60,000	600	£7,400
Secretarial staff	12,000	72,000	800	3,300
Artwork and printing		3,000		300
Copying		1,000		100
Travel		8,000		400
Other		56,000		4,700
Total		£200,000		£16,200

(a) Prepare a predetermined hourly rate for indirect costs.

(b) The following direct cost data were recorded during February for one of the company's contracts. How much cost was assigned to this contract during February?

	£
Professional staff (70 hours)	910
Secretarial staff (10 hours)	65
Artwork and printing	60
Copying	10
Travel	280

(c) Would this contract have been more profitable or less profitable if the overhead rate had been based on the company's actual cost experience in February?

5. *An exercise on segmental analysis* The profit and loss account for last month's operations of ABC Ltd is given below, showing a net profit of £14,070.

		£
Sales revenue		255,000
Cost of goods sold		178,500
Gross profit		76,500
Expenses		
Salaries	37,500	
Rent	7,500	
Packaging materials	15,180	
Postage and stationery	750	
Hire of office equipment	1,500	
		62,430
Net Profit		£14,070

Figure 1 *ABC Ltd: profit and loss account*

Alan Rothwell, ABC's chief executive, is interested in knowing the profitability of the company's three customers. Since this cannot be known from Figure 1 as it stands he asks his management accountant, David Simpson, to carry out the necessary analysis.

In addition to the five *natural* accounts shown in the profit and loss account, Mr Simpson has identified four *functional* accounts:

- Personal selling
- Packaging and despatch
- Advertising
- Invoicing and collection

His investigations have revealed that:
(i) Salaries are attributable as follows:

Sales personnel	£15,000
Packaging labour	£13,500
Office staff	£9,000

Salesmen seldom visit the offices. Office staff time is divided equally between promotional activities on the one hand and invoicing/collecting on the other.

(ii) The rent charge relates to the whole building, of which 20 per cent is occupied by offices and the remainder by packing/despatch.

(iii) All the advertising expenditure related to product C.

(iv) ABC Ltd markets three products, as shown in Fig. 2. These products vary in their manufactured cost (worked out on absorption lines), selling price, and volume sold during the month. Moreover, their relative bulk varies: product A is much smaller than product B, which in turn is only half the size of product C. Details are given in Figure 2.

Product	Manufactured cost per unit	Selling price per unit	Number of units sold last month	Sales revenue	Relative bulk per unit
A	£105	£150	1,000	£150,000	1
B	£525	£750	100	75,000	3
C	£2,100	£3,000	10	30,000	6
			1,110	£255,000	

Figure 2 *ABC Ltd: basic product data*

(v) ABC's three customers each requires different product combinations, places a different number of orders, and requires a different amount of sales effort. As Figure 3 shows, James received more sales calls, Charles placed more orders, and Hugh made up most of the demand for product C.

Customer	Number of sales calls in period	Number of orders placed in period	No. of units of each product ordered in period		
			A	B	C
Charles	30	30	900	30	0
James	40	3	90	30	3
Hugh	30	1	10	40	7
Totals	100	34	1,000	100	10

Figure 3 *ABC Ltd: basic customer data*

(a) Using the data that has been presented, and making any assumptions you feel to be appropriate (which must be stated and justified), apply absorption costing principles in order to determine the net profit or loss attributable to each of ABC's customers.

(b) On the basis of your answer to (a), what course of action would you propose? Give your reasons.

10.9 Further Reading

Boyce, R.O., & H. Eisen (1972), *Management Diagnosis: A Practical Guide*, London: Longman.
  A well-written, down-to-earth book that looks at a broad range of corporate ills.

Ingham, H., & L.T. Harrington (1980), *Interfirm Comparison*, London: Heinemann.
A very useful guide written by two long-standing (but now retired) experts from the
Centre for Inter-Firm Comparison. However, less comprehensive than that by their
erstwhile colleague, Westwick (see below).

Sevin, C.H. (1965), *Marketing Productivity Analysis*, New York: McGraw-Hill.
This short volume embodies a wealth of commonsense and valuable insights into
the effective application of financial analysis in planning—with an emphasis on
marketing.

Welsch, G.A. (1976), *Budgeting*, Englewood Cliffs, N.J.: Prentice-Hall. (Rev.
edition)
The standard work on the subject, this is a detailed and comprehensive book.

Westwick, C.A. (1973), *How to Use Management Ratios*, Aldershot: Gower.
An excellent and practical book that reflects the author's eight years at CIFC.

Wilson, R.M.S. (1979), *Management Controls and Marketing Planning*, London:
Heinemann. (2nd edition)
The method adopted in this text is to develop an approach to management control
and then to demonstrate its application to marketing planning.

Chapter 11

———————Decision-making———————

11.1 Introduction

The essence of management is decision-making—the process of choosing among various courses of action. Such decisions relate to *future* outcomes and therefore involve considerations relating to uncertainty.

For rational decision-making some form of information is necessary, which presupposes some means of measurement. Preferably, the information will be in quantitative terms, and should relate to the objective: it is easier to make the correct choice when keeping in mind what one is trying to accomplish. (If there exists more than one objective the decision-maker must balance one against another by making a *trade off*. For example, the decision-maker may trade off speed for quality in deciding on a particular means of production, if this appears to reflect accurately the relative importance of multiple objectives.)

An essential requirement in decision-making is the removal of doubt. Decisions are made in relation to objectives, and are well made if the objectives are attained. However, the uncertainty of the future means that a choice can be wrong. It also means that a single choice has several possible outcomes. (For example, if the decision is made to launch a new product, its sales may be at any one of several levels estimated before the event.) This demands that decisions be reached through systematic analysis.

It will be seen later that views of the future are of four types:
- ignorance
- certainty of outcomes (although choices must still be made among various strategies);
- risk—probabilities being assignable to possible outcomes;
- uncertainty—unable to assign probabilities.

The latter two views are the most usual and in the case of uncertainty, the decision-maker requires reliable criteria in order to choose among options since their consequences cannot be predicted with confidence. This problem can often be solved through the collection of more information, which means that the cost of this information must be balanced with the possible losses due to uncertainty if it is not collected. Further assistance is given by the adoption of a systematic approach to decision-making, such as that contained in the following steps:
1. Define the problem to be solved, and the specific desired objectives.
2. Determine alternative solutions (i.e. possible courses of action).
3. Analyse the consequences of each alternative by computing (in so far as possible) the costs and revenues of each.
4. Select the alternative that is most desirable.

5. Transform the decision into effective action.
6. Appraise the results.
We will develop this theme of decision-making by looking, in turn at cost-profit-volume analysis, differential cost analysis and risk analysis.

11.2 Cost-Volume-Profit Analysis

In making decisions management pays a great deal of attention to the profit opportunities of alternative courses of action. However, in the case of alternatives that involve changes in the level of business, profit does not usually vary in direct proportion to these changes in volume. This is a result of the cost behaviour patterns that were discussed in Chapter 9. Consequently, managers must realize that better evaluations can be made of profit opportunities by studying the relationships among costs, volume, and profits. Such studies lead to better decisions.

Profit is clearly a function of sales volume, selling prices, and costs. The non-uniform response of certain costs to changes in the volume of business can have a serious impact upon profit. For example, in a firm having a high proportion of fixed costs, a seemingly insignificant decline in sales volume from the expected level may be accompanied by a major drop in expected profit. The *profitgraph* is a simple way of illustrating the interrelationships of costs, profits, and levels of business. (This relates to *short-run* relationships only.)

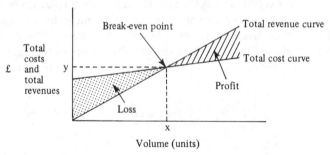

Figure 11.1 *Profitgraph*

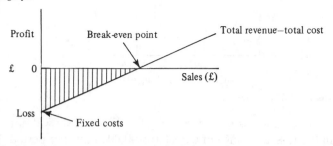

Figure 11.2 *Profit-volume chart*

Fig. 11.1 shows a simple profitgraph. Another name for this is a break-even chart, but this emphasizes one aspect of the total analysis—and not the most important aspect in most instances. Thus, in Fig. 11.1, point x indicates the units that must be sold in order that total revenue may be equated with total costs—at point y.

It is perhaps simpler to show the same relationships by netting total costs and total revenue for each level of activity. This is done in Fig. 11.2.

The reason why the total cost curve in Fig. 11.1 does not pass through the origin is the same as the reason why the profit curve of Figure 11.2 cuts the vertical axis below the point of zero profit: even when there are no sales the fixed costs must be paid and, consequently, the area below the break-even sales volume represents one of loss (being at its greatest at zero sales).

It has been mentioned that fixed costs are only fixed in relation to time and through a range of activity, termed *the relevant range*. A managing director's salary may be £50,000 in 19x1 as suggested in Chapter 9, and this represents a fixed cost of that period. But if the company he or she directs only operates at 10 per cent of expected activity, or alternatively operates at 200 per cent of expected activity, the level of remuneration or the director's continued presence at the helm may require further consideration. This could change the level of fixed costs.

Salaries are a good example of a cost that is related closely to responsibility and the size of an undertaking. For this reason top management in a large company earns more than its counterpart in a small one. Costs of an establishment nature are related to the size (hence, capacity) of an organization, and this relationship can be expressed in the concept of the relevant range.

A factory may be geared up to producing between 60,000 and 100,000 units of output per period, and its fixed costs will be a major determinant of this potential. However, if output falls below 60,000 units it may be necessary to close down part of the plant, dismiss executive staff, and cut fixed costs in other ways as well. On the other hand, if output exceeds 100,000 units, the need for further investment in plant and equipment, executive recruitment, and so forth must be considered; i.e. an increase in the level of fixed costs must be contemplated. (Obviously temporary fluctuations in demand will not result in drastic alterations in the capacity base, but prevailing trends over several periods are likely to have this outcome.)

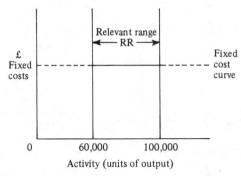

Figure 11.3 *Relevant range-fixed costs*

Graphically, the situation is shown in Fig. 11.3. Fixed costs will not change when output is within the relevant range of 60,000 to 100,000 units per period. However, at either end of this range a change in the level of fixed costs is quite possible. From this it will be appreciated that discussions of capacity (other than those concerned with further investment in new capacity or, alternatively, divestment of existing capacity) will be in relation to the relevant range.

Within the context of variable costs there is also a relevant range. Fig. 9.5 (p. 150) illustrated variable cost behaviour in a very fundamental way. However, the variable cost curve is likely to be curvilinear (as in Fig. 11.4) rather than linear (as in Fig. 9.5).

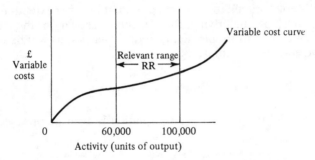

Figure 11.4 *Relevant range-variable costs*

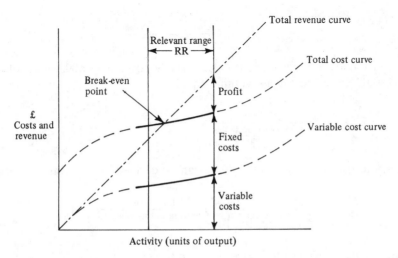

Figure 11.5 *Relevant range profitgraph*

It is conventional practice to treat variable costs as a linear function of output within the relevant range on the basis that a section from a curvilinear function approximates to a straight line. The section on which attention is focused is the relevant range representing the extremes of expected activity: a high of 100,000 units and a low of 60,000 units.

If the curves of Figs 11.3 and 11.4 are superimposed on a revenue curve (Fig. 11.1) we have the relevant range break-even chart of Fig. 11.5. This acknowledges the fact that a wide range of activity is possible, but concentrates on the cost behaviour patterns, revenue function and profit picture within the relevant range. Since the relevant range is related to available capacity and its efficient utilization, Fig. 11.5 is a more realistic device than is Fig. 11.1.

The activity level that is the basis of the measure of capacity in use (e.g. normal activity, practical capacity) bears no relationship to the break-even volume. If normal volume is the capacity measure used in connection with spreading fixed overheads it should be considerably higher than the break-even point—hopefully towards the right-hand side of the relevant range in Fig. 11.5.

C-V-P analysis is not confined to graphical presentations, but extends to the analysis of the cost relationships underlying the functions shown in the charts. These relationships are amenable to simple mathematical analysis, as will be demonstrated shortly. The basic equation is simple:*

$$\text{Sales revenue} = \text{Variable costs} + \text{Fixed costs} + \text{Profit}$$

At the break-even point profit is nil so the equation is even simpler:

$$\text{Sales revenue} = \text{Variable costs} + \text{Fixed costs}$$

In physical volume terms the break-even point can be calculated as follows:

$$\text{B-E volume} = \frac{\text{Fixed costs}}{\left(\dfrac{\text{Sales revenue} - \text{Variable costs}}{\text{Units sold}}\right)}$$

Thus, if a firm had fixed costs of £10,000, variable costs of £15,000, and sold 5,000 units for £30,000, the break-even volume equals:

$$\frac{10,000}{\left(\dfrac{30,000 - 15,000}{5,000}\right)} = 3,333 \text{ units}$$

In monetary terms the break-even volume can be derived by applying the formula:

$$\frac{\text{Fixed costs}}{1 - \left(\dfrac{\text{Variable costs}}{\text{Sales revenue}}\right)} = \frac{\text{Fixed costs}}{\text{Contribution margin ratio}}$$

and, using the data referred to above, is equal to:

$$\frac{10,000}{1 - \left(\dfrac{15,000}{30,000}\right)} = \frac{10,000}{0.5} = £20,000$$

The proof is simple. The unit price is £30,000/5,000 or £6, and the unit variable cost is £15,000/5,000 or £3. The unit *contribution* is therefore £3 (i.e. £6–£3) and sufficient units must be sold to cover the fixed costs: £10,000/3 = 3,333 units. At a selling price of £6 each the break-even sales revenue is 3,333 × £6 = £20,000.

The contribution concept is of vital importance in C-V-P analysis and marginal costing, and represents the difference between the selling price and the variable cost of an item. It is, in fact, the contribution that the sale of a product makes to fixed costs and profits *after* having covered the *avoidable* costs of that product. This point indicates the realistic perspective of C-V-P analysis in not attempting to allocate common costs to units of output since the possibility of volume variations renders a unit total cost, with its associated gross profit margin, meaningless.

*It is assumed that any mixed costs have been split into their fixed and variable elements, and shown as such.

The *contribution margin ratio* is the percentage of a volume change that is composed of variable costs. In our example the revenue from an additional sale is £6 and the additional costs, all variable, amount to £3. The contribution margin ratio is, therefore, $1 - 3/6 = 0.5$, or 50 per cent. In other words, half the revenue from changes in volume is sufficient to cover the variable costs, and the other half contributes to fixed costs and profits.

The slope of the profit curve in Fig. 11.2 is given by this ratio, indicating that (for this example) a given change in volume will cause the profit to vary accordingly by 50 per cent of the change. The assumption underlying this ratio's application is that other factors must remain constant, and it should be evident that this is a somewhat unrealistic assumption. Nevertheless, if a change in sales (in the above example) of £10,000 takes place, the change in profits will be as shown in Fig. 11.6.

	Original volume 30,000	Increase in volume +10,000	Decrease in volume −10,000
Sales	30,000	+10,000	−10,000
Variable costs	15,000	+5,000	−5,000
Fixed costs	10,000	Unchanged	Unchanged
Total costs	25,000	+5,000	−5,000
PROFIT	£5,000	£+5,000	£−5,000

Figure 11.6 *Profit-volume variations*

This shows clearly that, with a contribution margin (or profit-volume) ratio of 50 per cent, the profit variation for an upward movement is the same as that for a downward movement, except that it is positive in the former and negative in the latter, and is equal to one half of the change.

A further equation can be devised to measure the *margin of safety*. This is the excess of actual (or budgeted) sales over the break-even volume. The relevant equation is:

$$\frac{\text{Actual sales} - \text{Sales at break-even point}}{\text{Actual sales}}$$

Again, the data given earlier can be used to demonstrate the application of this equation. In monetary terms, the margin of safety is:

$$£\ \frac{30,000 - 20,000}{30,000} = \frac{1}{3} \text{ or } 33\frac{1}{3}\%$$

This ratio means that sales can fall by one-third before a loss will be incurred—assuming that the other relationships are accurately measured and remain constant.

If one considers the case of a firm with a high level of fixed costs, a small contribution margin ratio, and a low margin of safety, it is apparent that this is not a very healthy situation. Attempts should, perhaps, be made to reduce the fixed costs (i.e. the *programmed* rather than the *committed* costs), and also to increase the level of sales activity, or at least consider an increase in selling prices along with the possibility of a reduction in variable costs.

Before C-V-P analysis can be applied to particular problems it will usually be necessary to modify and manipulate the static charts such as those shown in Figs 11.1 and 11.5. This modification will centre upon the selection of the costs to be included in the analysis as this will be governed entirely by the managerial purpose of the analysis.

One of the major purposes of C-V-P analysis is to enable management to select the most desirable operating plans for achieving the firm's profit objective—under the circumstances foreseeable at the time the decision is to be made. Indeed, C-V-P analysis can be viewed as a way of translating a given objective (e.g. profit level) into a more operational sub-objective (e.g. sales volume), and thus aids planning considerably.

More specifically, C-V-P analysis can aid decision-making in the following typical areas:

- the identification of the minimum volume of business that the firm must achieve to prevent the incurrence of a loss;
- the identification of the minimum volume of business that the firm must achieve to attain its profit objective;
- the provision of an estimate of the probable profit or loss at different volumes of business within the range reasonably expected;
- the provision of data on relevant costs for special decisions relating to pricing, keeping or dropping product lines, accepting or rejecting particular orders, make or buy decisions, sales mix planning, altering plant layout, channels of distribution specification, promotional activities, and so on;
- the improving of profit performance, since the concept and behaviour of controllable profits are formulated precisely so that their practical usefulness in managerial control is clear; decisions can then be made in relation to raising/lowering selling prices, increasing volume, decreasing variable costs, and/or decreasing fixed costs;
- the formulating of long-range plans (via the insight given into cost behaviour and cost reduction possibilities rather than via profit forecasting: C-V-P analysis in this context is too simple and restrictive for longer term profit projections as it tends to assume that profit is a single-valued function of the activity rate with static conditions);
- the determining of functional relationships between activity rates, revenues, costs, and profits in such a way that standards may be set in terms of profit targets, cost levels, and contributions to facilitate subsequent control efforts.

The combination of C-V-P studies and budgets is of value in considering the range of possible outcomes. This is readily done by using preliminary budget figures as the basis for a profitgraph. If a particular budget is shown to be unsatisfactory, then the parameters can be recast until a more suitable budget results. In this way the profitgraph can conveniently report the overall profit plan to interested parties in a vivid way. One graph is easier to appreciate than is a sheet full of numbers, and has the added advantage of portraying the essential relationships in a straightforward manner.

When numerical budget statements are used for short term planning purposes, it is often helpful if they highlight the contribution margins of the various products. This is simply done by distinguishing between the variable costs and the fixed costs, with the latter being shown as a single figure, as in Fig. 11.7, which shows that the contribution margin statement can explain the cost-volume-profit behaviour in away that is not possible in the traditional 'full cost' type of statement.

	Total	Product X	Product Y	Product Z
Sales: Units	—	100	250	150
Sales revenue	£4,750	£1,000	£3,000	£750
Variable costs	£1,950	£300	£1,400	£250
Contribution	£2,800	£700	£1,600	£500
Fixed costs	£2,000			
PROFIT	£800			

Figure 11.7 *Contribution and profit statement*

Let us consider the application of C-V-P analysis to CKD Ltd. From Tables 17 and 19 (pp. 54 and 56) we can derive Fig. 11.8 which shows, for 19x5, the overall relationships among costs, volume, and profit for the company.

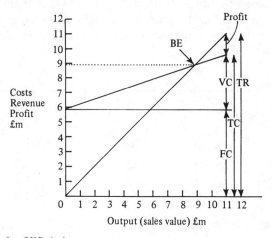

Figure 11.8 *Profitgraph for CKD Ltd*

In arithmetic terms we have:
SR = VC + FC + Profit
Where   SR = £11,007,500
           VC = £3,669,271
           FC = £5,815,889
        Profit = £1,492,340

Variable cost per £ of sales revenue is £0.336 so the break-even point is:

$$\frac{FC}{£(1.00 - 0.336)} = \frac{5,815,889}{0.664}$$

which gives us £8,758,869.
The margin of safety with which CKD is operating is:

$$\frac{£(11,007,500 - 8,758,869)}{£11,007,500} = 20\%$$

This means that sales could fall by a one-fifth before a loss would be in prospect.

With a little manipulation of data we can produce separate profitgraphs for the manufacturing and design sides of CKD's business. Using the 19x5 data, as we can see from Table 19, the costs directly attributable to these activities are:

	Manufacturing £	*Design* £
Variable costs	2,980,160	106,591
Fixed costs	2,547,940	969,809
TOTAL	5,528,100	1,076,400

However, it is necessary to split the other costs (marketing, distribution, administration, financial) between manufacturing and design to get the full picture.

We know that all the distribution and marketing costs specified in Tables 18 and 19 (pp. 55–6) are incurred for the benefit of manufacturing operations rather than design. But the costs of administration and financing are less straightforward. In Chapter 10 we assumed (see Fig. 10.10, p. 181) that £142,350 of these expenses were attributable to design services. If we assume further that 25 per cent of this total refers to variable costs and the remainder to fixed costs we can compile Fig. 11.9.

	Manufacturing operations		*Design services*	
	VC(£)	FC(£)	VC(£)	FC(£)
Manufacturing	2,980,160	2,547,940		
Design			106,591	969,809
Marketing	198,970	697,200		
Distribution	169,240	467,590		
Administration / Financial	208,723	1,026,587	35,587	106,763
TOTAL	3,557,093	4,739,317	142,178	1,076,572

Figure 11.9 *Costs by major activities, 19x5*

These calculations can then be used to produce Figs 11.10 and 11.11 when supplemented by the revenue details given in Table 17.

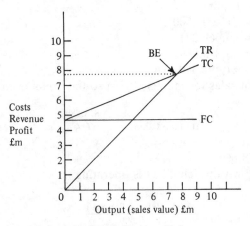

Figure 11.10 *Profitgraph for manufacturing-based activities, 19x5*

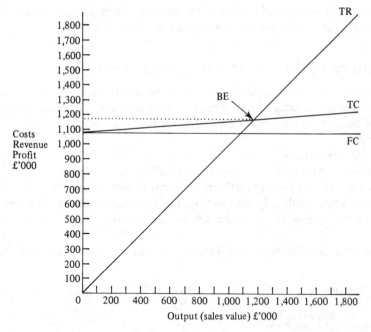

Figure 11.11 *Profitgraph for design services, 19x5*

For manufacturing-based activities the relevant figures are:
SR   £9,131,750
VC   £3,557,093
FC   £4,739,317
Profit £835,340

A break-even point can be worked out as follows:

$$\frac{FC}{\left(1 - \dfrac{VC}{SR}\right)} = \frac{4,739,317}{\left(1 - \dfrac{3,557,093}{9,131,750}\right)}$$

which gives us £7,763,009, and this in turn gives a margin of safety of

$$\frac{£(9,131,750 - 7,763,009)}{£9,131,750} = 15\%$$

By comparison, the break-even point for design services gives a much higher margin of safety. The break-even point is given by:

$$\frac{1,076,572}{\left(1 - \dfrac{142,178}{1,875,750}\right)} = £1,164,869$$

and the corresponding margin of safety is:

$$\frac{£(1,875,750 - 1,164,869)}{£1,875,750} = 38\%$$

These figures present a broad picture of the 19x5 activities, but we need to see how to proceed to generate more detailed data for decision-making.

11.3 Differential Cost and Revenue Analysis

As we saw in Chapter 9, differential costs are expected costs that differ among alternative courses of action, and similarly with revenues. It is appropriate to use differential analysis in any choice among alternatives, such as:
- make or buy
- maintain or raise prices
- accept/reject a special order below normal selling price
- retain mainframe computing facilities or adopt micro-computers.

One or two examples will help demonstrate the approach to adopt. The first relates to the costs of running a car and the second to a choice between two production methods.

Let us assume the following are the costs of running your car for 15,000 miles a year:

Petrol 750 gallons @ £2.00	£1,500
Oil changes, etc. 6 @ £10	60
Tyre wear (based on life of 20,000	
miles; a new set of 4 costs £160)	120
Regular maintenance and repair	330
Insurance	250
Washing and waxing	50
Tax	75
Garage rent and parking charges	300
Depreciation (£10,000 ÷ 4 year life)	2,500
	£5,185

Unit cost = 34.53p per mile (i.e. £5,185 ÷ 15,000)

The following questions might be posed:
1. If you drove 10,000 miles per year, what would be the average unit cost per mile? And if you drove 20,000 miles per year?
2. If you went on a 200 mile journey with a friend who agrees to share the cost of the trip, how much should the friend pay?
3. Your spouse wants a similar car for shopping and other errands that you now carry out. If you buy a second car it will be driven 3,000 miles per year, but the total mileage for both cars will still be 15,000 per year. What will be the annual cost of operating the second car? What will be the average unit cost?
4. Identify other costs of car ownership not identified so far.
5. What costs are relevant to the question of selling the car at the end of one year and using other means of transport? (Assume market value is £6,000).

The first step is to consider the behaviour patterns of the costs involved. If it is assumed that the car goes through a car wash once a week, and that parking charges are a function of mileage, we can classify costs in the following way:

Variable	*Fixed*	*Stepped*
Petrol	Insurance	Tyres
Parking charges	Tax	
Oil	Depreciation	
Maintenance	Garage rent	
	Washing	

This gives a basis for calculating the average cost per mile over a year, which, as Fig. 11.12 illustrates, is 45.1p when the annual mileage is 10,000 and 29.275p when the mileage is 20,000. In fact, the variable cost per mile is 13.4p which is the same irrespective of annual mileage. In total the fixed costs are the same (£3,175), but their impact on average unit cost depends upon the annual mileage.

	10,000 miles p.a.		20,000 miles p.a.	
Petrol	500 gals. @ £2,00	1,000	1,000 gals. @ £2.00	2,000
Oil	4 @ £10	40	8 @ £10	80
Tyre wear		80		160
Maintenance		220		440
Total VC		£1,340		£2,680
VC per mile		13.4p		13.4p
Insurance				
Washing and waxing				
Tax		3,175		3,175
Rent				
Depreciation				
Total Costs		£4,515		£5,855
Average cost per mile		45.1p		29,275p

Cost behaviour = £3,175 p.a. plus 13.4p per mile.

Figure 11.12 *Cost per mile*

The decision concerning the amount a friend should pay for a 200 mile journey is not as straightforward as it might initially appear. As a *minimum* it might reasonably be set at 50 per cent of the variable costs: $200 \times 13.4p/2 = £13.40$. On the other hand, unless the fixed costs are incurred it is impossible to use the car, so a portion of these costs might reasonably be included. As a *maximum* the figure would be:

$$\frac{\left(\dfrac{200}{15,000} \times £3,175\right) + (200 \times £0.134)}{2} = £34.53$$

This gives a range from £13.40 to £34.53 within which a choice must be made. If the trip would be undertaken with or without the friend it may be appropriate to go for the lower end of the range, but if it is being made at the friend's instigation perhaps the contribution should be towards the upper end.

Moving on to question 3, we can see from Fig. 11.13 that the variable costs are not relevant to the decision since they do not vary between owning one car or owning two cars (given the constant annual mileage). It is the fixed costs that vary: they double if one buys a second car, with the result that the cost per mile increases by a substantial amount for the second car and as an average for both cars.

	Car 1	Car 2	Total
Miles	12,000	3,000	15,000
FC	£3,175	£3,175	£6,350
VC @ £0.134	£1,608	£402	£2,010
TC	£4,783	£3,577	£8,360
Average cost per mile:	39.86p	119.23p	55.73p

In this example VC are *not* relevant: they are not affected.

Figure 11.13 *Costs of car ownership*

Apart from the costs shown in Figs 11.12 and 11.13, we need to consider the opportunity costs of travelling (e.g. whether other forms of transport exist in the locality, at what cost, and at what speed/convenience); the alternative use of the funds tied up in the car; the collision cost risk if one is only insured for fire and theft; breakdown costs (e.g. RAC or AA membership); and so on.

Finally, in response to question 6, the initial cost of the car (£10,000) is *sunk* and hence irrelevant to any subsequent decision. The relevant sum is the £6,000 that could be obtained from selling the car, and the decision about whether or not to sell must take into account the use to which this money might be put and the relative cost/convenience of travelling by car as opposed to other forms of transport.

Our second illustration concerns a toy manufacturing enterprise which plans to produce a plastic dump truck to sell at £5.00 and which has a choice of two alternative (i.e. mutually exclusive) methods of producing it.

1. Method A involves leasing a plastic moulding machine at a cost of £6,000 p.a. and entering into an annual maintenance contract which will cost £2,000 p.a.
2. Method B involves the leasing of a more expensive machine at £29,000 p.a. with an annual maintenance contract costing £3,000 p.a. However, this alternative uses less labour than Method A.

The expected costs of the two alternatives are given in Fig. 11.14.

	Method A £	Method B £	Differential cost
Annual fixed costs			
Occupancy costs	4,000	4,000	—
Lease cost	6,000	29,000	23,000
Maintenance contract	2,000	3,000	1,000
	12,000	36,000	24,000
Variable cost per unit			
Material	1.00	1.00	—
Labour	2.50	1.00	1.50
	3.50	2.00	1.50

Figure 11.14 *Costs of alternatives*

All these costs are future costs but not all are differential. Costs that do not vary between alternatives are not relevant to decision-making, so we can ignore occupancy costs (i.e. rent, etc.) and material costs. The truth of this can readily be proven, so let us do so by approaching the choice between Method A and Method B on the basis of all the available data.

If we take a pessimistic estimate of the annual sales volume for the dumper truck as being 13,000 units, the picture emerges as in Fig. 11.15.

	Method A		Method B	
Sales 13,000 @ £5.00		65,000		65,000
Fixed costs	12,000		36,000	
Variable costs:				
13,000 @ £3.50	45,500			
13,000 @ £2.00			26,000	
Total costs		57,500		62,000
PROFIT		£7,500		£3,000

Figure 11.15 *Comparative profit – 1*

In contrast, if a more optimistic sales estimate was 18,000 units p.a., this would produce a different picture as in Fig. 11.16.

	Method A		Method B	
Sales 18,000 @ £5.00		90,000		90,000
Fixed costs	12,000		36,000	
Variable costs:				
18,000 @ £3.50	63,000			
18,000 @ £2.00			36,000	
Total costs		75,000		72,000
PROFIT		£15,000		£18,000

Figure 11.16 *Comparative profit – 2*

At an annual sales volume of 13,000 units Method A is to be preferred, whereas Method B is preferable at a volume of 18,000 units p.a. This approach fails to yield a general solution, but such a solution can be achieved using differential data. In principle what we wish to identify is the *point of cost indifference*, at which the lower fixed costs of Method A are exactly offset by the lower variable costs of Method B. It is clear that A is preferable up to this point and B is preferable beyond it. Let us call this point X.

At X, the point of cost indifference, the total costs of A will equal those of B:

$$TC (A) = TC (B)$$

Since total costs consist of fixed and variable elements we have:

$$FC (A) + VC (A) = FC (B) + VC (B)$$

(We can show this graphically, as in Fig. 11.17.)

If we substitute the data from Fig. 11.14 into this equation we get:

$$£12,000 + £3.50 X = £36,000 + £2.00 X$$

which reduces to:

$$£1.50 X = £24,000$$

Therefore X = 16,000 units.

At volumes in excess of 16,000 units p.a. Method B is the best but at lower volumes Method A is the best.

However, we can prove this rather more efficiently by using the differential costs on their own:

$$X = \frac{\text{Differential FC}}{\text{Differential unit VC}} = \frac{£24,000}{£1.50} = 16,000 \text{ units.}$$

Fig. 11.18 gives a graphical portrayal of the differential cost solution.

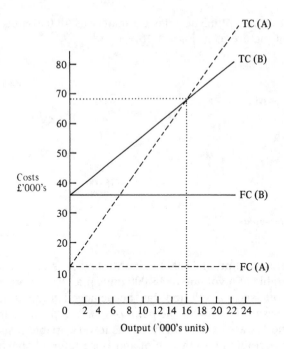

Figure 11.17 *Comparative costs*

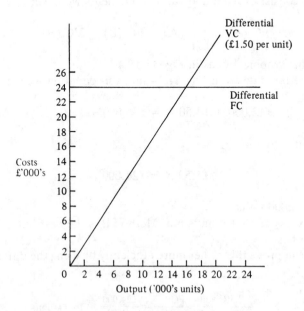

Figure 11.18 *Differential costs*

As a final aspect of this illustration we can contrast the point of cost indifference with the break-even point.

If Method A is chosen the break-even point is given by:

$$\frac{FC}{\left(\dfrac{\text{Unit SP} - \text{Unit VC}}{\text{Unit SP}}\right)} = \frac{£12,000}{£\left(\dfrac{5.00 - 3.50}{5.00}\right)}$$

which gives the BEP as £40,000 or 8,000 units.

On the other hand, for Method B the BEP is given by:

$$\frac{£36,000}{£\left(\dfrac{5.00 - 2.00}{5.00}\right)} = £60,000 \text{ or } 12,000 \text{ units.}$$

However, the point of cost indifference corresponds with neither 8,000 nor 12,000 units, being 16,000 units. At an annual sales volume of 16,000 the respective margins of safety are:

$$\text{Method A:} \quad \frac{16,000 - 8,000}{16,000} = 50\%$$

$$\text{Method B:} \quad \frac{16,000 - 12,000}{16,000} = 25\%$$

which seems to favour the former.

Apart from choosing between different ways of doing things another common decision relates to product lines—especially when a particular product line looks to be unprofitable. We may have a situation in which an enterprise has three product lines, X, Y and Z, with the cost/revenue characteristics as in Fig. 11.19.

	Product X	Product Y	Product Z	
Unit selling price	4.86	3.70	9.87	
Unit cost (fully absorbed)	4.51	3.92	7.43	
UNIT NET PROFIT	£0.35	£(0.22)	£2.42	
Annual volume (units)	15,000	12,000	9,000	*Total*
Total sales revenue	72,900	44,400	88,830	206,130
Total costs	67,650	47,040	66,870	181,560
NET PROFIT	£5,250	£(2,640)	£21,960	£ 24,570

Figure 11.19 *Net profit by product line*

The overall picture is that total revenue (£206,130) exceeds total costs (£181,560) by £24,570, but when costs are spread across the product lines it appears that product Y is unprofitable. The question, therefore, is whether or not to delete Y from the range in order to improve overall profit performance.

An answer to this question cannot be provided from the data in Fig. 11.19 since that data fails to identify the differential costs and revenues on which sound decisions must be based. A fuller breakdown of costs is needed, and this is offered in Fig. 11.20.

	Product X £	Product Y £	Product Z £	TOTAL £
DIRECT COSTS:				
Variable:				
Direct material	17,100	8,760	19,620	45,480
Direct labour	16,500	14,880	15,840	47,220
Distribution	6,750	3,000	6,750	16,500
Administration	3,450	2,040	2,790	8,280
Fixed:				
Depreciation	4,950	4,440	4,770	14,160
Total direct costs	48,750	33,120	49,770	131,640
INDIRECT COSTS:				
Variable:				
Manufacturing	8,250	7,440	7,920	23,610
Fixed:				
	10,650	6,480	9,180	26,310
Total indirect costs	18,900	13,920	17,100	49,920
Total costs	67,650	47,040	66,870	181,560

Figure 11.20 *Analysis of annual total costs by product line*

What we really need to know is: which categories of cost are differential? (Or, to put it another way, if product Y is deleted which costs will be avoided?) Taking the categories one by one it is probable that all the direct material costs can be avoided, and if specialist machinery is used for producing Y with a depreciation cost of £4,950 p.a., this can be avoided if the equipment is sold. But direct labour may not be so easy to eliminate: employees may be made redundant—at a cost—or transferred to other duties. If we assume that half these costs are avoidable then the net annual savings on direct labour would amount to £7,440. Similarly, the labour element within distribution and administration may not be wholly avoidable, so let us again assume annual savings of less than the full amount—say, 40 per cent.

Of the indirect categories of cost it is likely that some of the variable overheads (exclusive of labour) will be avoidable—75 per cent, say, of the sum apportioned to product Y. And of the remaining fixed costs, it may not be possible to avoid any in a small enterprise if just one product line is deleted.

On the basis of these assumptions and data we can present the financial evidence in a way that helps lead to a sensible decision. This is given in Fig. 11.21 which reveals that if product Y is deleted, annual sales revenue of £44,400 will no longer be received while costs of only £28,236 will be saved, thereby losing a profit contribution from Y of £16,164.

			£
Forgone revenue from product Y			
COST SAVINGS:			44,400
Direct material	(100%)	8,760	
Direct labour	(50%)	7,440	
Distribution	(40%)	1,200	
Administration	(40%)	816	
Depreciation	(100%)	4,440	
Variable overheads	(75%)	5,580	

	28,236
FORGONE PROFIT CONTRIBUTION	16,164

Figure 11.21 *Consequences of deleting product Y—1*

	Product X	Product Z	TOTAL
Sales revenue	72,900	88,830	161,730
Costs (as in Figs 11.19 and 11.20)	67,650	66,870	134,520
Unavoidable costs following deletion of Product Y: £(47,040 − 28,236)			18,804
NET PROFIT			£ 8,406

Figure 11.22 *Consequences of deleting product Y—2*

The impact of this on the overall picture is shown by a comparison of Figs 11.19 and 11.22: the original net profit of £21,960 would fall to £8,406 if product Y were deleted. This is quite a vivid illustration of how misleading cost apportionments can be in decision-making. A full cost analysis can draw one's attention (as in Fig. 11.19) to the allocation of effort among an enterprise's activities, but it does not specify the differential (or avoidable) costs and revenues of continuing to offer product Y versus deleting it from the range. It is the latter that we need to have if poor decisions are not to result.

In developing the above discussion we have not considered all the relevant issues; such as the interdependence of sales of X, Y and Z; the ability of the company to increase sales of X or Z if Y is deleted; and so forth. Obviously these matters must be taken into account. We can consider two specific issues that may be relevant in this type of context.

Assuming that the decision was made to delete product Y and that this would leave an inventory of 100 kilos of raw material A (which cost £1.00 per kilo to acquire), there may be two available alternatives:
1. sell material A back to the supplier at £0.50 per kilo;
2. use A in manufacturing product X in place of material B which is in stock (at a cost of £0.45 per kilo) and which can be purchased at £0.60 per kilo.

On the basis of costs the best solution is clear: use A as a substitute for B. The logic is simple: if A is sold back to the supplier when it could be used for making product X the company incurs an *opportunity cost* of £0.10 (i.e. £0.60 replacement cost less the sum of £0.50 per kilo that could be obtained by selling A back to the supplier). The cost of £0.45 per kilo that was paid for the inventory of B and the cost of £1.00 per kilo paid for A are good examples of *sunk costs*—they are not relevant to the decision at hand.

The other issue to consider concerns the availability of capacity. If product Y were deleted then additional capacity would become available to increase the output of X and Z. But if the company was already operating at full capacity and decided not to delete product Y, it would wish to know how best to utilize its capacity. The solution to this type of problem requires us to identify *the limiting factor* and to use this as a basis for maximizing profit per unit of the limiting factor.

Two points need to be emphasized. Firstly, the appropriate profit measure is the *contribution* (i.e. sales revenue minus variable costs) rather than the net profit figures we have seen in Fig. 11.19. Any apportionment of indirect costs will distort the picture. Secondly, consideration needs to be given to the particular factor providing the constraint which limits the enterprise's output. It could be sales potential (i.e. market capacity); or the availability of raw materials, skilled labour, machine hours, funds, and so on. (At different points in time different factors will tend to set the constraint as circumstances change).

If plant capacity (expressed in terms of machine hours) sets the constraint in our example, we need to identify the relative profit contribution of each product line per machine hour. This can be done from the data in Fig. 11.23 and the knowledge that the machine hours required to produce one unit of each product line are:

Product	Machine hours
X	1.21
Y	1.36
Z	1.94

The profit contribution per machine hour is:

Product	
X	£1.39 ÷ 1.21 = £1.15
Y	£0.69 ÷ 1.36 = £0.51
Z	£3.99 ÷ 1.94 = £2.06

from which it is evident that the manufacture and sales of Z should be favoured over X and Y because Z generates a much higher rate of profit contribution per machine hour than do the other product lines. Similarly, X would be favoured over Y even though Y itself generates a positive contribution.

	Product X £		Product Y £		Product Z £	
Selling price per unit		4.86		3.70		9.87
Variable costs per unit:						
Direct material	1.14		0.73		2.18	
Direct labour	1.10		1.24		1.76	
Manufacturing overheads	0.55		0.62		0.88	
Distribution	0.45		0.25		0.75	
Administration	0.23		0.17		0.31	
		3.47		3.01		5.88
Contribution per unit		1.39		0.69		3.99

Figure 11.23 *Profit contribution by product line*

11.4 Allowing for Risk and Uncertainty

As mentioned in the introduction to this chapter, decisions must be made in the face of imperfect knowledge about the future. One's view of the future may be characterized in terms of:

Ignorance: where the future is seen as a blank.

Assumed certainty: which is a pretence, for all practical purposes, that the future is known exactly, and estimates become deterministic.

Probability: where it is not known exactly what will happen in the future, but the various possibilities are weighted by their assumed probability of occurrence.

Uncertainty: where a variety of outcomes is possible, but probabilities cannot be assigned.

There is little that can be done in cases of ignorance other than to follow a systematic approach and attempt to delay making the decision until further information has been gathered. In cases of certainty, of course, there is no such need for delay. This covers situations in which the decision-maker has full knowledge.

In relation to decision-making under conditions of risk and uncertainty, the purpose of expressing an opinion about the likelihood of an event occurring is to facilitate the development of decision-making procedures that are explicit and consistent with the decision-maker's beliefs.

Allowing For Risk

In the risk situation *probability theory* is central in rational decision-making. The probability of a particular outcome of an event is simply the proportion of times this outcome would occur if the event were repeated a great number of times. Thus the probability of the outcome 'heads' in tossing a coin is 0.5 since a large number of tosses would result in 50 per cent heads and 50 per cent tails.

By convention, probabilities follow certain rules, such as:

- The probability assigned to each possible future event must be a positive number between zero and unity, where zero represents an impossible event and unity represents a certain one.
- If a set of events is mutually exclusive (i.e. only one will come about) and exhaustive (i.e. covers all possible outcomes), then the total of the probabilities of the events must add to one.

The probability of an outcome is a measure of the certainty of that outcome. If, for instance, a sales manager is fairly confident that his division will be able to sell 10,000 units in the forthcoming period, he may accord a probability of 0.8 to this outcome (i.e. he is 80 per cent certain that 10,000 units will be sold). By simple deduction, there is a 20 per cent probability that the outcome will be something other than 10,000 units (i.e. $100 - 80 = 20$ per cent).

One development from probability theory is the concept of *expected value*. This results from the multiplication of each possible outcome of an event by the probability of that outcome occurring, and gives a measure of the *payoff* of each choice. An example should make this situation clear.

A company has two new marketable products, but only sufficient resources to manufacture and market one of these. Estimates of sales, costs, and profits are as shown in Fig. 11.24.

	Sales £	Costs £	Profit £	Probability	Expected value £
PRODUCT A	1,000	500	500	0.1	50
	1,250	600	650	0.4	260
	1,500	700	800	0.3	240
	1,750	800	950	0.2	190
				1.0	£740
PRODUCT B	2,000	800	1,200	0.2	240
	2,300	950	1,350	0.4	540
	2,500	1,050	1,450	0.2	290
	2,700	1,150	1,550	0.1	155
	3,000	1,300	1,700	0.1	170
				1.0	£1,395

Figure 11.24 *Decision information*

The calculations are very simple. If sales of product A amount to £1,000, the associated costs as shown are £500, and thus the profit is also £500. But there is only a probability of 0.1 that this outcome will eventuate, giving an *expected value* of £50 (i.e. £500 × 0.1).

This procedure is followed for the other possible outcomes of product A sales, costs and profits, and the expected values of each outcome summated to give an expected payoff of £740. (This is nothing more than a weighted arithmetic average of the data given in Fig. 11.24).

In contrast, product B has an expected payoff of £1,395 and this choice is, therefore, the better one of the two—provided that profit is the desired objective, as measured by the payoff computation.

Apart from the externally given economic and physical conditions surrounding a decision (i.e. the 'states of nature'), the decision-maker's own attitudes towards the alternatives must also be taken into account. His or her scale of values will determine the *desirability* of each possible course of action, whereas the conventional prediction systems merely assign probabilities.

The application of simple risk analysis is best illustrated by means of an example. Let it be assumed that RST Limited has two new products, A and B, but only sufficient resources to launch one of these. The relevant states of nature relate to competitive activity: no matter which product is launched, it may be assumed that the competition will:

• do nothing; or
• introduce a comparable product; or
• introduce a superior product.

On the basis of past experience and current knowledge the management of RST Limited attach probabilities of 0.25, 0.5 and 0.25 respectively to these states of nature. In the light of these alternative conditions the profit of each strategy can be shown in a *payoff matrix* (Fig. 11.25).

This matrix shows that if product B is launched and a comparable competitive product is introduced, a profit of £20,000 will be made, and so forth for the other five possible outcomes. The best decision would appear to be to introduce product B and hope that competitive action does not change. But is this so?

STRATEGY	STATE OF NATURE		
	Do nothing	Introduce comparable product	Introduce superior product
Launch A	£40,000	£30,000	£20,000
Launch B	£70,000	£20,000	£0

Figure 11.25 *Payoff matrix*

By using the concept of expected value, it is possible to calculate the expected profit (or payoff) from each strategy by multiplying the probability of each outcome by the profit from that outcome. Thus, for strategy A (the introduction of product A), the expected payoff is given by:

$$(40,000 \times 0.25) + (30,000 \times 0.5) = (20,000 \times 0.25)$$

and is equal to £30,000.

Similarly, for strategy B the expected pay-off is:

$$(70,000 \times 0.25) + (20,000 \times 0.5) + (0 \times 0.25)$$

which equals £27,500.

This analysis clearly shows that strategy A is to be preferred as it has a larger expected profit or payoff. It is vital, however, that the distinction between the *expected* payoff and the *most probable* payoff is understood and attention focused on the former rather than the latter. The most probable payoff for strategy A is that with the competitive introduction of a comparable product, which has a probability of 0.5 and a profit estimated at £30,000. The most probable payoff for strategy B has the same state of nature, and a profit of £20,000. But the most probable outcome cannot be used as the basis for decision-making because it ignores the other possible outcomes. It is thought to be 50 per cent certain that a comparable competitive product will be launched, which means it is also 50 per cent *uncertain* that this will occur, and allowance for this eventuality should accordingly be made. The use of expected payoffs allows for this.

Allowing for Uncertainty

Uncertainty arises from a lack of previous experience and knowledge. In a new venture it is possible for uncertainty to be attached to the following factors:
• date of completion;
• level of capital outlay required;
• level of sales prices;
• level of revenue;
• level of sales volume;
• level of operating costs; and
• taxation rules.

Inevitably, decision-making under conditions of uncertainty is more complicated than is the case under risk conditions. In fact, there is no single *best* criterion (such as expected payoff) that should be used in selecting a strategy. Of the various available techniques, company policy or the decision-maker's attitude will determine that which is selected. Four possible criteria are given below.

Maximin—Criterion of Pessimism

The assumption underlying this technique is that the worst outcome will always come about and the decision-maker should therefore select the largest payoff under this assumption.

In the payoff table (Fig. 11.25) the worst outcomes are £20,000 for strategy A and £0 for strategy B. It follows that strategy A should be pursued—it is the maximum minimum (maximin). The philosophy is that the actual outcome can only be an improvement on the profit from this choice.

Maximax—Criterion of Optimism

This is the opposite of maximin and is based on the assumption that the best payoff will result from the selected strategy. Referring again to Fig. 11.25, the highest payoffs are £40,000 and £70,000 for A and B respectively. Strategy B has the highest maximum payoff and will be selected under the maximax criterion.

Criterion of Regret

This criterion is based on the fact that, having selected a strategy that does not turn out to be the best one, the decision-maker will regret not having chosen another strategy when the opportunity was available.

Thus, if strategy B had been adopted (see Fig. 11.26) on the maximax assumption that competition would do nothing, and competition actually did nothing, there would be no regret; but if strategy A had been selected the company would have lost £70,000 − £40,000 = £30,000. This measures the *regret* and the aim of the regret criterion is to minimize the maximum possible regret. A regret matrix ((Fig. 11.26) can be constructed on the above basis.

The maximum regret is, for strategy A £30,000, and for strategy B £20,000. The choice is therefore B if the maximum regret is to be minimized.

STRATEGY	STATE OF NATURE		
	Do nothing	Introduce comparable product	Introduce superior product
Launch A	£30,000	£0	£0
Launch B	£0	£10,000	£20,000

Figure 11.26 *Regret matrix*

Criterion of Rationality—Laplace Criterion

The assumption behind this criterion is that, since the probabilities of the various states of nature are not known, each state of nature is equally likely. The expected payoff from each strategy is then calculated and the one with the largest expected payoff selected.

For strategy A the expected payoff under this criterion is:

$$(40,000 \times 0.33) + (30,000 \times 0.33) + (20,000 \times 0.33)$$

which equals £30,000; and for strategy B it is:

$$(70,000 \times 0.33) + (20,000 \times 0.33) + (0 \times 0.33)$$

which is also equal to £30,000. In this example neither strategy is therefore preferable under the Laplace criterion.

Although analytical methods can be applied to the evaluation of risk and uncertainty, management may prefer to take other courses of action to reduce risk and uncertainty. Perhaps the best method is to increase the information available to the decision-maker prior to a decision being made. For instance, marketing research can supply further information prior to new product launches via product testing or test marketing.

Alternatively, the scale of operations may be increased, or product diversification pursued. Fig. 11.27 illustrates the case of two products, with product A having a seasonal demand pattern that is the opposite of the pattern of product B. But in combination Fig. 11.28 shows that the overall result is one of continuous profitability, whereas either product in isolation would result in a loss during part of its demand cycle.

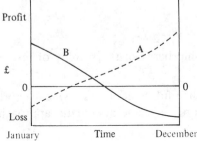

Figure 11.27 *Diversified products*

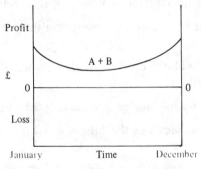

Figure 11.28 *Combined profitability*

11.5 Summary

In this chapter we have looked at the approaches to financial analysis that are intended to help managers in their decision-making endeavours.

The interplay of costs, revenue, profits and the impact of the volume of activity on these variables was discussed under the heading of cost-volume-profit analysis. In addition to having potential value for a range of specific decisions, this technique can be used to give an overview of the full range of an enterprise's activities. From it we can derive the contribution, the profit-volume ratio, the break-even point, and the margin of safety, but one does need to bear in mind the assumptions on which C-V-P analysis is based, and hence its limitations.

One significant limitation is its emphasis on the fixed-variable split. A more important distinction is that between avoidable and unavoidable costs, and this (along with revenue issues) was dealt with under the heading of differential analysis. Examples were given to show that fixed *and* variable costs can be differential, and that attempting to make decisions on the basis of full cost data is potentially very misleading. Full cost analysis can raise questions, but one needs differential analysis to provide the answers. Through this approach one can see the relevance of opportunity cost and constraining factors and the irrelevance of sunk costs.

Whatever the decision it will have implications for the future, and this requires that we tackle the problems of risk and/or uncertainty. Various approaches to these issues were discussed and illustrated.

Once decisions have been made they need to be controlled, which takes us to Chapter 12.

11.6 Exercises

Review Questions

1. Explain the relationship between the scarcity of resources and the difficulty of decision-making.

2. Is it (a) possible; (b) helpful, to adopt a *systematic* approach to decision-making? (Base your answer on a specific systematic approach that you should make explicit.)

3. What assumptions underlie cost-volume-profit analysis? Do you think that these assumptions limit the managerial usefulness of this technique?

4. Define what is meant by 'the relevant range' in the context of decision-making. Why is this significant?

5. In what ways is cost-volume-profit analysis helpful? Illustrate your answer by reference to CKD Ltd.

6. Are 'full' costs more useful for decision-making than differential costs?

7. How many alternative 'views of the future' can you propose? In what ways do they differ?

8. Are 'sunk costs' ever relevant to decision-making?

9. If it was suggested to you that you should use expected values in place of single point estimates for decision-making purposes, how would you react?

10. From a decision-making point of view, what is the distinction between the long-run and the short-run?

Problems

1. Rho Ltd—*Cost-Volume-Profit Analysis*
   Assume the following:

Present sales:	£400,000
Variable cost:	£0.75 per £ of sales
Fixed cost:	£80,000

   (a) Find the effect on profit of:
      (i) a decrease of 20 per cent in sales;
      (ii) an increase of 20 per cent in sales.

   (b) Same as (a) above except that the variable costs equal £0.60 per £ of sales.

   (c) Assuming the same data as in (a), what is the effect on profit at present unit volume of:
      (i) an increase in sales price of 10 per cent, other factors remaining the same?
      (ii) a decrease in sales price of 10 per cent, other factors remaining the same?

   (d) Assuming the same data as in (a), what is the effect on profit at present unit volume of:
      (i) an increase of 6 per cent in the variable cost?
      (ii) a decrease of 6 per cent in the variable cost?

   (e) Assuming the same data as in (a), what is the effect on profit at present unit volume of:
      (i) an increase of 10 per cent in the fixed cost?
      (ii) a decrease of 10 per cent in the fixed cost?

2. Production and other operating data for Kay (Chronometers) Ltd last year was as follows:

Sales (units)	100,000
Selling price per unit	£16
Production (units)	120,000
Opening inventory	0
Manufacturing cost per unit:	
Direct material	£4
Direct labour	£6
Variable overheads	£1
Fixed overheads	£3
Marketing & Administrative costs:	
Variable	£50,000
Fixed	£80,000

   (a) Calculate the company's profit under:
      (i) absorption costing;
      (ii) variable costing;
   and explain the difference.

   (b) Determine the company's:
       (i)   break-even point;
       (ii) margin of safety.

3. Briar Ltd manufacture high-quality, hand-made pipes, and have experienced a
   steady growth in sales over the past 5 years. However, increased competition has
   led the managing director, Mr Bruno Condor, to believe that an aggressive
   advertising campaign will be necessary in 1988 to maintain Briar's present growth
   rate.
       To prepare for next year's advertising campaign, the company's accountant has
   prepared the following data for Mr Condor relating to 1987. (Briar Ltd operates on
   a calendar year basis).

Cost schedule

	£
Variable costs:	
Direct labour	8.00 per pipe
Direct materials	3.25 per pipe
Variable overheads	2.50 per pipe
Total variable costs	£13.75 per pipe
Fixed costs:	
Manufacturing	25,000
Selling	40,000
Administrative	70,000
Total fixed costs	£135,000
Selling price	£25.00 per pipe
Expected sales (1987) 20,000 units	£500,000
Tax rate: 40%	

Bruno Condor has set the sales target for 1988 at a level of £550,000 (i.e. 22,000
pipes @ £25.00).
(a) What is the projected after-tax net income of Briar Ltd for each of 1983 and
    1988?
(b) What is the break-even point (in units) for each of 1987 and 1988?
(c) Mr Condor believes that an additional outlay of £11,250 for advertising in 1988
    (with other costs remaining constant) will be needed to achieve the sales
    target set for that year. What will be the after-tax net income for 1988 if this
    additional £11,250 is spent?
(d) What will be the break-even point (in £s) for 1988 if the additional £11,250 is
    spent?
(e) Assuming the advertising campaign is undertaken, what is the required 1988
    sales level (in £s) to equal 1987's after-tax net income?
(f) At a sales level of 22,000 units, what is the maximum amount that can be spent
    on advertising if an after-tax net income of £60,000 is desired?
(g) What are the major weaknesses in the approaches you have adopted in
    answering (a) to (f) above?

4. The Capital Motor Co. Ltd recently suffered a strike that lasted for two weeks.
   During that time no motor cars were produced. The company issued a press
   statement to the effect that the cost of the strike was £5,000,000. This figure was
   estimated on the basis of lost production of 1,000 vehicles, each of which could
   have been sold for £5,000, a total loss of turnover of £5,000,000.

The company's accountant, however, feels that this figure overstates the cost of the strike, and produced the following statement to support his view:

Expenses avoided	£
Materials (£1,000 per car)	1,000,000
Production labour (£500 per car)	500,000
Depreciation of machinery	1,750,000
Overheads: 200% on production labour	1,000,000
	4,250,000
Loss of sales revenue	5,000,000
Cost of strike	£750,000

The following additional information is available:

(i) Depreciation of machinery is based on the straight-line method of calculation. However, the plant manager estimates that the machinery will fall in value by £200,000 each week regardless of the level of production. He feels that, in addition, its value will fall by £150,000 for each 100 cars that are produced.

(ii) Overhead expenses are recovered at the rate of 200 per cent on production labour. Most of the overhead expenses are unaffected by the level of production, for example rent, rates, maintenance and staff wages, but some, such as power and lighting, vary directly with production. The general manager estimates that the latter type of overhead expense amounts to £10,000 for every 100 cars produced.

(iii) During the period of the strike the maintenance staff, whose wages are included in the fixed overhead expense, carried out a major overhaul on one of the company's machines using materials costing £10,000. This overhaul would normally have been performed by an outside contractor at a price, including materials, of £100,000.

(iv) The sales manager feels that about one half of the production lost could be made up and sold in the next month by the production labour working overtime. Labour is paid at the rate of time and one half for overtime working.

Does the press statement or the accountant's revised statement properly reflect the cost of the strike to Capital Motor Co Ltd?

5. Stanbridge & Partners manufacture rotary clothes driers. Last July the firm made a batch of 10,000 units that turned out to be defective. The total cost of the batch was £50,000.
   Two options seem to be available:
   (i) to sell the batch in its present state for £2.50 per unit; or
   (ii) to correct the defects at an estimated unit cost of £3.00 and then to sell the batch at the normal price of £7.50 per unit.
   (a) State (with reasons) which option the firm should choose.
   (b) If the correcting of defective units meant forgoing the manufacture of a further batch of 20,000 units, which option would you then favour?

6. Woodhouse & Co. manufacture a range of kitchen utensils. The firm's approach to setting prices is to add a profit mark-up to the full cost of each product line, and data relating to the year just finishing is given below for item X (which sells at a steady rate of 5,000 units p.a.):

	Unit cost
Direct materials cost	1.50
Direct labour cost	3.00
Indirect manufacturing cost	2.50
Marketing and administrative cost	1.50
Full cost	8.50
Profit mark-up (10% of full cost)	0.85
Selling price	£9.35

It is estimated that the direct costs will increase next year by 10 per cent for materials and 5 per cent for labour, while indirect manufacturing costs are likely to increase by £4,000 in total. Marketing and administrative costs are not expected to change, and the level of demand for item X is expected to remain at 5,000 units.

Using the same approach to pricing as shown above, what will be the price of item X next year?

11.7 Further Reading

Cooke, S., & N. Slack (1984) *Making Management Decisions*, London: Prentice-Hall International.
A broad-based text that encompasses behavioural and quantitative approaches to decision-making.

De Coster, D.T., & E.L. Schafer (1979), *Management Accounting: A Decision Emphasis*, New York: Wiley. (2nd edition)
This is a well-written book with clear explanations and illustrations showing how to use management accounting data in decision-making.

Moore, P.G., & H. Thomas (1976), *The Anatomy of Decisions*, Harmondsworth: Penguin.
An excellent introductory text dealing with quantitative approaches to decision-making.

Rappaport, A. (editor) (1975), *Information for Decision-Making*, Englewood Cliffs, N.J.: Prentice-Hall. (2nd edition)
This is a valuable anthology of authoritative contributions—both behavioural and quantitative—to decision-making.

Tucker, S.A. (1980), *Profit Planning through the Break-Even System*, Aldershot: Gower.
This text shows how to apply cost-volume-profit analysis in a wide range of business situations.

Welsch, L.A., & R.M. Cyert (eds.) (1970), *Management Decision Making*, Harmondsworth: Penguin.
A collection of influential articles that emphasize a behavioural approach to decision-making.

Chapter 12

———Control———

12.1 Introduction

If progress towards the attainment of objectives is to be achieved it must be observed and measured: there must be some idea of where an enterprise is relative to where it ought to be, thus giving a basis for corrective action. This is the domain of control.

Control can be facilitated by responsibility accounting (which was introduced in Chapter 9). In essence, this is an approach in which costs, revenues and profits are monitored in accordance with organizational responsibilities.

The fact that control is one of the most pervasive elements in business success requires that it be soundly based on:

- a clearly-defined organizational structure;
- equitable standards of performance; and
- regular and constructive appraisal of attainment.

Any manager seeking to exercise control must appreciate that any particular system only serves to assist. The system itself is *not* control, and for any control system to be effective it is necessary for those who will be held accountable to be given every opportunity to contribute to the formulation of their own commitments (by which their performance will be evaluated).

Complete control can never be achieved purely on the strength of quantitative information. However, financial analysis does provide a suitable quantitative base to which the manager can add both qualitative data and other quantitative factors to help formulate control action.

Accounting is useful in the control process in three major ways:

- as a means of *communicating* information on what management wants done;
- as a means of *motivating* the organization to act in ways most likely to attain the objectives of the business; and
- as a means of *appraising performance* and *reporting* on performance to those concerned.

In addition, control information can be used as a basis for future planning (but it must be emphasized that the aim of control is not to correct past mistakes: it is rather to guide current and future activities to achieve corporate objectives).

In control accounting the criterion of comparability is important. This demands uniformity and consistency in the accounting system in order that co-ordination may be established between goals and control feedbacks. Given this co-ordination and comparability, the extraction of variances will permit:

- self-appraisal by lower management;
- subordinate appraisal by top management; and

- activity appraisal by top management (to evaluate the performance of the overall range of corporate activities).

The need for delegation of responsibility in an organization leads to the presumption that a good control system should rely heavily on self-correction.

These introductory remarks can be summarized in the following keys to control:

What to Measure

Many companies tend only to measure material factors (such as time and physical quantities) that can readily be expressed in production or financial terms. However, it is important that certain non-material factors should also be measured—especially those indicating the performance of responsible individuals throughout the company. (Relevant examples would be quality levels, the number of new customer accounts opened, the speed of service, market share details, productivity, absenteeism, etc.) Apart from including non-financial data as well as financial data, it is equally important that information relating to external matters be collected as rigorously as internally generated data. Moreover, an obvious requirement in any system is that measurement must be designed to aid interpretation.

Interpretation

This is the essential link between reporting and decision-making. The demands on top management's time are such that reports should both present and interpret the exception. Where practicable, trends should be displayed graphically—for instance, the level of manufacturing overheads in relation to productive activity—to permit instant appreciation.

Selectivity

Control can break down because management attempts to control too much, with the really important issues becoming submerged in a mass of irrelevancies. In any series of elements to be controlled a small fraction (in terms of elements) will always account for a large fraction (in terms of effects). This tendency is known as *Pareto's law*, one example being the frequently met 80/20 rule in which, say, 80 per cent of a company's sales are accounted for by 20 per cent of its customers. Identifying the critical elements of performance that exert the greatest influence on the attainment of objectives is a basic task in management control. It is generally considered that between four and six factors constitute the causes of corporate success—provided the company is able to select the appropriate factors, and do these four to six things extremely well. In practice, many companies attempt to control many factors that are unimportant in a control sense because their behaviour patterns follow those of other more essential factors. Information systems must highlight the critical factors that govern the company's success.

Accountability and Controllability

Information must be keyed to those individuals who are responsible for achieving results. It has been emphasized in the sections on responsibility accounting that an individual should only be held responsible (i.e. accountable) for results when the following conditions prevail:

- he or she knows what achievements are expected;
- he or she knows what is actually being achieved; and, of greatest importance,
- it is within the individual's power to regulate what is happening.

When all these conditions do not exist simultaneously it may be unjust and ineffective to hold an individual responsible for the level of costs, revenue, or profit that has been achieved.

With these four keys as the background, the financial analyst's responsibilities in relation to control procedures will centre upon:

- the selection of key factors and control points;
- the segregation of non-controllable factors so that the picture of the controllable aspects is not confused;
- relating the plans and controls to individual accountability at the various managerial levels;
- ensuring that the setting of standards meets the needs of the control system, and can be built into departmental plans;
- designing the financial reporting system for the effective display of feed-back data.

From a planning point of view responsibility accounting is important because, being based on clearly defined areas of responsibility, it enables responsible individuals to play the major role in planning. Regardless of size, planning only makes sense if all levels of management are involved. Thus the managers who are held responsible for performance have a right to participate in setting the goals and levels of performance that they must achieve as part of the overall corporate effort. In this way, human relations should be improved through greater involvement, more job satisfaction, and the avoidance of duplicated effort which may otherwise create clashes.

12.2 Organizational Issues

The implications of fixing responsibility are as follows:

- The organizational structure must be clearly defined, and responsibility delegated so that each person knows his or her role.
- The extent and limits of functional control must be determined.
- The responsible individuals should be fully involved in preparing plans if they are to be held responsible for results.
- Responsible individuals must be serviced with regular performance reports.
- Means must be established to enable plans to be revised in line with actual performance in such a way that responsible individuals are involved.
- Every item should be the responsibility of some individual within the organization.

The ability to delegate is a sign of a good manager, and responsibility accounting facilitates this. Specfically, charging managers with responsibility for a segment of the business is the best known way of ensuring that they perform satisfactorily.

A responsibility centre is made up of various cost and revenue items for which a given individual is responsible. It is consequently a personalized concept that may be made up of one or more of the following:

- a cost centre;
- a profit centre;

- an investment centre.

Let us look at each of these in turn.

A cost (or expense) centre is the smallest segment of activity, or area of responsibility, for which costs are accumulated. In some cases the cost centre may correspond with a department, but in others a department may contain several cost centres. The milling machines in a machine shop can be viewed as one cost centre of an engineering company, but the machine shop will also have other cost centres within it (such as turret lathes and auto-robots). A cost centre is not essentially a personalized concept, but it may be any specified area of activity for which it is desired to accumulate cost data, and may be of any of the following types:

- Production cost centre, such as assembly departments and finishing departments.
- Service cost centre, such as personnel, accounting, and utility departments that are necessary but not directly productive.
- Ancillary manufacturing centres, such as those concerned with producing packing materials.

A cost centre may be created for cost control purposes whenever management feels that the usefulness of accumulating costs for the activity in question justifies the necessary effort.

Only input costs are measured for this organizational unit: even though there is some output, this is not measured in revenue terms. Thus a production unit will produce x units at a given total (or unit) cost, with the output being expressed either as a quantity or in terms of input costs.

A profit centre is a segment, department, or division of an enterprise that is responsible for both revenue and expenditure. This is the major organizational device employed to facilitate decentralization (the essence of which is the freedom to make decisions).

Among the arguments favouring decentralized profit responsibility are:

- a divisional manager is only in a position to make satisfactory trade-offs between revenues and costs when expected to take responsibility for the profit outcome of his or her decisions (failing which it is necessary for many day-to-day decisions to be centrally regulated);
- a manager's performance can be evaluated more precisely if he or she has complete operating responsibility;
- managers' motivation will be higher if they have greater autonomy;
- the contribution of each division to corporate profit can be seen via divisional profit reports.

The advantages of profit centres are that they resemble miniature businesses and are a good training ground for potential general managers.

An investment centre is a segment, department, or division of an enterprise that is not only responsible for profit (i.e. for revenue and expenditure) but which also has its success measured by the relationship of its profit to the capital invested within it (i.e. profitability). This is most commonly measured by means of the rate of return on investment (ROI).

The logic behind this concept is that assets are used to generate profits, and the decentralizing of profit responsibility usually requires the decentralization of control over many of a company's assets. The ultimate test, therefore, is the relationship of profit to invested capital within a division. Much of its appeal lies in the apparent ease with which one can compare a division's ROI with earnings opportunities elsewhere—inside or outside the company. However, ROI is an imperfect measure and needs to be used with some scepticism, and in conjunction with other performance measurements.

Apart from ROI an investment centre may be assessed on the basis of *residual income*. This can be defined as the operating profit, or income, of an investment centre less the imputed interest on the assets used by the centre. An example can indicate the difference between the two approaches. If Division A and Division B operate in the same type of business with the same circumstances, but Division A's performance is assessed by ROI and Division B's by residual income, we might have the picture shown in Fig. 12.1. If the manager of Division B was to maximize residual income, his activities would expand as long as the division earned a rate in excess of the imputed charge for invested capital. In other words, the manager of Division B would expand as long as his incremental opportunities earned 16 per cent or more on his incremental assets.

	Division A	Division B
	£	£
(1) Operating income	25,000	25,000
(2) Imputed interest at 16% of assets		16,000
(3) Operating assets	100,000	100,000
ROI [(1) ÷ (3)]	25%	
Residual income [(1) − (2)]		9,000

Figure 12.1 *Residual income* vs *ROI*

In contrast, if managers are expected to maximize ROI this could induce managers of highly profitable divisions to reject projects that might be highly acceptable from the point of view of the organization as a whole. Thus the manager of Division A would be unhappy to accept a new project returning less than 25 per cent, since this would reduce the average ROI even though 16 per cent is regarded by top management as an acceptable rate. The residual income manager, as we have seen, would accept all projects earning 16 per cent or more.

Before moving on to consider the setting of standards perhaps a few words should be said concerning controllable *vs* uncontrollable costs within the context of responsibility accounting.

Controllable costs (and controllable revenues or profits) are those that can be directly regulated by a given individual within a given period of time.

The division of costs into controllable and uncontrollable categories is important in order that performance levels may be evaluated and also for securing the co-operation of managers at all levels. The manager who is involved in planning his performance level in the knowledge that those controllable costs for which he or she is responsible will be monitored, accumulated, and reported is likely to be motivated towards attaining the predetermined level of performance. In this way it can be seen that the collecting of controllable costs by responsibility centres serves as a motivating force as well as an appraisal mechanism.

While the ideal procedure is for each responsibility centre to be assigned those costs over which it has sole control and for which it is therefore responsible, in practical terms this cannot usually be achieved. It is rare for an individual to have complete control over all the factors that influence a given cost element. For example, a foreman cannot have control over wage rates since these are typically determined through negotiations between unions and management. Nevertheless, the foreman will be held responsible for the total wages bill of his department which means that he must attempt to control his costs by limiting overtime and otherwise regulating the number of hours worked.

Apart from those costs over which a responsible individual actually has control, the responsibility centre may be charged with costs that are beyond that individual's direct control and influence but about which management wishes him or her to be concerned. A good example is the cost of a company's personnel department: an operating manager may be charged with a proportion of the personnel department's costs on the grounds that either:

- He or she will be careful about making unnecessary requests for the services of the personnel department if made to feel somewhat responsible for its level of costs; or
- He or she may try to influence the personnel manager to exercise firm control over the department's costs.

Allocating general overheads to responsibility centres is done by many companies which practise responsibility accounting (and which therefore recognize that such costs are beyond the control of those to whom they are allocated) on the grounds that each responsible individual will be able to see the magnitude of the indirect costs that are incurred to support the unit. There is a major disadvantage that should be seriously considered: the manager of a small responsibility centre incurring directly controllable costs at his or her level in a given time period of, say, £10,000 may be allocated £45,000 of general overhead costs. In relation to the overall level of overhead costs, the manager may feel that those costs for which he or she is responsible are so insignificant that he or she may give up trying to control them. The point to note is that each cost must be made the responsibility of whoever can best influence its behaviour, and allocating costs beyond this achieves at best very little from a control viewpoint and may be distinctly harmful to the cost control effort.

Guidelines that have been established for deciding which costs can appropriately be charged to a responsibility centre are:

1. If an individual has authority over both the acquisition and the use of a cost incurring activity, then his or her responsibility centre should bear the cost of that activity.
2. If an individual does not have sole responsibility for a given cost item but is able to influence to a significant extent the amount of cost incurred through his or her own actions, then he or she may reasonably be charged with the cost.
3. Even if an individual cannot significantly influence the amount of cost through direct action, he or she may be charged with a portion of those elements of cost with which management wishes that individual to be concerned, in order that he or she may help influence those who are more directly responsible.

12.3 Setting Standards

We have seen that control involves guiding current and future activities in the light of desired outcomes, expectations regarding the future, and experience from the past. These desired outcomes are represented by the enterprise's objectives and the plan by which the objectives might be attained. Their specification enables the individual to know in advance what is expected and how performance will be assessed.

Establishing standards of performance is part of the larger problem of motivating individuals towards goal-striving behaviour. The standards and plans are not the goals—they are the agreed means by which the goals may be achieved. The ideal situation is that in which a control system is so designed that it leads people to take actions that are not only in their own self-interests but also in the interests of the company.

This process is facilitated by considering the *aspiration levels* of the firm's decision-makers. The relationship between motivation and levels of aspiration is fairly clear, and revolves around past success/failures and future hopes. Sufficient flexibility should therefore be built into the setting of standards to improve motivation by either upwards or downwards movements of targets in order to achieve continuous improvements in performance.

For example, a manager may fail to reach the established plan for reasons beyond his or her control. As a result, the level of aspiration will tend to fall, and motivation will drop accordingly. If this process is to be reversed, a new standard should be set that is attainable (while maintaining an efficient level of performance). If this is done realistically, it should improve the manager's motivation by equating a reasonable standard with his or her aspiration level.

In essence, the standard should specify what the performance should be under prevailing conditions. For deriving company-wide ROI standards the emphasis should be on *external* parameters taking account of:

- the achieved ROI of successful competitors in the same industry;
- the ROI of other leading companies, operating under similar risk and skill circumstances;
- the position of the company in its own industry, bearing in mind the degree of competitiveness;
- the level of risk faced, with higher risk usually requiring a higher ROI from the investor's point of view; and
- the 'expected' ROI—as seen by such groups as trade unions, the financial establishment, creditors, etc.

The actual determination of a specific ROI is not easy, especially in view of the weaknesses of some of the above items of comparison. The average ROI for the industry, or even the ROI of the most successful member firm, is not necessarily *efficient*. This requires that the individual firm also considers its own *internal* abilities and resources in arriving at the final standard.

In connection with more detailed standards of performance, the bases should emphasize *internal* parameters. If this is not so, the standards will not reflect the firm's particular operating circumstances.

Past performance may be a useful basis for determining operating standards, but the danger is that it includes inefficiencies that should not be perpetuated. Current conditions and future expectations are of greater relevance since an attainable level of efficiency can be incorporated into the standards as these conditions dictate.

Attainability is an important dimension of any realistic standard. If standards do not reflect both current and efficient levels of performance, as well as individual aspiration levels, they are not likely to be attainable or to motivate.

The 'ideal' standard of the industrial engineer is not a reasonably attainable level of performance, as it describes a perfect situation. Real-life business conditions are anything but perfect, requiring that the ideal gives way to built-in flexibility to accommodate varying circumstances.

In summary, detailed standards for performance measurement should be internally derived, currently attainable, flexible, and agreed with those who are to be held responsible for their attainment.

Statistical methods have proved to be helpful in setting standards involving a high degree of precision (e.g. for repetitive but small tasks as in a manufacturing situation relating to material or labour input). However, the tendency to use such techniques to set standards that are too tight for a reasonable expectation of achievement is similar to the mistake of the industrial engineer in setting ideal standards (by, for instance, over-precise work study methods). The aim is presumably to reduce costs, but the result is a confusion of the objectives of cost reduction and cost control. *Cost reduction* is practised through value analysis, improved factory layout, the introduction of superior working methods, and so on. On the other hand, *cost control* exists to maintain conformity between actual and planned results. Standards must be amended to reflect the results of cost reduction efforts whereas cost control takes place within the framework of established standards.

In building up budgets (whether they are based on the aggregation of detailed cost standards or on larger 'building blocks', such as charges for rent, rates, and so on) it will be necessary to make assumptions regarding the level of activity/capacity utilization that is likely to be experienced during the period to which the budget will relate. A problem arises here due to the uncertainty surrounding the level of activity that may be experienced: a 'good' budget should be able to accommodate varying circumstances by adapting to significant changes in the enterprise's operating conditions. If this is not done it will mean that a manager's actual performance at an achieved level of activity will be compared with a budget relating to a different level of activity. While this is informative in connection with assessing the accuracy of forecasts, it is not very helpful in appraising the efficiency of performance. What is needed is a *flexible budget* which can be contrasted with a *fixed budget*.

Fixed budget

The fixed (or static) budget is the easiest to prepare, with the costs for the period being budgeted on the basis of some chosen level of (expected) activity. The actual costs are then compared with the budget, and the variances reported to the managers

	Budget	Actual	Variance
Sales (units)	10,000	11,000	+ 1,000
Sales revenue	£15,000	£16,500	+£1,500
Expenditure:			
Direct	10,000	11,000	+ 1,000
Indirect	4,000	4,200	+ 200
Profit	£1,000	£1,300	+£ 300

Figure 12.2 *Fixed budget*

concerned. No matter what the actual level of activity, the fixed budget remains unmodified and therefore the comparison may be between widely differing levels of activity. This is illustrated in Fig. 12.2.

It is obviously inappropriate to compare the costs for sales of 10,000 units with those for 11,000 units, as some of the costs will vary with the level of activity. The basis for true comparison, hence control, should be the flexible budget.

Flexible Budget

The word 'flexible' refers to the fact that the budgeted cost is adjusted according to the level of activity experienced in the budget period. This provides management with several estimates of expense (and revenue) for varying volumes of sales and production. In essence, a flexible budget is a series of fixed budgets for the range of possible levels of activity that are most likely to arise. The first estimate will usually be based on *normal* activity and the other estimates will be for levels above and below this norm: e.g., 10, 15 and 20 per cent above/below normal volume.

The major advantage of the flexible budget over the fixed is its ability to specify the budgeted level of costs *without revision* when sales and production programmes are changed. It does this (as shown in Fig. 12.3) by distinguishing between those costs that vary with changes in the level of activity and those that do not. In other words, it is based on a thorough knowledge of cost behaviour patterns.

	Fixed budget	Flexible budget	Actual	Variance
Sales (units)	10,000	11,000	11,000	—
Sales revenue	£15,000	£16,500	£16,500	—
Expenditure:				
Direct	10,000	11,000	11,000	—
Fixed indirect	1,500	1,500	1,500	—
Variable indirect	2,000	2,200	2,190	−10
Mixed indirect	500	520	510	−10
Profit	£ 1,000	£ 1,280	£ 1,300	+20

Figure 12.3 *Flexible budget*

This improved way of showing actual versus budgeted results illustrates that the excess indirect expenditure of £200 shown in Fig. 12.2 is, in fact, a cost *saving* of £20. It is vital to look at the constituent elements of indirect expense to arrive at this conclusion. Variable costs will tend to remain constant *per unit of output* whereas fixed costs will tend to remain constant *in total*.

Although they do provide a dynamic base for comparative purposes, flexible budgets are usually only valid within the relevant range. Within this range, the straightforward comparison of 'actual' with 'budget for actual' (i.e. the use of a flexible budget) indicates an achieved level of efficiency but does not indicate the target level that should have been achieved. In Fig. 12.3 the full picture is given because the *target* sales level is shown (i.e. 10,000 units) as well as the control information revealed by the use of the flexible budget for the *actual* level of 11,000 units.

Flexible budgets are usually only applied to overhead items since direct material and direct labour expenditure will usually be based on standard costs. Nevertheless, it is possible to construct an overall flexible budget that includes direct as well as indirect costs. Additional flexibility can be achieved via factors that are collateral to the budget, such as maximum and minimum limits on finished stock levels.

It is not surprising that C-V-P analysis has been compared with flexible budgeting in being able to show what the cost picture should be for a given sales volume. There is no doubt that in association with flexible budgeting, C-V-P analysis is very much strengthened as a management tool, but the two techniques should be distinguished from each other.

12.4 Variance Analysis

When actual results are compared with budgeted figures any discrepancy is called a *variance*. The identification and investigation of variances is of managerial concern for such reasons as:

- to highlight errors in budgeting procedures (e.g. the use of fixed budgets);
- to indicate the need for budget revisions (e.g. inappropriate standards);
- to pinpoint those activities requiring remedial attention.

The principle of *management by exception* should be applied in analysing variances to ensure that it is only the significant variances that are investigated.

Management by exception is a principle that stands out in a systematic approach to control. A control system operated on this principle is one in which management's attention is drawn to the relatively small number of items having significant variances from plan. Consequently, little attention needs to be paid to the relatively large number of items conforming to plan. This permits managers to focus their attention on planning for the future, instead of becoming submerged in day-to-day trivia. Past events cannot be altered—only their impact on the future can be affected by management action. Management by exception is the means to optimizing future operations on the basis of knowledge from the past.

It cannot be expected that standards will be met perfectly, so some measure of the significance of results *vis-à-vis* standards must be developed. This involves the setting of *tolerance limits* with results falling beyond these limits being the subject of control and investigation, while those falling within the limits are accepted as being satisfactory.

The tolerance range should not be so broad as to excuse all levels of performance, nor so narrow as to cause control action to be instigated too frequently.

The basic instrument of control in this respect is the statistical control chart (see Fig. 12.4). This allows successive levels of performance for a particular factor to be observed in relation to standards and tolerance limits. The example given in Fig. 12.4 illustrates the control of advertising expenditure. As a percentage of sales revenue this is allowed to fluctuate around a standard of 10 per cent, but as soon as it exceeds a tolerance of 2 per cent either way it is investigated to identify the cause. The reason may be, in this example, the entry into the market of a new competitor causing an increase in advertising effort on the part of the company to regain lost sales. (The ratio can vary through either constant sales levels with varying advertising expenditure, or constant advertising with changing sales.) A change in prevailing conditions should result in a reassessment of the standard and a modification of the levels of tolerance.

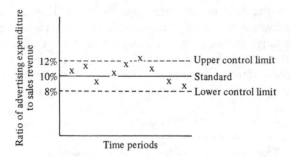

Figure 12.4 *Statistical control chart*

The statistical control chart is based on the well-known statistical principle that *significant variances* are those that do not arise purely through chance circumstances. Consequently, the tolerance range should be sufficiently wide to accommodate variations from standard that are purely due to chance. The assumption is that results falling beyond the tolerance limits are attributable to controllable causes and not to chance, and are therefore worthy of investigation.

Standards and budget allowances are both measures of what costs should be, and the variance between the standard or budget figure and the actual figure is an indication of the level of efficiency that has been achieved.

However, if the standard was not set properly, or conditions have changed since it was set, then any comparison with actual may result in variances that are meaningless. Having determined that standards are acceptable, the analyst should separate, for each level to which he or she reports, the controllable from the uncontrollable variances. Only the controllable variances should be reported to operating management, and reported in such a way that it is clear *where* each variance arose, *who* was responsible, and *why* it happened.

The two most important requirements of variance analysis as an aid to the control effort are to personalize the variances according to responsibility and to have some measure of the significance of each variance (i.e. the tolerance limits discussed above).

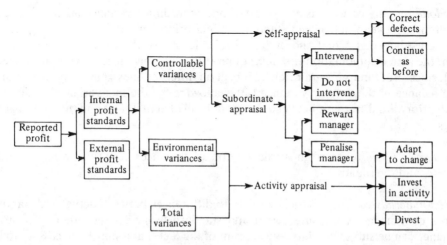

Figure 12.5 *Appraisal of profit performance*

This emphasizes the role of variance analysis in motivating and evaluating the performance of individual managers, but variance analysis is also important in a wider respect in controlling profits. Fig. 12.5 indicates how these two purposes are interrelated. (It also shows the way in which inter-firm comparisons may be made.)

Taking the box of 'controllable variances' from Fig. 12.5, these can be classified into four groups, relating to materials, labour, overheads, and sales.

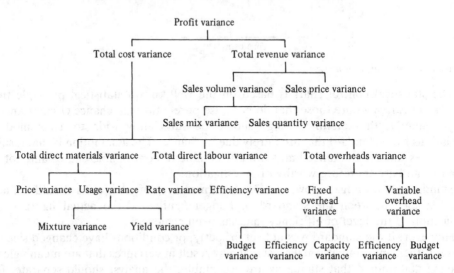

Figure 12.6 *Hierarchy of variances*

Diagrammatically, the variances are detailed in Fig. 12.6. (This selection, while not exhaustive, indicates the most frequently used variances.) The nature of each is briefly outlined below:

The profit variance is the total difference between the actual and the budgeted profit for the budgeted level of activity.

The total revenue variance is composed of one subordinate variance arising through a difference between actual and standard selling prices and another resulting from a difference between actual and budgeted sales levels. In the case of a multi-product firm, the actual combination (i.e. mix) of products sold may differ from that budgeted and, since profit margins are rarely identical on different lines, a mix variance results. The balance of the volume variance (after allowing for the mix variance) is due to a straightforward difference between the profit level of actual sales and that of budgeted sales.

The total cost variance is an amalgamation of variances resulting from materials, labour, and overheads.

Direct materials variances basically relate to differences between actual and standard prices on the one hand, and actual and standard usage on the other. The usage variance can be sub-divided to take account of the fact that it may be necessary to use a non-standard mix (e.g. when there is a shortage of standard materials, substitute materials costing either more or less may be used), and also that losses arise in certain manufacturing processes (such as chemical production) so that a yield of 100 per cent of the inputs is not obtained.

Direct labour variances are similar to the major direct material variances. If the actual rate differs from the standard labour rate then a rate variance will arise. If more (or less) labour hours are used than should have been used, an efficiency variance will result. (Of course, when more hours are used than standard this is strictly an *inefficiency* variance.)

Overhead variances relate to either variable or fixed overheads. In the case of either, however, a budget variance arises when the actual price paid for a factor is other than the budgeted price. In addition, since separate rates will have to be calculated, separate efficiency variances can be reported. The difference between actual hours (either machine or labour) and standard hours will result in a fixed overhead efficiency variance. This is derived from the formula:

$$(\text{Actual hours} - \text{Standard hours}) \times \text{Fixed overhead rate}$$

The variable overhead efficiency variance is analogous to the labour efficiency and material usage variances, and arises when a larger than standard 'dose' of variable overheads is consumed. The capacity (or volume) variance is purely a function of fixed costs and arises when the level of activity exceeds or falls short of normal volume.

Before variances can be used in the control process, management must understand what they mean. The direct materials price variance indicates that the terms the firm actually received in purchasing raw materials differed from those it expected. This may be good or bad, depending on whether the actual terms were better or worse than anticipated, and on how much they were better or worse. If the variance exceeds its tolerance (say 2 per cent of standard price, or £10, whichever is the smaller), then the chief purchasing officer is the only person who can be held responsible. Similarly, the direct labour rate variance is the responsibility of either the works manager (in so far as it relates to the working of more or less overtime than was budgeted) or the personnel officer (in so far as it relates to negotiated changes in labour rates that have not yet been incorporated into the standards).

Direct material usage, direct labour efficiency and variable overhead efficiency variances are all *prima facie* the responsibility of works management, as is the fixed overhead efficiency variance.

The most difficult variance to assign to any one individual is the capacity variance. It could not be held to be the responsibility of the works manager, since he or she is only expected to produce that which the marketing function requests, and any variation from normal demand will result in a capacity variance. But if the marketing department is adhering to its predetermined plans, no-one in it can be held responsible for the vagaries of consumer demand that lead to fluctuations in the level of productive output, and hence to capacity variances.

In the same way that standards can be set for non-productive items, so variance analysis can be carried out for non-production items as suggested above. When actual selling prices differ from standard selling prices a *sales price variance* can be computed. Standard selling prices will be used in compiling budgets, but it may be necessary to adapt to changing market conditions by raising or lowering prices, so it becomes desirable to segregate variances due to price changes from variances due to quantity and product mix.

The formulae for computing sales variances are:

Sales price variance = actual units sold × (actual price − standard price)
Sales volume variance = sales quantity variance + sales mix variance
Sales quantity variance = budgeted profit on budgeted sales − expected profit on actual sales
Sales mix variance = expected profit on actual sales − standard profit on actual sales

'Expected profit on actual sales' is calculated as though profit increases or decreases proportionately with changes in the level of sales. 'Standard profit on actual sales' is the sum of the standard profit per unit for all units sold. (For a single product firm, or in one where the profit per unit of sales is constant over the product range, the standard profit on actual sales is equal to the expected profit on actual sales, and the sales mix variance will necessarily be nil.)

The following example should make the methodology clear. Budgeted sales of a company's two products for a forthcoming period were as follows:

Product A 500 units @ £2.00 per unit
Product B 700 units @ £1.50 per unit

and their costs were:

Product A £1.75 per unit
Product B £1.30 per unit

Actual sales for the period were:

Product A 560 units @ £1.95 per unit
Product B 710 units @ £1.40 per unit

Budgeted sales revenue	= £[(500 × 2.00) + (700 × 1.50)] = £2,050		
Actual sales revenue	= £[(560 × 1.95) + (710 × 1.40)] = £2,086		
Budgeted profit	= £[(500 × 0.25) + (700 × 0.20)] =	£265	
Actual profit	= £[(560 × 0.20) + (710 × 0.10)] =	£183	
Total sales variance			−£82
Sales price variance	= £[560 × (1.95 − 2.00)] + [710 × (1.40 − 1.50)]=		−£99
Sales volume variance:			
Quantity variance	= £265 − ($^{2086}/_{2050}$ × 265] =	+ £4	
Mix variance	= £269 − [(560 × 0.25) + (710 × 0.20)] =	+£13	
∴ Sales volume variance =			+£17
Total sales variance			−£82

12.5 Summary

The process of controlling business operations depends in no small part on the devising, compiling, and constant revising of an adequate and up-to-date system of reports.

In developing reports and deciding on their frequency, the financial analyst must assess their ultimate utility to their recipients. Moreover, to achieve the aim of successfully communicating the essential facts about the business to management, the analyst must have a clear idea of the purposes, possibilities and limitations of the many different types of statements and reports. He or she must, therefore, understand the problems and viewpoints of those who receive the reports, and also ensure that they understand the true meaning and limitations of those reports.

The use to which reports are put normally falls into one of four categories:

1. To spot things that are going wrong, and permit corrective action to be taken before serious loss results—this is the most fruitful and constructive use of control information.
2. To spotlight what has actually gone wrong, and guide management in picking up the pieces and trying to cut the losses that result from failure.
3. To determine exactly how and why failure has occurred, and to suggest the steps that might be taken to prevent its recurrence—this is highly constructive since mistakes cannot always be avoided but they need not be repeated.
4. To find out who is to blame for failure—in general this is the least constructive use of reports.

In specifying what is to be reported at each level of management, especially at lower levels, the analyst must pose two questions:

- What are the necessary and controllable factors relevant to the level of authority in question?
- In what form are these factors best presented to aid in decision-making at this level?

The level of management in question will determine whether reports relate results to long-range objectives, expressed in aggregate terms, or whether they relate results to standard costs in great detail. The principles of control are the same for these extremes of top management and supervisory management, but the form of report is different.

The adoption of a structured approach to reporting, with results reported by areas of responsibility, will enable top management to view the results and efficiencies of individual departments in the light of their contribution to overall performance and objectives. It may be, however, that the need for control action on the part of top management indicates a failure to achieve control at a lower level.

Similarly, the existence of a long time-lag between actual events and the reporting of these events via the top management control system may create the need for corrective action that is more drastic, more complex, and which involves more people than if such action had been initiated at a lower level of control more closely associated with the actual events.

Within the control framework the characteristics of good reports are that they should:

- be oriented towards the user, taking into account both his or her level and function;
- give as much information as possible in quantitative terms, and flow both ways in the organization (i.e. up and down);
- be based on a flexible system that allows quick changes to meet new conditions;
- be oriented towards operations rather than towards accounting.

On a tangible plane, succinctness is a great virtue in reporting, while on an intangible plane, a major contribution made by an adequate reporting system is that the recipient of a report is made to pause and think over the contents of that report.

Typical reports include:

Profitability reports by:
  product;

division;
area;
customer group;
channel of distribution.

Cost reports:
labour analysis;
material analysis;
manufacturing overhead analysis;
administrative cost analysis;
selling cost analysis;
cost of production;
cost of sales.

Sundry reports:
orders received;
orders delivered;
cash receipts;
physical output;
value of inventories;
statistical analyses.

The particular reports produced in a given company will obviously depend on the activities and circumstances of that company.

Most of the reports suggested above can be generated by a budgetary control system. Although budgeting draws attention to the problems faced by the firm, and can help lead to their solution, it is not without its own problems. Essentially these relate to:

- gaining top management support;
- developing the sales forecast;
- educating all persons who are to be involved in the budgeting process;
- establishing realistic standards of desired performance;
- achieving flexibility in the application of budgeting; and
- maintaining effective follow-up procedures.

In addition to these problems there are specific limitations and dangers in developing and using budgetary procedures. In outline these limitations relate to the following:

1. The plan is based on estimates, which means that judgement is necessary in interpreting and using the results. There is always a need for judgement in management, and the adequacy of planning and controlling operations hinges upon the adequacy of the judgement.
2. The plan must be continually adapted to fit changing circumstances. This is only a limitation in the sense that it involves a constant monitoring of operating conditions, results, and expectations. The judgement requirement can be linked to (1) above.
3. The execution of a budget plan will not occur automatically. Full involvement by all levels of management is necessary—preferably as an on-going rather than spasmodic activity.
4. The budget will not take the place of management. This is the complement of (3),

indicating that management can be assisted by budgeting, but full effectiveness comes from the combination of the two.

The dangers or disadvantages of budgeting are also fourfold, as follows:

1. It can become so detailed and complex that it is meaningless and unduly expensive. The budget should be a framework that does not hinder through undue rigidity.
2. The budgetary goals (i.e. levels of performance) may come to supersede the aims of the firm. This confuses the *means* with the *end results*.
3. Budgets may hide inefficiencies by continuing initial expenditures in succeeding periods without proper evaluation. A good budgetary system should include means of re-examining the standards and other bases of planning.
4. The abuse of budgeting (e.g. by using the budget as a pressure device) defeats its purposes.

Ineffective budgetary systems are characterized by a failure to develop and use budgets to their fullest advantage. For example, the use of budgets for planning only is wasteful, as no procedure can exist for ensuring that performance conforms with the plan unless budgets for control are also developed.

12.6 Exercises

Review Questions

1. To what extent can financial systems be designed to accommodate the array of environmental factors that influence organizational performance?

2. How can budgeting systems help in securing organizational control?

3. What aspects of human behaviour do you think are important in the functioning of financial control systems?

4. Define the aims of responsibility accounting and outline its links to organizational structure.

5. 'Any manager worth his salt can find a good excuse for a variance'. Discuss.

6. Explain what is meant by 'management by exception'.

7. What does it mean for a system (organizational or otherwise) to be 'in control'?

8. How might a manager determine whether or not a variance should be investigated?

9. Assess the advantages/disadvantages of using last period's profit as a benchmark for gauging the adequacy of the current period's profit.

10. What are the keys to control?

Problems

1. *Profit Variance Analysis*. John Swann, Managing Director of Post Electric Corporation, glanced at the summary profit and loss statement for 1986, which he

was holding (Fig. 1), and tossed it to Sandy Cunningham. Swann looked out of the window of his office and declared, somewhat smugly,

'As you can see Sandy, we exceeded our sales goal for the year, improved our margin, and earned more profit than we had planned. Although some of our expenses seemed to grow a little faster than sales, 1986 was a pretty good year for us, don't you think?'

Sandy Cunningham, a recent graduate of a highly regarded business school, was serving a training period as executive assistant to Swann. He looked over the figures and nodded his agreement. Swann continued:

'Sandy, I'd like you to prepare a short report for the Board Meeting next week summarizing the key factors that account for the favourable overall profit variance of £70,000. I think you're about ready to make a presentation to the Board if you can pull together a good report. Check with the Controller's Office for any additional data you may want. Remember, the Board doesn't want a long complex presentation. See what you can come up with.'

Sandy Cunningham agreed to the assignment and gathered the data shown in Fig. 2. How can he present an analysis of 1986 operating results to the Board?

	Budget	Actual
Sales	£5,400	£5,710
Manufacturing costs	2,000	2,090
	3,400	3,620
G and A Expenses	1,500	1,650
Net income before taxes	£1,900	£1,970

Figure 1 *Post Electric Corporation 1986—Operating results (000)*

	Meters		Generators	
	Budget	Actual	Budget	Actual
Price	£30	£29	£150	£153
Manufacturing cost	15	16	40	42
Margin	£15	£13	£110	£111
Units sold	80,000	65,000	20,000	25,000
Industry sales (units)	800,000	700,000	200,000	250,000

Figure 2 *Additional information**

*Post's products are grouped into two main lines of business for internal reporting purposes. Each line includes many separate products which are averaged together for purposes of this problem.

2. *Price and Quantity Variances for Transportation* The following standards have been established for the LMN Company for each detailed function of the transportation function:

	Product line A		Product line B	
	Unit Cost (£)	*Estimated Units of Variability*	*Unit Cost (£)*	*Estimated Units of Variability*
Handling claims (per shipment)	1.00	180	1.10	200
Loading and unloading (per pound loaded)	0.60	1,000	0.50	800
Drivers' and helpers' wages (per truck-mile)	0.70	700	0.40	680

The following actual units of variability and actual costs were incurred for the company's two product lines:

	Product line A		Product line B	
	Cost per Unit of Variability (£)	*Actual Units of Variability*	*Cost per Unit of Variability (£)*	*Actual Units of Variability*
Handling claims	1.20	160	1.15	220
Loading and unloading	0.70	1,100	0.65	900
Drivers' and helpers' wages	0.74	710	0.48	710

Prepare variance analysis statements for each product line.

3. *Quantity and Price Variances for Transportation.* The ABC Company provides you with information concerning the detailed standards established for the transportation function. Actual data is also included in the following:

Function	Budgeted cost	Standard cost per unit	Actual cost	Actual cost per unit
Clerical work (per shipment)	£1,000	£2.00	£1,350	£2.25
Planning and supervision (per unit shipped)	8,000	0.50 + £4,000 per period	8,880	0.60 + £4,020 per period
Loading and unloading (per pound loaded)	975	0.65	1,131	0.78
Drivers' and helpers' wages (per truck-mile)	2,400	0.80	2,646	0.84

Calculate variances for each of the functions detailed.

4.

XYZ Ltd.: Data for 19x9

Profit	£ 20,000,000
Sales	£300,000,000
Investment	£100,000,000

Calculate:
   (a) Investment turnover
   (b) Margin on sales
   (c) Return on investment
and (d) Show how (a), (b) and (c) interrelate.

5. The following schedule of investment possibilities has been drawn up by the manager of the Marsupial Division of the Marsfield Company to show the required investment and anticipated annual operating profit from each potential project:

Project	Required investment	Anticipated operating profit
A	£ 500,000	£ 90,000
B	700,000	200,000
C	1,000,000	230,000
D	1,100,000	300,000
E	1,200,000	280,000

At present the total investment in the Marsupial Division amounts to £5,000,000 and the annual operating profit for the current year is expected to be £1,250,000.

(a) If the manager of the Marsupial Division wishes to maximize his ROI:
    (i)   Which projects will he select?
    (ii) What ROI will he earn?

(b) If the manager of the Marsupial Division wishes to maximize RI for that division with a minimum ROI requirement of 15 per cent:
    (i)   Which projects will he select?
    (ii) What RI will he earn?
    (iii) Will your answers to (i) and (ii) differ if the minimum ROI requirement was 20 per cent?

6. The Doddery Company has two divisions, Lorst and Gawn, and evaluates its managers on the ROI criterion.
    Budgets for next year are as follows:

	Lorst	Gawn	Total
Investment	£1,200,000	£1,000,000	£2,200,000
Revenue	£ 600,000	£ 300,000	£ 900,000
Operating expenses	£ 300,000	£ 200,000	£ 500,000
Profit	£ 300,000	£ 100,000	£ 400,000

A new investment opportunity has arisen and could be adopted by either division. It requires an investment of £200,000 and promises annual operating profits of £40,000.

(a) Which (if either) of the divisional managers would accept the new project? Why?

(b) If an RI criterion (with minimum ROI of 18 per cent) were in use, which manager (if either) would accept the new project? Why?

(c) With minimum ROI of 18 per cent, should the new project be accepted from the viewpoint of the Doddery Company as a whole? Why?

12.7 Further Reading

Anthony, R.N., J. Dearden, & N.M. Bedford (1984), *Management Control Systems*, Homewood, Illinois: Irwin. (5th edition)
    A pioneering text that looks at the control process in a broad, organizational way rather than in a narrow, technical manner.
Hofstede, G.H. (1968), *The Game of Budget Control*, London: Tavistock.

This widely acclaimed book looks at the ways in which budgetary control systems actually operate, and offers critical insights.

Houck, L.D. (1979), *A Practical Guide to Budgetary and Management Control Systems*, Lexington, Mass.: D.C. Heath.

In this practically-oriented book the author shows how to combine financial analysis with industrial engineering.

McCosh, A.M., M. Rahman, & M.J. Earl (1981), *Developing Managerial Information Systems*, London: Macmillan.

The emphasis in this book is on the design of information systems to facilitate control within the framework initially put forward by Anthony, et al.

Tricker, R.I., & R.J. Boland (1982), *Management Information & Control Systems*, Chichester: Wiley. (2nd edition)

This book consists of a balanced blend of 'briefings' (on the design and operation of information and control systems) and 'cases' (covering actual applications).

Wilson, R.M.S. (1983), *Cost Control Handbook*, Aldershot: Gower. (2nd edition)

A comprehensive handbook aimed at manufacturing enterprises that seeks to illustrate how cost control might be achieved (covering an array of approaches and applications).

—Part 4—

Long-Term Considerations

Chapter 13

—————The Nature of Investment—————

13.1 Introduction

Investment is one of the main sources of economic growth in an enterprise. It is required not only to increase the total capital stock of plant, equipment and buildings but also to employ labour in productive activity. In that sense, one way of seeing an enterprise is as a collection of investment projects, each covering one aspect of the business involving the use of resources with the expectation of receiving a return commensurate with the risk involved. This return must repay the original outlay as well as providing a minimum annual rate of return (or interest) on that outlay. In the same way, an individual who invests £1,000 in a building society will expect to receive that £1,000 back at some future time along with compound interest thereon in the meantime. This is a typical investment situation.

The essence of investment is to give up current resources in anticipation of generating a larger quantity of future resources. Note that not all investments are made with the intention of securing a return in excess of cost. Some investments are made to meet legal and safety criteria. Others, such as investment in the arts and in education, may be made for more public-spirited motives. Moreover, even where investments do present a strong financial inducement there are often other benefits which may be seen as more important determinants of the choice.

An example of this might be where an enterprise has to choose among three mutually exclusive cost-saving projects. The enterprise may decide that there are three important criteria influencing the decision: annual cost savings, staff redundancies resulting, and improved safety. The analysis of the projects is as presented in Fig. 13.1.

Project Criterion	A	B	C
Cost savings	£1,000	£500	£200
Staff redundancies	5	3	4
Safety change	0	−5%	+5%

Figure 13.1 *Multiple criteria for investment choice*

We can see from Fig. 13.1 that each criterion ranks the investment projects differently as follows:

Ranking Criterion	1	2	3
Cost savings	A	B	C
Staff redundancies	B	C	A
Safety	C	A	B

The manager can only resolve the problem of choice by assigning relative weights to the different criteria. This of course depends on the goals and objectives of the enterprise. In this book we limit ourselves to examining the financial criteria for choosing particular investments ahead of others, so we consider only investments which are intended to have a financial inducement. The investor's aim in these cases will be to secure the maximum net cash flow (after tax) from the investment, and this will be achieved only from investments having the highest rate of return of those available. In this chapter we shall consider some preliminary issues relating to the investment decision and in the subsequent chapter examine some of the main measurement techniques used in project appraisal.

13.2 The Nature of Investment

When we speak of investment it is common for us to assume that we mean investment in capital assets (such as plant and machinery) or long term projects (such as a proposal to expand into a new market). This is a restricted and flawed understanding of the nature of investment. As pointed out in Chapter 3, an enterprise is a collection of investments comprised of trading assets (materials, cash, debtors) and capital assets (buildings, plant, machinery) and companies expect to earn a return on all of these investments. The distinction, of course, is that we expect to earn the benefit or return on the investment in materials quickly—usually within a few months—whereas in the case of plant we expect it over a number of years. Thus the idea of investment should not be conceived of too narrowly.

In this chapter, however, we are limiting our discussion to investment in capital assets and projects. Characteristically, a decision to invest in a capital project involves a largely irreversible commitment of resources that is generally subject to a significant degree of risk. Such decisions have far-reaching effects on a company's profitability and flexibility over the long term, thus requiring that they be part of a carefully developed strategy that is based on reliable appraisal and forecasting procedures. Typical examples of projects might be:
- expansion projects (such as breaking into a new market);
- replacement projects (replacing a fleet of salesmen's cars);
- projects aimed at reducing the cost of production processes.

Projects for analysis do not just appear: a continuing stream of good investment opportunities results from careful business planning and research and development. Accordingly, a well managed enterprise will go to some lengths to create an environment where there will be a constant flow of good investment ideas. This can be done formally and informally. The enterprise's formal system for generating investment proposals will usually be found in its marketing and research and development departments. It is also desirable that capable and imaginative employees be encouraged to advance ideas.

Since some ideas will be good and others not, procedures must be established for screening projects. Fig. 13.2 illustrates a possible cycle for new product development.

Ths figure shows the development of a new product beginning with an assessment of market demand and passing through the screening, proposal, development and review stages until finally the product is launched. (Perhaps only one proposal in ten will get through all stages.)

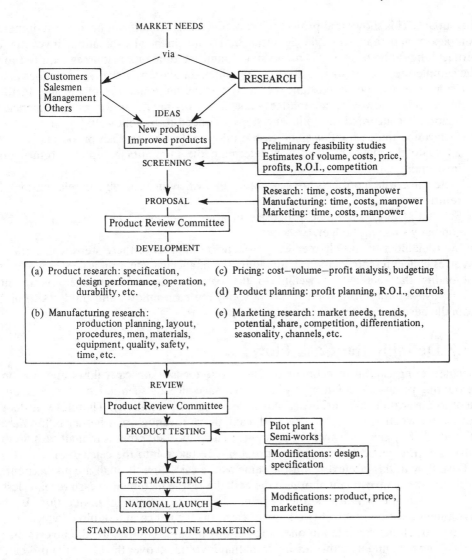

MARKET NEEDS

via

Customers
Salesmen
Management
Others

RESEARCH

IDEAS

New products
Improved products

SCREENING

Preliminary feasibility studies
Estimates of volume, costs, price,
profits, R.O.I., competition

PROPOSAL

Research: time, costs, manpower
Manufacturing: time, costs, manpower
Marketing: time, costs, manpower

Product Review Committee

DEVELOPMENT

(a) Product research: specification,
     design performance, operation,
     durability, etc.

(b) Manufacturing research:
     production planning, layout,
     procedures, men, materials,
     equipment, quality, safety,
     time, etc.

(c) Pricing: cost—volume—profit analysis, budgeting

(d) Product planning: profit planning, R.O.I., controls

(e) Marketing research: market needs, trends,
     potential, share, competition, differentiation,
     seasonality, channels, etc.

REVIEW

Product Review Committee

PRODUCT TESTING

Pilot plant
Semi-works

Modifications: design,
specification

TEST MARKETING

NATIONAL LAUNCH

Modifications: product, price,
marketing

STANDARD PRODUCT LINE MARKETING

Figure 13.2 *New product development cycle*

This model shows that the appraisal process is continuous and involves both quantitative and qualitative analysis. Some aspects of investment proposals can be expressed in financial terms (e.g. costs and revenues) while others must be decided more subjectively (e.g. purchasing supplies locally or from abroad). Qualitative issues can be very complex and, while we do not wish to understate their importance, we do not deal with them in detail here as they are usually specific to particular proposals and the enterprise in question. Here we wish to concentrate on just one part of project appraisal—the financial evaluation.

Realistic investment appraisal requires the financial evaluation of many factors, such as choice of size, type, location and timing of investments, giving due consideration to the effects of taxation and alternative forms of financing (or funding) the outlays. This shows that project selection decisions are difficult on account of their complexity and their strategic significance. To aid financial evaluation, investment projects should be broken down into stages, and the time and resources required for the completion of each stage assessed. Computer simulation, network techniques and decision trees can be of assistance in analysing the large number of possible factor combinations. However, no matter what the investment, as far as the financial evaluation is concerned the following steps will need to be followed:

1. Determine the cash inflows and cash outflows attaching to each proposal.
2. Evaluate the risks involved and determine the minimum acceptable return on investment.
3. Determine which projects are acceptable and which unacceptable in relation to the return required.
4. Select the most profitable proposals in accordance with the constraints of the company's capital budget.

In the remainder of this chapter we will focus on the first of these steps which really involves collecting information. Ultimately, the financial evaluation is concerned with estimating the increase in wealth to the company from alternative investment proposals. We therefore want to know about the cash inflows and outflows to and from the business arising from the investments.

13.3 Defining the Cash Flows

In considering capital investment decisions our focus is on cash flows and not on accounting profits. Accounting profits, as we have already seen in Chapters 3 and 6, incorporate within them arbitrary allocations (e.g. depreciation). Therefore, it does not matter whether outlays are termed 'capital' or 'revenue', or whether inflows are termed 'profit', 'tax allowance' or whatever. The important point is that all cash flows relating to the particular investment proposal are taken into the calculation.

Cash flow in this context is not the same as the cash flow through a bank account. For purposes of investment appraisal the cash flow is the incremental cash receipts less the incremental expenditures solely attributable to the investment in question. Each investment decision involves two flows of cash: (a) the net capital outflow (which may or may not all be expended in one time period) of cash required for the investment; and (b) the net annual inflows arising from that investment over the life of the project.

An investment appraisal implies the ability to quantify these cash inflows and outflows with some degree of confidence. Let us consider these two flows in turn.

Estimating the Net Capital Outflow

In some instances the net capital outflow will be synonymous with initial investment required. That is, the complete outlay on the investment may be required at the beginning of the project before any inflows can be generated. Even where this is not strictly the case it is still common for the larger proportion of investment outlay to be expended at the initial stage of a project.

Long Term Capital Outlay

The outlays/capital costs of a project are two: the long term capital outlays necessary to finance a project, and working capital. Typically, additional working capital will be required to cover a higher inventory, or a larger number of debtors, and to be worthwhile the project must earn a return on this capital as well as on the long term capital.

All cash receipts and expenditures associated with the net long term capital outflow must be considered. For example, let us say CKD Ltd is planning to acquire new wood-carving machinery with a basic cost of £25,000. If in addition to this there are transport costs of £1,500 and installation costs of £2,000, the net capital outlay is £28,500.

It is also possible that this cost may be partially offset. In some regions it is possible to obtain government or regional development grant aid for investment in certain classes of fixed assets and in such cases the value of the grant should be deducted. A second factor affecting the size of the initial outlay is the early taxation relief which the government gives for certain fixed asset purchases. The government grants this early taxation relief by allowing the company to write off a large part of the full cost of the asset purchase against profits in the year of acquisition before calculating the taxation liability. This has the effect of delaying the taxation liability until later years (a timing benefit). It differs from the government grant, which is a straightforward cash payment to the company. The implication of the early taxation relief is best illustrated by an example.

Assume a company annually earns a profit before depreciation of £15,000. In 19x1 it acquires for £10,000 a fixed asset which qualifies for early taxation relief. The asset has an expected life of five years and no residual value. The calculation of the company's taxation liabilities from years 19x1 to 19x5 would be as shown in Fig. 13.3.

Year	19x1 £000	19x2 £000	19x3 £000	19x4 £000	19x5 £000
Profit before depreciation	15	15	15	15	15
less: qualifying asset	10	—	—	—	—
Taxable profit	5	15	15	15	15
Tax at 50%	2.5	7.5	7.5	7.5	7.5
Tax payable one year in arrears	—	2.5	7.5	7.5	7.5

Figure 13.3 *Taxation computation—1*

Now, if this early taxation relief were not available, an alternative would be for the asset to be written off over its expected useful life (i.e. £10,000 ÷ 5 = £2,000 per annum). While the rules of the Inland Revenue are somewhat more complex than this, the point which is being made does not change. On the basis outlined the calculation of the company's taxation liability might appear as shown in Fig. 13.4.

Year	19x1 £000	19x2 £000	19x3 £000	19x4 £000	19x5 £000
Profit before depreciation	15	15	15	15	15
less: write off of fixed asset	2	2	2	2	2
Taxable profit	13	13	13	13	13
Tax at 50%	6.5	6.5	6.5	6.5	6.5
Tax payable one year in arrears	—	6.5	6.5	6.5	6.5

Figure 13.4 *Taxation computation—2*

In both cases we can see that tax relief is given for the purchase of the fixed asset and in both cases a total of £32,500 tax is payable on the company's profits. However, we also see that in the first case, where early relief is granted, the charge to taxation is lower in the first year and higher in the later years. In the second case an even amount of £6,500 is charged each year. At this stage it is sufficient to point out the benefit to the tax payer in having the taxation liability delayed. The benefit arises in having additional cash flow which can be put to productive use in the intervening period.

Working Capital Outlay

In addition to the initial investment for new machinery, CKD Ltd should also calculate the need for increased working capital. If additional sales are expected it usually goes without saying that the working capital requirement will alter in some way because increased sales can involve increased stock holding, increased debtors and a higher cash requirement. It may mean that the company needs to raise additional finance. However, a satisfactory arrangement can often be reached by more efficient management of existing resources. Having estimated the net capital outlay as accurately as possible the company can then proceed to estimate the net annual inflows from the project.

Estimating Net Inflows

This is normally a much more difficult task than estimating net cash outlay. It is difficult because where new products, markets or production methods are involved, the ability to provide accurate future estimates of cash flow will be reduced. There are two reasons for this. One is that there is an uncertainty about the future which makes it difficult to predict accurately: factors such as the expected level of selling prices, sales volume and operating costs all combine to create uncertainty where new projects are being assessed. The second is that there are risks attaching to projects which can only be assessed in probabilistic terms, particularly the risk from a changing external economic environment.

For the moment we shall ignore risk and assume a reasonable degree of certainty about the project's attributes. (We discuss the implications of risk in projects in Chapters 11 and 13). Notwithstanding risk, the task for the financial analyst is to estimate as accurately as possible the initial capital outlay and incremental annual cash inflows (sales), the incremental annual cash outflows (operating costs), the rate of taxation, and thus an estimate for annual net cash flow. There are a number of procedural issues to be considered in attempting to estimate cash flows.

Project's Life

An investment decision implies a length of service—the project's life. The project must be related to a definite period of time. In a static world, that period would quite naturally be taken as being equal to the physical life of the asset that is the purpose of the investment, which may be known with a good deal of certainty on the basis of past experience. However, in a dynamic world the life of the project may be determined by:
• technological obsolescence; or

- physical deterioration; or
- a decline in demand for the output of the project, such as a change in taste away from the product manufactured.

No matter how good a company's maintenance policy, its technological forecasting ability, or its demand forecasting ability, uncertainty will always be present because of the difficulty of predicting the length of the project's life. If this period is incorrectly estimated the whole analysis will be wrong, or at least grossly inaccurate. Every attempt should therefore be made to obtain expert advice.

Depreciation

In investment appraisal there is no need to make provision for depreciation from the cash inflows expected from the project. This is because the recovery of capital is automatically allowed for via the cash inflows. This has the important advantage in that the profitability assessment is not affected by the pattern of accounting depreciation chosen or, for that matter, any other accounting allocation technique.

Taxation

The calculation of taxation liability is subject to the detailed rules of taxation law. Briefly, a liability to taxation is computed as a particular percentage of 'taxable profit' and taxable profit is variously defined depending on the particular situation. As far as most companies are concerned their liability to corporation taxation will be based on accounting profit adjusted as required by taxation legislation. Therefore, in establishing the after-tax annual net cash inflows, the analyst must perform some detailed calculations to estimate the tax liability. It is not simply a case of applying the taxation rate to the net cash inflow, though in some cases (say a preliminary assessment of an investment) such a procedure may be acceptable.

Residual Values and Costs

The residual assets of the project may have a value either as scrap or in an alternative use or location. There may also be residual costs associated with a project (e.g. making good the landscape after opencast mining or removing North Sea drilling platforms). These residual values and costs must be taken into account when computing the net cash inflows from a project. Note also that at the end of the project the additional working capital which was needed to finance the increased level of activity will be released. This residual working capital is thus recoverable at the termination of the project's life and this net terminal value should be taken into account in the cash flow calculations.

Thus, the actual assessment of a project's profitability is a team exercise in which the expertise of the economist, the market researcher, the engineer and the financial analyst must all be brought together. The outcome of their collaboration will be a phased forecast of the cash flow (in the form of inflows and outflows) over a period of years.

13.4 Time Value of Money

To permit realistic appraisal, the value of a cash payment or receipt must be related to the time when the transfer takes place. In particular, it must be recognized that £1 received today is worth more than £1 receivable at some future date. This arises firstly because £1 received today could be earning interest in the intervening period and, secondly, to the extent that there is inflation in the economy the value of money will decrease over time. This is the concept of *the time value of money*.

Let us examine a very simple compound interest example. An individual invests £100 at 10 per cent for two years, interest to be compounded annually. The calculation of the sum to be received in two years' time is calculated as in Fig. 13.5.

	£
Investment at time 0	100.00
Interest for year 1 at 10%	10.00
Investment at time 1	110.00
Interest for year 2 at 10%	11.00
Sum at end of year 2	£121.00

Figure 13.5 *Future value calculation*

This calculation can be generalized into the following formula:

$$A = P(1 + r)^n$$

Where A = Sum to be received at time n
       P = Initial investment
       r = Interest rate
       n = Time/compounding period

Inserting the details from the above example we get:

$$A = 100(1 + 0.1)^2 = £121$$

So, £100 invested today at 10 per cent per annum compound interest would accumulate to £110 at the end of one year and to £121 at the end of two years. This is what we mean by compounding.

However, if we reverse the above notion we are saying that £121 receivable in two years' time is worth £100 today if 10 per cent is the prevailing rate of interest. The process of converting future sums into their present equivalents is known as *discounting* which is simply the opposite of compounding. (Compounding is used to determine the future value of present cash flows whereas discounting is used to determine the present value of future cash flows.)

Thus in the previous example, if we wish to know the present (today's) value of £121 to be received in two years' time, given an interest rate of 10 per cent, we reverse the compounding process and divide the terminal sum of £121 by 1.21, bringing it back to £100. The more usual way to compute this is to multiply the future amount by the discount factor $1/1.21$ (i.e. 0.8264) also giving £100. Tables exist which give these discount factors for a wide range of interest rates and time periods. Fig. 13.6 presents an extract from these tables.

Period	1%	5%	8%	10%
1	0.9901	0.9524	0.9259	0.9091
2	0.9803	0.9070	0.8573	0.8264
3	0.9706	0.8638	0.7938	0.7513

Figure 13.6 *Extract from discount tables*

Another example will help to clarify this further. An investor who can normally obtain 8 per cent on his investments is considering whether or not to invest in a project that gives rise to £388 at the end of each of the next three years. The present value of the sums is shown in Fig. 13.7.

Year	Inflow £ (1)	8% Discount factor (2)	Net present value £ (1) × (2) = (3)
1	388	0.9259	359
2	388	0.8573	333
3	388	0.7938	308
			1,000

Figure 13.7 *NPV evaluation working schedule*

If the investment's capital cost is less than the present value of its returns, say £800, then it should be accepted. Since the present value of the returns on this outlay is a larger amount (i.e. £1,000 − £800 = £200 gain from the investment) then this project should be undertaken. The gain of £200 is the *net present value* of the investment.

13.5 Summary

In this chapter we have examined some of the basic concepts associated with investment appraisal. We saw that capital investment projects have a major impact on the future well-being of the firm. We also saw that one of the main tasks in appraising an investment is making accurate estimates of the cash inflows and outflows. Lastly, we examined the idea of the time value of money which is one of the cornerstones of good appraisal techniques. In the next chapter we shall expand on the ideas presented here.

13.6 Exercises

Review Questions

1. From an investment decision-making point of view, what aspects of a business enterprise are decision-makers concerned about?

2. What is project risk? Discuss the main risks associated with setting up a kitchen furniture business. Consider how you might go about attempting to measure the risks which you have identified.

3. Explain why in the evaluation of project cash flows the depreciation expense can be ignored yet other expenses (for example, rent) cannot.

4. If a high percentage of an enterprise's total costs are fixed costs this usually indicates exposure to a high degree of business risk. Discuss.

5. Discuss in general terms the risk profile one might expect in an enterprise running a successful weekly current affairs magazine.

6. Draft an explanatory note on the concept of present value to someone with limited business experience.

7. You have been trying to select a building society in which to deposit excess funds. The main difference you find between them is that some compound interest annually, some semi-annually, and others quarterly. With which will you deposit your funds? Explain your choice.

8. If you have £600 on 1 January 1987, what interest rate compounded annually would you have to obtain to ensure that you have £1,800 on 31 December 1992?

9. What does it mean if the net present value of an investment project is exactly equal to zero?

10. Your employer explains to you that because of cash shortages he is unable to pay your £500 monthly salary for March. Instead he offers to pay you £110 each month from April to August. Choose a discount rate and evaluate his proposal, then explain your choice.

Problems

1. Along with four business colleagues you set up Busybee Shoes Ltd to operate a chain of retail shoe stores. You appoint Patricia McHugh, a bright young graduate, to manage the operation and it is agreed that in addition to her salary she is to be paid an annual bonus of 2 per cent of the net cash flow into the business. Ms McHugh had a very successful first year; five stores were opened and two further outlets are planned. The following is a summary of the events for the first year:

(i)   Purchased five leasehold properties for five stores for a total of £120,000. Each lease has a 25 year life.

(ii)   Alterations to existing properties to make them suitable as shoe stores—total cost £66,000. The alterations are expected to last for 10 years.

(iii)   Ms McHugh employed 1 manager and 2 sales assistants for each store. Managers are paid £7,500 p.a. and assistants are paid £4,000 p.a.

(iv)   The cost of goods sold was £73,000. Trade creditors at the end of the year were £5,000.

(v)   Sales during the first year amounted to £218,000. Debtors at the end of the year were £8,000.

(vi) Other operating expenses paid in cash amounted to £28,000.

(vii) On 30 November 19x8 Busybee signed leasehold agreements for two new premises.

(a) Prepare a cash flow statement for the first year of operations and calculate Ms McHugh's bonus.

(b) Discuss the measure for evaluating performance on which Ms McHugh's bonus is based.

2. Kieran Creaner and Peter Driscoll have been operating a food processing business for the past two years. They rent a small farm and employ one farm assistant. They process only their own produce which they sell mainly to hospitals and schools. Net cash flow in the first two years was −£1,000 and +£5,000 respectively. Peter now wishes to leave the business and offers to sell his half share to Kieran. Kieran argues that Peter has nothing to sell because they have not begun to generate profits yet. He suggests that Peter just leave the business with no obligations. Peter argues that he is selling his rights to future income and predicts net cash flow over the next ten years as follows:

Year	£
1	8,000
2	12,000
3	15,000
4	15,000
5	15,000
6	18,000
7	18,000
8	20,000
9	20,000
10	20,000

Kieran is confused and comes to you seeking advice. He also tells you that Peter's estimates of future cash flow are 50 per cent overstated. Draft a letter to Kieran setting out your views regarding the sale of the business.

13.7 Further Reading

Franks, J.R., & J.E. Broyles (1979): *Modern Managerial Finance*, Chichester: John Wiley & Sons.
  An excellent book on finance which is readable and non-mathematical. It is specifically directed at a managerial audience.
Merrett, A.J., & A. Sykes (1973): *The Finance and Analysis of Capital Projects*, London: Longman (2nd edition)
  A classic text devoted to the questions of selection and financing of capital projects.
Samuels, J.M., & F.M. Wilkes (1986): *Management of Company Finance*, Wokingham: Van Nostrand. (4th edition)
  A good introduction to finance for managers who wish to gain a deeper understanding of modern developments.

Chapter 14

—————————Investment Appraisal—————————

14.1 Introduction

In the last chapter we discussed the nature of investment and touched on some aspects of the evaluation procedure. However, in order to keep the presentation simple, we ignored the problem of risk and uncertainty and assumed that the cash flows could be accurately calculated and were sure to occur. Clearly, these assumptions are unlikely to be appropriate in real business situations. In this chapter, therefore, we develop a more in-depth understanding of investment analysis techniques as the business manager might use them in practice.

We assume in this chapter that the company has selected projects for investment which satisfy its qualitative investment criteria but which remain to be evaluated financially. There are three main issues to be addressed in this chapter. The first concerns the treatment of risk in evaluating capital projects. The second is the selection and application of an appropriate evaluation technique to assist in making a choice. The third is the selection of the most efficient portfolio given an enterprise's budget constraints. Before turning to these questions we take a brief look at the nature of financial appraisal.

14.2 The Nature of Financial Appraisal

An investment decision implies the existence of an objective. It implies that a certain objective is desired and that a particular investment strategy will achieve it. From our discussion in the last chapter it should be clear that one very important input to the investment decision model is financial appraisal. In some instances (e.g. the choice between two or more replacement machines where both are equal in all respects except price) the financial appraisal may be the most important element in the evaluation process.

Various criticisms have been put forward in relation to the methods of appraisal that many enterprises employ. Among the most important are:

1. Although most enterprises only make investment decisions after careful consideration of the likely costs and benefits as they see them, these decisions are often reached in ways that are unlikely to produce the pattern or level of investment that is most favourable to economic growth—or even most profitable to the enterprise.
2. Many enterprises apply criteria for assessing investment projects that have little relevance to the measurement of the expected rate of return on capital invested (ROI).
3. Even though a calculation of the ROI of each project may be made, the methods used vary widely and are sometimes so arbitrary as to give almost meaningless

results. (For example, a failure to assess returns *after* tax is a frequent weakness of many widely-used methods since alternative opportunities can only be effectively compared and appraised on an after-tax basis.)

Careless means of investment appraisal may result in over-cautious investment decisions in which too high a rate of return is demanded before a project is undertaken. This causes delay in economic growth. Alternatively, careless appraisal may mean that investment decisions are made which result in the selection of projects that yield an unduly low ROI. This causes a waste of scarce capital resources which is also unfavourable to economic growth.

From the information point of view, the use of inadequate means of investment appraisal results in a damaging restriction in the flow of information to top management, since these methods are incapable of fully exploiting data. Because an enterprise's future is inextricably linked to its investments, poor methods that give poor information and lead to poor decisions are likely to result in many mistakes.

We have already observed that the purpose of investment is primarily to ensure the long-term growth and survival of the company. Therefore, where a choice among alternatives is to be made on the basis of a financial evaluation, the criterion should be the increase in value to the company. Projects should be ranked on that basis and those resulting in higher increases in value should be selected first.

The first step in making this assessment of the increase in value to the company (i.e. estimating the cash inflows and outflows associated with the project) was considered in the last chapter. We now know that the appraisal is not a simple matter of listing net cash flows; the presence of risk means that there is likely to be a number of possible outcomes that could occur. It is important for appraisal to consider the variability of these outcomes.

14.3 Variability of Cash Flows

In Chapter 13 we examined the process of estimating the net cash flows associated with a capital project. We did not consider the situation where the actual cash flows turned out to be different from the anticipated cash flows. This situation is, of course, the one we would expect in business and the expectation of differences between the anticipated and actual cash flows indicates that there is risk present in a project.

Risk is used to describe the type of situation in which there are a number of possible states of nature and hence outcomes as outlined in Chapter 11 (pp. 225–227). In investment decision-making, risk generally derives from five sources:
1. Risk from undertaking insufficient numbers of diversified investments.
2. Risk from misinterpretation of data.
3. Risk from bias in the data and their assessment.
4. Risk from error of analysis.
5. Risk from changing environmental factors (such as changes due to inflation, technology, variations in market demand, etc.).

Let us examine a practical example. Where a businessman is launching a new product he will have to estimate future sales volumes, sales prices and manufacturing costs. Some of these estimates can only be guesses based on past information and assumptions about the future. In such cases the business manager will usually be able to envisage a number of alternative possible outcomes contingent upon the occurrence or non-occurrence of certain internal and external events in relation to the project. Thus, the risk present in the project (arising from one or more of the above five sources) prevents the manager predicting precisely the outcome of an investment decision.

It is crucial that the management of an enterprise understands the sources of risk which may affect the outcome of an investment project; it is only by knowing these that the risk can be managed effectively. The significance of particular risks must be determined when the project is being analysed and they must be taken into account in the evaluation process.

Where a number of possible outcomes to a project are envisaged one way of managing this variability as far as the investment appraisal is concerned is to assign probabilities to the possible outcomes and calculate the expected outcome of the project. This concept was introduced in Chapter 11 (pp. 225–227).

The application of this is best illustrated via the example given on p. 226 of Chapter 11, with certain modifications as shown in Fig. 14.1.

STRATEGY	STATE OF NATURE		
	Do Nothing	Introduce comparable product	Introduce superior product
Launch A	£40,000	£30,000	£20,000
Launch B	£80,000	£15,000	£10,000

Figure 14.1 *Payoff matrix*

(It is assumed that the states of nature and their probability of occurrence are as given in Chapter 11.)

This matrix shows that if product A is launched and a comparable competitive product is introduced, a profit of £30,000 will be made, and so forth for the other five possible outcomes. The best decision would appear to be to introduce product B and hope that competitive action does not change. But is this necessarily so?

In Chapter 11 the concept of expected value was introduced. (This is nothing more than the weighted arithmetic average of the possible outcomes for each strategy.) By using this concept it is possible to calculate the expected profit (or payoff) from each strategy by multiplying the probability of each outcome by the profit from that outcome. Thus for strategy A (the introduction of product A) the expected payoff is given by:

$$(£40,000 \times 0.25) + (£30,000 \times 0.5) + (£20,000 \times 0.25)$$

and is equal to £30,000.
Similarly, for strategy B the expected payoff is:

$$(£80,000 \times 0.25) + (£15,000 \times 0.5) + (£10,000 \times 0.25)$$

which also equals £30,000.
There are two features of note from this example. Firstly, the expected value technique has reduced the mathematical complexity of the investment problem by producing a point estimate of expected cash flow which can now be discounted. The

second and more important point is that the calculations indicate that the expected value for each project is the same, i.e. £30,000. Does this mean that either project is equally desirable to the management of CKD Ltd? The answer to this question is 'no'. It is not enough simply to calculate the expected value of the cash flows—this just gives a point estimate. In order to take account of the risk in the project, management must make an assessment of the variability of the cash flows (i.e. the range between the higher and lower possible values for each project).

In the above example the relative riskiness of each project has been made obvious; the risk associated with project B is greater than that with project A. The reason for this is that the variability in the possible outcomes for project B is far greater than the variability associated with project A. If product B is launched, it is possible to earn a very high return of £80,000 if the competition does nothing: however, there is only a 25 per cent chance of this occurring. If the competition introduces a comparable product the profit will be much smaller at £15,000. On the other hand, if product A is launched and the competition introduces a superior product (i.e. the worst possible outcome) the firm will still earn a profit of £20,000. The decision as to which project to select will depend on management's attitude to risk. On the assumption that management is risk averse it will launch product A, and vice versa.

The riskiness of a project as measured by the variability of cash flows will not in all cases be immediately obvious from the payoff matrix. A procedure does exist for calculating the variability. The measure is the statistical standard deviation. The standard deviation is simple to calculate and provides a measure of variability or range of the possible outcomes around the expected value.

However, we must stress that point estimates of risk (such as the standard deviation) should be used with caution. Essentially, they are useful in that they make the calculations associated with project appraisal more manageable. What is far more important in business is that management understand the sources of risk associated with investment projects, so that effective managerial action can be taken either to control or reduce the risk.

We now turn to consider how management should incorporate risk in evaluating investment projects.

14.4 Risk and Selecting a Discount Rate

The amount of risk an enterprise is willing to accept to obtain a given financial return is a general question of values that cannot wholly be rationally determined. An enterprise may, for instance, opt for a policy of conservatism and require a very high return for risk or, alternatively, for a policy of taking greater risks.

Clearly a policy must be determined and it must then be translated into specific rate of return requirements for different types of projects. The categories of project might be:

- cost saving investment;
- replacement investment;
- market expansion investment;
- investment required by regulations;
- welfare amenity investments.

Each category will involve different types of risk, and the aim of classifying the various proposals by type is to ensure that they all receive equal consideration once due allowance has been made for the differential risks involved.

The basic technique is to discount the future cash flows to their present values using the expected return on the particular projects. Below we examine two methods which have been developed to deal with this. The first and more traditional method uses the weighted average cost of capital to discount the cash flows, whereas the second uses a capital market discount rate.

The Weighted Average Cost of Capital

The weighted average cost of capital is a traditional basis for calculating the discount rate. In Chapter 7 we defined a company's cost of capital as the weighted average cost of the various elements in its capital structure. The WACC is intended to reflect the cost of the company's capital given its existing risk profile. Thus an investment project will only add to the value of the company when the expected return from the project is greater than the company's cost of capital. This makes intuitive sense; if the cost of the company's capital which is being used to finance the investment is higher than the expected return from that investment, then the effect of making that investment will be to reduce the value of the company.

In Chapter 7 we estimated the cost of capital of CKD Ltd as 14 per cent. Thus in evaluating the financial aspects of an investment decision the board of CKD must ensure that its approved projects at least earn a return of 14 per cent. This percentage is often referred to as the *hurdle rate* or the *cut-off rate*.

However, there is one serious problem underlying the use of the WACC as a discount rate for capital projects. This is that it assumes that the project being evaluated has the same risk profile as the company's existing projects, and clearly there is no universal basis for such an assumption. There are many capital projects which will have risk profiles differing from the average of the company's projects. Nevertheless, it is accepted that the WACC might be considered useful where the rates of return on debt or equity are the same as those required for the project; i.e. where their risk profiles are the same.

Capital Market Discount Rate

The underlying rationale for a capital market discount rate rests on the above criticism of the WACC. That is, if risk and return are related, it does not make sound financial sense to use a single discount rate (such as WACC) to assess the attractiveness of all projects which a company might undertake. If we do use the WACC there is a chance that we might reject projects which give adequate return relative to the risks involved.

Therefore, if we accept that the securities market approximates the correct relationship between risk and return then it would seem appropriate to use measures based on it in assessing capital projects. The problem for the financial analyst, of course, is to find this rate. If the risk profile of a possible investment project was identical to a security already valued in the market it would be a simple case of using the rate of return on that security to discount the project's expected cash flows. Unfortunately, it is not easy to find such correspondence between the market and projects for investment, so an attempt must be made to compute the risk profile of the project.

We shall not go into this calculation here, but it is as well for the manager to know that this discount rate will comprise an allowance for three things:

- the risk free rate of interest (i.e. that available on short-term government securities which have no risk);
- an allowance for the risks in the economy as a whole which may affect the particular investment;
- an allowance for the risks to the company itself in taking on the investment.

At this point we can summarize the steps to date in our evaluation process as follows:

1. Management should estimate the expected cash inflows and outflows from a given investment project over the expected life of the project.
2. Next, management should estimate the minimum acceptable rate of return on investment (i.e. cost of capital, capital market rate, or cut-off rate).
3. The next stage is to use a measurement technique (such as discounting) to decide which projects satisfy the financial criterion.

We proceed now to examine this third stage.

14.5 Financial Evaluation

The purpose of the financial evaluation is to rank each project in terms of its financial desirability (i.e. its contribution to increasing the value of the company). To do this we need a technique which will help us compare the expected return on the investment project with the company's cost of capital. This is achieved by discounting methods of evaluation.

Discounting Methods of Evaluation

The basic idea behind any financial evaluation procedure is usually to relate estimates of annual cash outlays on an investment to the annual after-tax cash receipts generated by it. Discounting techniques do this by ensuring that the time value of cash inflows and outflows is taken account of. We examine two discounting techniques below, the net present value technique and the internal rate of return technique.

Net Present Value

The net present value technique discounts the net cash flows from an investment by the company's minimum acceptable rate of return (which we can take as being the weighted average cost of capital) and deducts the initial investment to give the yield from the funds invested. If the yield is positive then the investment is *prima facie* worthwhile, but if it is negative the project is unable to pay for itself and is thus unacceptable. An index can be developed for comparative purposes by relating the yield to the investment to give the yield per £1 invested. This is the *excess present value index* and facilitates the ranking of competing proposals in order of acceptability.

We can illustrate this with an example from CKD Ltd. Suppose that CKD Ltd identifies some spare manufacturing capacity and that, for an initial outlay of £50,000, it could use this capacity to manufacture a new product with an anticipated life cycle of five years. The alternative is to use the extra capacity to manufacture more of their existing product B for which they expect very high demand over the next three years. For convenience, it is assumed that neither product will generate any income after five years. CKD Ltd calculates its WACC at 14 per cent and estimates net after-tax cash flows for each product as shown in Fig. 14.2.

Year	Product B £	New product £
1	30,000	5,000
2	25,000	25,000
3	25,000	25,000
4	5,000	25,000
5	5,000	20,000

Figure 14.2 *Estimated cash flow for each product*

Fig. 14.3 sets out a present value analysis of the alternatives. The factors used to discount the cash flows are taken from discount tables and the rate used is 14 per cent (CKD Ltd's WACC).

	Product B			New product		
Year	Net cash flow	Discount rate	NPV	Net cash flow	Discount rate	NPV
	(1)	(2)	(1) ×(2)	(4)	(5)	(4) × (5)
0	(50,000)	1.0	(50,000)	(50,000)	1.0	(50,000)
1	30,000	.8772	26,316	5,000	.8772	4,386
2	25,000	.7695	19,238	25,000	.7695	19,237
3	25,000	.6750	16,875	25,000	.6750	16,875
4	5,000	.5921	2,960	25,000	.5921	14,802
5	5,000	.5194	2,597	20,000	.5194	10,388
TOTAL			17,986			15,688

Excess present value index: $\dfrac{£17,986}{£50,000} = 0.36$ $\dfrac{£15,688}{£50,000} = 0.31$

Figure 14.3 *NPV evaluation of the two projects*

We can see that both these projects have positive net present values when discounted at 14 per cent and therefore are both acceptable using the criterion of adding wealth to the business. However, if only one of the projects can be undertaken (for whatever reason), as far as the financial evaluation is concerned CKD Ltd should use the extra capacity to increase production of product B. The excess present value index indicates that each £1 invested in producing product B generates £1.36 of present value (i.e. the original £1 plus an excess of £0.36). The corresponding excess for the new product is £0.27. Thus, manufacturing and selling additional quantities of product B will result in a greater increase in the value of CKD Ltd than will the new product.

Internal Rate of Return

The second of the two discounting methods is called the internal rate of return (IRR). The NPV method, as we have seen, measures the addition a project makes to the value of the company by discounting the cash flows at the cost of capital. The IRR is often defined as the rate of return on an investment which equates the present value of the future cash flows to the capital cost of the investment. It seeks to establish the interest rate which, if it were used to discount the cash flows, would produce a net present value of zero. If the internal rate of return exceeds the financial standard (i.e. the cost of capital) then the project is *prima facie* acceptable.

The actual calculation of the IRR must be done by trial and error because the rate is unknown at the outset. Again, tables and computer packages are available to aid the analyst and it is not a very difficult exercise. We do not wish to confuse the reader with the calculation in this book. In the main, both the IRR and NPV will rank projects in the same way, resulting in the same choice of project. However, there are some instances where the IRR may indicate a rank ordering that could lead to an incorrect decision. It is preferable in general to use the NPV method where possible.

Traditional Methods of Evaluation

There are some other more traditional methods of evaluation in use. These do not have the theoretical rigour of the discounting techniques and, if used alone, can result in bad decisions. We outline two of these: the payback period and the average rate of return.

The Payback Period

The payback period is the most widely used technique and can be defined as the number of years required to recover the cost of the investment. This is easy to calculate but is often calculated before tax and after accounting depreciation. There is no reason why this should be so and it is preferable to make adjustments for these items. Despite this, there are still weaknesses which the following example helps to illustrate. Let us assume that CKD Ltd is facing a choice between two machines, each requiring an initial capital outlay of £20,000. Malcolm Sand, CKD Ltd's Financial Director, having discussed the situation with Philip Randall, the company's Director of Operations, calculates that both machines will pay for themselves in three years from the after-tax cash flows shown in Fig. 14.4.

		Cash flows	
Year	Machine X		Machine Y
	£		£
1	10,000		2,000
2	8,000		4,000
3	2,000		14,000
4	1,000		2,000
5	1,000		1,000
6	1,000		—
Total	£23,000		£23,000

Figure 14.4 *After-tax net cash flows on two machine investments*

Both these investment projects show the same after-tax cash flows of £23,000. Moreover, each machine pays back the initial investment within the first three years (i.e. £20,000 in each case). However, this does not mean that the investments are equally attractive. In fact, financially, machine X is the more attractive project because of the earlier return: £18,000 in the first two years compared with £6,000 in the case of machine Y. Thus, the payback method has the serious defect of ignoring the time value of money.

Secondly, by definition the payback method ignores the cash flows extending beyond the payback period. Ironically, it is projects with long payback periods which are characteristically involved in long-range planning and which determine an enterprise's future. However, they may not yield their highest returns for a number of years and the result is that the payback method is biased against the very investments that may well be the most important to long term success. Associated with this, the payback method ignores the different sizes/scales of investment projects and thus cannot provide any guide to a rate of return. It can therefore be seen more as a measure of liquidity than profitability. On that basis the payback method—if used at all—should only be a preliminary screening device where an enterprise is desperately short of cash.

Average Rate of Return

The average rate of return (alternatively known as the *accounting rate of return*) may be defined as the ratio of the average annual net income after taxes to the average investment over the life of the project. It is calculated as follows: assume that a company proposes to invest £12,000 in a new machine which is expected to increase productive capacity and thus sales, resulting in additional annual earnings of £1,800 for four years. In addition, the company expects to have to invest a further £2,000 in working capital. The return of £1,800 must be related to the average investment in the project. Assuming that the machine has a zero scrap value the annual average investment in the project will be:

$$£2,000 + \tfrac{1}{2} (£12,000 - £0) = £8,000.$$

By comparing this with the average annual return of £1,800 we can compute the average rate of return on the investment as:

$$\frac{£1,800}{£8,000} \times 100 = 22.5\%$$

The net income in the average rate of return calculation is not cash flow but rather the reported accounting income. While the method is superior to the payback method in that it takes account of earnings over the economic life of the asset, it is also flawed for failing to take account of the timing of the cash flow. This weakness is made worse by the failure to specify adequately the relative attractiveness of alternative proposals. The method is biased against short term projects in the same way that payback is biased against longer ones. Also, there are many different ways of calculating the average rate of return.

14.6 Capital Rationing

In terms of financing investment projects three essential questions may be asked:

1. How much money is needed for capital expenditure in the forthcoming planning period?
2. How much money is available for investment?
3. How are the funds to be assigned when the acceptable proposals require more money than is available?

The first and third questions are resolved by reference to the discounted return on the various proposals since it will be known which are acceptable, and in which order of preference.

The second question is answered by reference to the capital budget. The level of this budget will tend to depend on the quality of the investment proposals submitted to top management. In addition, it will also tend to depend on:

- top management's philosophy towards capital spending (e.g. is it growth minded or cautious?);
- the outlook for future investment opportunities that may be unavailable if extensive current commitments are undertaken;
- the funds provided by current operations; and
- the feasibility of acquiring additional capital through borrowing or share issues.

It is not always necessary, of course, to limit the spending on projects to internally-generated funds. Theoretically, projects should be undertaken on the point where the return is just equal to the cost of financing these projects.

If safety and the maintaining of, say, family control are considered to be more important than additional profits, there may be a marked unwillingness to engage in external financing and hence a limit will be placed on the amounts available for investment.

Even though the enterprise may wish to raise external finance for its investment programme, there are many reasons why it may be unable to do this. Examples include:

- The enterprise's past record and its present capital structure (i.e. gearing) may make it impossible—or extremely costly—to raise additional debt capital.
- The enterprise's record may make it impossible to raise new equity because of low yields.
- Covenants in existing loan agreements may restrict future borrowings.

Furthermore, in the typical company, one would expect capital rationing to be largely self-imposed.

14.7 Post Audit

The management of investment projects does not end when the decision to invest has been made. In fact, one might argue that it is only beginning. Each major project should be followed up to ensure that it conforms to the conditions on which it was accepted, as well as being subject to cost control procedures.

14.8 Summary

In Chapters 13 and 14 we have considered the financial evaluation of capital investment projects. Taken together, these chapters should provide the manager with an appreciation of how capital investment decisions should be made in practice. The key message for the manager is that the most difficult task is estimating the benefits (in the form of net cash flows). This is a far more important task than choosing the most appropriate ranking and selection techniques. If reasonably correct estimates of the future benefits are available, then common sense can often be brought to bear in ranking and selecting. On the other hand, no number of sophisticated selection techniques can overcome the problem of careless estimates, though they may certainly trap the manager into relying on those estimates.

14.9 Exercises

Review Questions

1. Is the capital budgeting decision the most important one the financial manager has to make? Justify your answer.

2. What are the main problems associated with making decisions on the basis of comparisons between expected monetary values of alternative courses of action?

3. Why is it critical for companies to monitor and control capital expenditures?

4. Discuss the differences between uncertainty and risk as these concepts relate to investment appraisal.

5. Even where projects are not characterized by certainty, we often simplify them by assuming certainty. Is it reasonable to make such simplifications? Consider the advantages and disadvantages.

6. Assess the primary strengths and weaknesses of the payback method as the criterion for selecting investment projects.

7. What factors should be considered in deciding whether to scrap or sell an asset?

8. Explain how a substantial profit on the sale of plant and machinery might be dealt with in a replacement decision analysis.

9. Consider how a computer might be useful in project appraisal.

10. What is meant by capital rationing? How should enterprises ration capital?

Problems

1. The Boston Bakery Ltd plans to open a second retail outlet. Two locations are being considered. The first, a city centre location, will cost £50,000 for a ten year lease and the expected annual net cash flows from trading are £10,000 for each of the first five years and £12,400 for years six to ten.

   The second location is in a busy suburban shopping centre. A ten year lease there will also cost £50,000. Trading cash flows are expected to be £10,500 for each of the first four years and £11,000 for years five to ten.

   The company's weighted average cost of capital is 12 per cent. However, the proprietor believes that the city centre location may be a riskier project and suggests that you increase the discount rate by 2 per cent to take account of this.

   Advise the Boston Bakery Ltd.

2. Tricolor Travel Agency Ltd is reviewing its trade credit policies. The company has

projected sales for 19x8 at £1m. The annual fixed costs are £52,000 and the variable costs are 75 per cent of sales. Bad debts represent on average 5 per cent of sales. The present period of credit given to customers is 30 days and the managing director believes that if this is increased to 60 days sales would increase by 20 per cent. The company estimates its cost of capital at 12 per cent.

Advise the managing director.

3. Carrickmines plc has £1m available for immediate investment. The company is considering a range of possible projects and has calculated the internal rate of return on each as set out below:

Project	Cost £000	IRR %
A	200	24
B	400	23
C	300	20
D	300	19
E	500	17

Carrickmines has the following capital structure:

Share capital (ordinary shares pf £1)	10.0m
Revenue reserves	7.0m
10% Debenture stock	6.0m
	─────
	23.0m

The ordinary shares have a market value of £1.80 each and the debenture stock is quoted at £83 per £100 of stock. The annual earnings per share are expected to remain stable at 36p.

(a) Decide which projects should be accepted on the basis of the above information.

(b) Explain how your answer would be affected if you are told that projects A and B are mutually exclusive and that projects D and E are mutually exclusive also.

(c) Explain how your answer would be affected if Carrickmines could raise an additional £3m by the issue of debentures.

4. The Maryland Dairy has a machine which cost £40,000 four years ago. Its net book value is now £24,000 and it could be sold for £15,000. The company plans to purchase a new machine costing £55,000 which will have an estimated useful life of 10 years. Shipping and installation costs are expected to be approximately £1,500. The new machinery is expected to produce additional annual profits of £8,000 p.a. over its expected life, before charging depreciation on a straight line basis. However, an additional investment in working capital will also be required of £3,500. The enterprise's cost of capital is estimated at 12 per cent.

Evaluate the proposed investment in the new machinery. (Ignore taxation.)

14.10 Further Reading

Bierman, H., & S. Smidt (1980), *The Capital Budgeting Decision: Economic Analysis of Investment Projects*, New York: Macmillan. (5th edition)

This is an excellent book which deals with the practical and theoretical issues of investment appraisal. Complex ideas are left until later chapters so that an intuitive understanding of important ideas can be gained earlier.

Wilkes, F.M., & R. Brayshaw (1986), *Company Finance and its Management*, Wokingham: Van Nostrand Reinhold.
A major workbook and study guide that combines summaries of key concepts and worked solutions to a range of financing problems.

Chapter 15

————————Outlook for the Future————

15.1 Introduction

In this concluding chapter we wish to examine how the skills we have developed in this book can help us view the future outlook for CKD Ltd. We do this by using information presented earlier in the book (Chapters 2 and 3) to prepare a forecast financial plan for the coming year, 19x6.

Before doing this it seems appropriate to reassess how far we have come in the previous chapters, and in so doing to set the context for our examination of the future outlook of CKD Ltd.

15.2 The Position to Date

We stressed in the Preface to the book that our aims in writing it were twofold: to show readers how to make better decisions by encouraging them to obtain better financial information, and to explain some of the jargon associated with financial matters. We have tried to do this by elaborating the very basic idea that financial information within the business enterprise is centrally concerned with planning, decision-making and control.

Thus, in Part 2 we introduced a range of ideas associated with the evaluation of an enterprise's financial performance. The examination of these ideas was presented in the context of the five year historical financial information of CKD Ltd. We looked at ways of analysing liquidity, profitability and capital structure. There are two important things we would like the reader to take away from this part of the book. Firstly, we would wish that the reader develop a familiarity with the concepts of liquidity, profitability and capital structure and the associated measuring techniques. Secondly, we would wish the reader to develop a sense of 'comfort' with financial data, i.e. a grounded belief that financial data is not some esoteric art or craft understood only by accountants but, rather, that it represents information which is accessible to anyone provided certain basic relationships are understood.

Part 3 developed the idea that financial information can be useful in the planning, decision-making and control processes within enterprises. Indeed, it stressed that financial information is central in this process. As with Part 2, Chapters 9 to 12 focused on particular aspects of the process in the context of the historic financial information of CKD Ltd.

In Part 4 we moved away from considering the information relating to CKD Ltd to address in more general terms the question of investment. This section introduced the core ideas in project and investment appraisal. We examined those issues surrounding proposed projects which should concern those charged with making investments decisions. We also looked at some simple techniques for carrying out the appraisal.

Despite the fact that many of the previous chapters have used the historical financial information of CKD Ltd to explicate ideas presented, we hope that the point of all this analysis has not been lost. The purpose of financial analysis must be action-oriented. It should help managers to design strategies which will improve performance in the broadest sense. In Chapter 11 we referred to this design process in the context of our discussion of budgeting. However, we did not present a budget or forecast for CKD Ltd for any future period of time.

In the remainder of this chapter we present a forecast of the financial performance and position of CKD Ltd for 19x6. The information is presented in the following manner. Firstly, in section 15.3 below we set out the main assumptions/decisions which CKD Ltd make about financial transactions for the year 19x6. These assumptions, together with the projected information presented in Chapter 2 (pp. 15–22), are used as a basis for preparing projected statements for the year 19x6. The projected financial statements (incorporating a profit and loss account, a balance sheet, a funds flow statement and a value added statement) are presented in section 15.4. In section 15.5 working notes are provided to explain the origin of amounts included in the projected statements where the sources are not already obvious.

15.3 Assumptions and Decisions Relating to Year 19x6

We detail below the assumptions made in order to prepare the financial statements of CKD Ltd for 19x6. The assumptions are divided between those relating to the balance sheet and those relating to the profit and loss account. The funds flow statement and the value added statement are abstractions from the profit and loss account and the balance sheet and no additional assumptions need to be made in relation to these statements.

Balance Sheet

The following assumptions are made in order that a projected balance sheet can be prepared:

Investments At the end of 19x6 a further £400,000 will be invested in marketable securities increasing the total investment to £800,000.

Debtors and prepayments CKD Ltd plans to control more efficiently the amount of credit taken by its customers. The company plans to reduce the collection period to 50 days. Prepayments are expected to be approximately £100,000.

Inventories CKD Ltd plans to exercise tighter control over the level of inventories which have been increasing over the past number of years. The company plans to reduce the inventory holding to four months (i.e. an inventory turnover ratio of 3). The relative size which each component of inventory bears to the total should be:

Raw material	20%
Work in progress	30%
Finished goods	50%

Creditors and accruals CKD Ltd plans to reduce the period of credit which it is taking from its suppliers. This has been very variable for some time and the company plans to adopt a consistent policy of taking 60 days' credit. Accrued expenses are expected to be approximately £142,000.

Share capital and reserves There will be no new issues of share capital during 19x6. The revenue reserves will increase by the amount of retained profit for the year 19x6.

Long term loans On 1 January 19x6, CKD Ltd will make the first repayment of £360,000 on its 12 per cent long term loan, reducing the outstanding balance to £1,440,000.

Profit and Loss Account

In Chapter 2, most of the information needed to prepare the projected profit and loss account and value statement is provided (i.e. sales revenues and costs). However, there are two additional assumptions which we make here:
- that the rate of corporation tax on the company's profits will remain at 50 per cent for the coming year;
- that the dividend on the ordinary shares will be the same as for 19x5 (i.e. 15 per cent).

15.4 Projected Financial Statements

The projected financial statements follow.

FIXED ASSETS

	Cost	Dep.	WDV	£
Plant and machinery	2,200,000	760,000	1,440,000	
Land and buildings	3,000,000	906,000	2,094,000	
Fixtures and fittings	1,270,000	307,700	962,300	
Office equipment	459,000	395,800	63,200	
Motor vehicles	470,000	400,000	70,000	
	7,399,000	2,769,500	4,629,500	4,629,500

CURRENT ASSETS

Cash		402,210	
Investments		800,000	
Debtors		1,600,000	
Prepayments		100,000	
Inventories:			
Consumables	90,000		
Raw materials	372,000		
Work-in-progress	558,000		
Finished goods	930,000		
		1,950,000	
			4,852,210

CURRENT LIABILITIES

Creditors:			
Trade	650,000		
Taxation	937,165		
Dividends	450,000		
Accruals	142,000	2,179,165	
			2,179,165

NET CURRENT ASSETS	2,673,045
NET TOTAL ASSETS	£7,302,545

FINANCED BY

Share capital	3,000,000	
Capital reserve	23,680	
Revenue reserve	2,438,865	
Shareholders' funds		5,462,545
Long term loans		
12%	1,440,000	
15%	400,000	
	1,840,000	
		£7,302,545

Figure 15.1 *CKD Ltd—Projected balance sheet as at 31 December 19x6*

		£
Sales revenue		11,788,500
Cost of sales		6,837,400
Gross profit		4,951,100
Marketing expenses	989,840	
Distribution expenses	698,000	
Administrative expenses	1,079,630	
Financial expenses	264,300	
		3,031,770
Net operating profit		1,919,330
Loss on disposal	85,000	
Interest earned	(40,000)	45,000
Net profit before tax		1,874,330
Taxation at 50%		937,165
Net profit after tax		937,165
Dividends proposed (15%)		450,000
Retained earnings for year		£487,165

Figure 15.2 *CKD Ltd—Projected profit and loss account for the year ended 31 December 19x6*

		£
SOURCES OF FUNDS		
(a) OPERATIONS		
Net profit before tax	1,874,330	
Add: Depreciation	565,500	
Loss on sale	85,000	
		2,524,830
(b) PROCEEDS FROM SALE		75,000
(c) FINANCING		—
Total sources		2,599,830
USES OF FUNDS		
(a) ACQUISITION OF FIXED ASSETS		
Plant and machinery	400,000	
Fixtures and fittings	350,000	
Office equipment	50,000	
Motor vehicles	140,000	
		940,000
(b) TAXATION		937,165
(c) DIVIDENDS		450,000
Total uses		2,327,165
Funds flow during year		£272,665

Figure 15.3 *CKD Ltd—Projected funds flow statement for the year ended 31 December 19x6*

£

VALUE ADDED

Sales to customers	11,788,500	
Less: Bought in materials and services	3,973,755	
Value added		£7,814,745

APPLIED AS FOLLOWS:

TO EMPLOYEES: Wages, salaries, pensions, etc.	5,142,115	
TO GOVERNMENT: Taxes	937,165	
TO PROVIDERS OF CAPITAL:		
Interest	232,800	
Dividends	450,000	
TO PROVIDE FOR ASSETS:		
Depreciation	565,500	
TO PROVIDE FOR THE FUTURE:		
Retained earnings	487,165	
		£7,814,745

Figure 15.4 *CKD Ltd—Projected value added statement for the year ended 31 December 19x6.*

15.5 Working Notes to the Projected Financial Statements

Balance Sheet

Fixed assets	Plant and machinery	Land and buildings	Fixtures and fittings	Office equipment	Motor vehicles	Total
	£	£	£	£	£	£
COST						
Opening balance 1 January 19x6	2,000,000	3,000,000	1,170,000	409,000	330,000	6,909,000
Additions	400,000	—	350,000	50,000	140,000	940,000
Disposals	(200,000)	—	(250,000)	—	—	(450,000)
Closing balance 31 December 19x6	2,200,000	3,000,000	1,270,000	459,000	470,000	7,399,000
DEPRECIATION						
Opening balance 1 January 19x6	680,000	846,000	381,500	304,000	282,500	2,494,000
Depreciation for year	220,000	60,000	76,200	91,800	117,500	565,500
Eliminated in respect of disposals	(140,000)	—	(150,000)	—	—	(290,000)
Closing balance 31 December 19x6	760,000	906,000	307,700	395,800	400,000	2,769,500
WRITTEN DOWN VALUE 31 December 19x6	1,440,000	2,904,000	962,300	63,200	70,000	4,629,500

Debtors

As indicated in section 15.2 above, the debtors' collection period is to be reduced to 50 days' sales. Therefore debtors' balances at 31 December 19x6 can be calculated as follows:

> Projected sales revenues for year   £11,788,500
>
> Debtors 50 days' sales = £11,788,500 × $^{50}/_{365}$ = £1,614,863
>
> (say) £1,600,000

Inventories

An inventory turnover rate of 3 is planned for 19x6. On that basis CKD Ltd's inventory holding will be approximately one-third of its annual cost of sales. (Note that only the Manufacturing Division holds inventory.) We can calculate the projected level of inventory at the 31 December 19x6 as follows:

> Projected cost of goods sold (manufacturing) (from Chapter 2, p. 17)   £5,591,040
>
> Average inventory level £5,591,040 × $\frac{1}{3}$ = £1,863,680
>
> (say) £1,860,000 divided up as follows:

	£
Raw material (20%)	372,000
Work-in-progress (30%)	558,000
Finished goods (50%)	930,000
	£1,860,000

Creditors

CKD Ltd plans reducing the credit period taken from suppliers to 60 days. Using the figure for 'bought in materials and services' from the Value Added Statement as the best approximation to purchases, we calculate the year end creditors' balances as follows:

> Projected cost of bought in materials and services   £3,973,755
>
> Creditors 60 days' purchases = £3,973,755 × $^{60}/_{365}$ = £653,220
>
> (say) £650,000.

Cash Balance

The balance of cash £402,210 remaining at 31 December 19x6 is a 'balancing figure' in the Balance Sheet. That is, it is calculated by deduction. Given that all the other amounts in the Balance Sheet, except cash, are stated at planned levels it is simply a matter of inserting cash to make up the difference in the Balance Sheet. Of course, in practice the financial manager will be able to reconcile the projected closing balance of cash by reference to the detailed schedules of projected cash inflows and outflows during the planning period.

Profit and Loss Account

Loss on Disposal of Fixed Assets

The loss on the disposal of fixed assets of £85,000 is calculated as follows:

	Plant and machinery £	Fixtures and fittings £	Total £
Cost of assets disposed	200,000	250,000	450,000
Accumulated depreciation on assets disposed	140,000	150,000	290,000
Written down value	60,000	100,000	160,000
Proceeds from sale	20,000	55,000	75,000
Loss on disposal	40,000	45,000	85,000

Interest earned

The interest of £40,000 relates to the company's holding of marketable securities (£400,000 × 10%). It is assumed that the additional investment of £400,000 was made at the end of 19x6 and that there was no income arising on that portion of the investment for the current year.

Appendix

——Institutional Framework of Accounting——

A.1 Introduction

Throughout this book we have focused largely on financial analysis by managers in situations where the manager has an in-depth knowledge of the company's activities and where no restrictions are imposed on the style and format of information which he may request or prepare. However, we did make the point in Chapter 1 that as far as external publication is concerned, a legal, institutional and regulatory framework exists governing the form and content of financial reports.

In the course of his day-to-day activities, the manager may require some understanding of externally published information (for example, in discussions with other companies, with banks and other financial institutions). It is as well, therefore, for the manager to acquire some familiarity with the framework governing external financial reporting. This appendix provides a brief introduction to this framework.

A.2 Framework Governing External Financial Reporting

The presentation and content of financial information for external publication in the United Kingdom is governed principally by long-standing convention, company law and accounting standards. In addition, for listed companies, the Stock Exchange lays down some additional requirements mostly of a disclosure nature. We shall consider each of these sources of governance in turn.

Accounting Conventions

The origins of accounting date back thousands of years. Specimens of accounting records survive from ancient Egypt and Crete. We know that by the thirteenth century the elements of a system of double entry book-keeping existed and this is still in use today. However, it was the emergence of the joint stock company with its public ownership of shares, together with the rise of industrialization in the nineteenth century, which gave birth to the profession of accounting as we know it today.

Throughout its development as a professional craft, accounting has developed methods and procedures for measuring, recording, summarizing and classifying information. Some of these procedures and conventions have stood the test of time and become part and parcel of what we know accounting to be. The reader may recall that some of these conventions were discussed in Chapters 3 and 6. They are:
1. the business entity convention
2. the accounting period convention
3. the monetary measure convention

4. the historical cost convention
5. the going concern convention
6. the matching convention
7. the consistency convention
8. the prudence convention
9. the duality convention
10. the materiality convention.

There are other conventions and procedures in addition to the above. The common feature they all share is that they are recognized and accepted by accountants as the correct way to account. A number of these conventions are of such central importance to accounting (e.g., the conventions of going concern, matching, consistency and prudence) that they now have the status of professional standards which must be complied with by professional accountants. We examine this source of governance under *Professional Accounting Standards* below.

Company Legislation

Company legislation is devised by parliament to regulate the activities of incorporated bodies. The legislation is enacted usually in response to demand for improved legislation both nationally and internationally. For example, the EEC has been very active in improving and harmonizing company legislation within member states.

Until the beginning of 1985, there were in effect six companies acts in operation in the United Kingdom. These were the Companies Acts 1948, 1967, 1976, 1980 and 1981 and the Companies (Beneficial Interests) Act of 1983. In addition there were numerous statutory instruments affecting company law which had been issued under these and other acts. In March 1985, this legislation was consolidated into the Companies Act 1985. Although the intention was that all the legislation should be contained in one act, three much smaller acts were enacted dealing with very specific issues. These are the Business Names Act 1985, the Company Securities (Insider Dealing) Act 1985 and the Companies Consolidation (Consequential Provisions) Act 1985.

The Companies Act 1985 contains the over-riding requirement that the financial statements of limited companies must present a 'true and fair view' of the company's state of affairs and of its profit or loss for the reporting period. They also require specific additional disclosures; for example, a geographical analysis of turnover and details of transaction with directors of the company. These disclosure requirements are set out in the fourth schedule to the Companies Act 1985.

The legislation is detailed and complex and copies of the relevant Acts are available from Her Majesty's Stationery Office. However, perhaps more usefully, it is worth noting that professional accounting firms give specialist advice in this area and many have produced booklets summarizing the reporting requirements of the Acts. These are generally made available by the firms to client companies and other interested parties on request.

We should not overlook the importance of the EEC in relation to the development of company legislation. In its attempt to harmonize and improve company legislation within member states, the EEC has published a number of Directives which member states must eventually incorporate into their own national legislation. These

Directives deal with various aspects of the management and administration of companies.

As far as external financial reporting practices are concerned, it is the Fourth Directive (which was adopted by the Council of Ministers in July 1978) that has had the most impact. The Directive was implemented in the UK by the Companies Act 1981, now consolidated in the Companies Act 1985. The Directive deals, *inter alia*, with the layout of annual financial statements, valuation methods for assets and liabilities, and contents of the directors' report.

Looking ahead, it is likely that the EEC will continue to be a major source of improvement and change in company law. The EEC Seventh Directive (dealing with financial statements for groups of companies) was adopted by the Council of Ministers in June 1983. This legislation has to be implemented nationally by the end of 1987. Further developments are expected also.

Professional Accounting Standards

Accounting standards are professionally developed and professionally enforced accounting principles or conventions. Accounting standards have been codified in the United Kingdom only fairly recently—since 1970. In 1970, the Accounting Standards Committee (ASC) was formed to develop definitive standards of financial accounting and reporting.

The ASC is made up of representatives of the six major accountancy bodies in the United Kingdom and the Republic of Ireland, together with non-accounting representatives from commerce and industry. The accounting representatives (making up the majority of the Committee) are members of the Institutes of Chartered Accountants in England and Wales (ICAEW), Scotland (ICAS) and Ireland (ICAI); the Chartered Association of Certified Accountants (CACA); the Chartered Institute of Management Accountants (CIMA); and the Chartered Institute of Public Finance and Accountancy (CIPFA). Fig. A.1 gives an indication of the relative sizes of the bodies.

Professional body	Founded*	Approximate size (1986)
ICAEW	1880 (1870)	80,000
ICAS	1951 (1854)	11,000
ICAI	1888	5,000
CACA	1939 (1891)	27,000
CIMA	1919	25,000
CIPFA	1885	9,000
Total		157,000

(*Predecessor body in brackets)

Figure A.1 *Accounting bodies' membership*

At the time of writing twenty-three Statements of Standard Accounting Practice have been issued (two of which have been withdrawn) and a number of others are in draft stages. These standards set out how particular items should be treated in financial statements for external publication and should be followed by all members of the above named accounting bodies. A listing of the statements is provided in Fig. A.2.

1 Accounting for associated companies
2 Disclosure of accounting policies
3 Earnings per share
4 The accounting treatment of government grants
5 Accounting for value added tax
6 Extraordinary items and prior year adjustments
7 Changes in the purchasing power of money (*withdrawn*)
8 The treatment of taxation under the imputation system in the accounts of companies
9 Stocks and work in progress
10 Statements of source and application of funds
11 Accounting for deferred taxation (*superseded by SSAP 15*)
12 Accounting for depreciation
13 Accounting for research and development
14 Group accounts
15 Accounting for deferred taxation
16 Current Cost Accounting (*no longer compulsory*)
17 Accounting for post balance sheet events
18 Accounting for contingencies
19 Accounting for investment properties
20 Foreign currency translation
21 Accounting for leases and hire-purchase contracts
22 Accounting for goodwill
23 Accounting for acquisitions and mergers

Figure A.2 *Listing of statements of standard accounting practice, March 1986*

Copies of the statements are available from any of the main accounting bodies and any members of the bodies employed in business enterprises will have copies.

The Stock Exchange

For companies which are listed on the Stock Exchange, a fourth source of regulation exists. The Stock Exchange sets out in its book *Admission of Securities to Listing* (often referred to as 'the Yellow Book') the rules which must be followed by companies listed on the Exchange. The Yellow Book includes a number of rules in relation to the publication of financial information.

In general, the requirements of the Stock Exchange place additional disclosure requirements on the listed company. For example, the Stock Exchange requires listed companies to provide a geographical analysis of turnover and of contribution to trading results whereas the Companies Act 1985 only requires a geographical analysis of turnover. In addition, the Exchange reinforces the authority of the Accounting Standards Committee by requiring all listed companies to comply with the Statements of Standard Accounting Practice.

A.3 Conclusion

Over the past twenty years, the trend in external financial reporting has been for increased and improved disclosure. It is likely, given the demand for information in our society, that this trend will continue. It will be impossible for the business manager to develop an in-depth knowledge of the detailed financial reporting requirements; in fact it is already becoming an area of career specialization for some accountants and lawyers. The best the manager can do is to remain familiar with the sources of pronouncements regulating financial reporting and seek specialist advice as necessary.

A.4 Further Reading

Arthur Andersen (1986), *Accounting and Reporting Requirements*, London: Arthur Andersen & Co.

Bellamy, M.F. (1985), *Companies' Accounts Checklist* (Accountants Digest No. 181). London: ICAEW, Winter.

Coopers & Lybrand (1985), *Form and Content of Company Accounts*, London: Coopers & Lybrand.

Ernst & Whinney (1979), *The Fourth Directive*, London: Ernst & Whinney.

Ernst & Whinney (1985), *The Consolidation of Company Legislation*, London: Ernst & Whinney.

Glossary

Abandonment cost. The costs incurred in closing down a department or a division, or in withdrawing a product or ceasing to operate in a particular sales territory, etc.

Absorbed cost (full cost). That cost which is made up of direct costs plus overhead costs, the latter having been allotted to cost units by means of overhead absorption rates.

Absorption costing. The practice of charging all costs—both variable and fixed, and both direct and indirect—to operations, products, or processes or other segment.

Accounting period. That period of time over which costs and revenues are 'matched' in order to arrive at a profit figure, or the period of time between sets of accounts (e.g. 1 year, 1 month, etc.). This will also relate to the future periods for which budgets are compiled.

Accrued charges. Charges relating to benefits that have been received but not invoiced.

Acid test. The ratio of liquid assets (i.e. current assets net of stock) to current liabilities that represents an organization's ability to meet its immediate financial commitments.

Activity costing. The process of determining costs for activities (or segments) of a business other than manufacturing.

Actual cost. The cost incurred in carrying out an activity, running a process, manufacturing a product, etc., that is compared with a standard cost in order to determine a measure of efficiency.

Allocation. The charging of whole items of cost to cost centres or cost units. (This follows the responsibility criterion since allocated costs are direct costs of the cost centre or cost unit.)

Apportionment. The charging of proportions of items of cost to cost centres or cost units. (This is not in accordance with the responsibility criterion. Indirect costs need to be apportioned, e.g. in absorption costing systems.)

Appropriation. The funds allocated to a particular purpose (e.g. advertising appropriation, R & D appropriation) for a given period. Such funds represent the total budget for their purpose and are programmed costs.

Assets. The resources owned by an organization (both tangible and intangible) that are put to use in achieving organizational objectives.

Audit. An inspection of records, assets, activities and transactions in order to verify and validate their existence and accuracy.

Avoidable cost (escapable cost). A cost that will not be incurred if an activity is not undertaken or is discontinued. (Avoidable costs will often correspond with variable costs.)

Balance sheet. A classified statement of assets, liabilities, and ownership interest in an organization. This statement characterizes the 'accounting identity': A = C + E, where
    A = assets
    C = claims (or liabilities)
    E = equity (or ownership)

Batch costing. The technique and process of ascertaining costs for a group of identical items that maintains its identity throughout one or more stages of production.

Book value. See *Written Down Value*

Breakeven analysis. See *Cost-volume-profit analysis*

Breakeven point. The level of activity (output) at which profit is nil (i.e. total revenue is equal to total cost).

Budget. A financial and/or quantitative statement, prepared and approved prior to a defined period of time, of the policy to be pursued during that period for the purpose of attaining a given objective.

Budgetary control. The process of establishing financial limits to component parts of individual enterprises so that responsibilities are related to the requirements of policy; and the continuous comparison in accounting for outlays, etc., between actual and budgeted results so that remedial action, if necessary, may be taken at an early stage.

Capacity. The level of output that can be achieved with existing facilities in a given period of time.

Capital employed. The sum of share capital, reserves, and loan capital. (This is equivalent to total assets net of current liabilities and is also termed 'net worth'.)

Capital expenditure. Outlays on assets that are required and held for the purpose of generating income (e.g. plant and machinery, motor vehicles, premises). Contrast with *Revenue expenditure*.

Cash flow. In its simplest sense, the change in an enterprise's bank account during a period. More precisely, the cash flow is the after-tax earnings of the enterprise, net of dividends, plus depreciation charges of the period.

Committed cost. A cost that is primarily associated with maintaining the organization's legal and physical existence (and over which management has little, if any, discretion).

Contribution. The difference between sales revenue and the variable cost of sales (i.e., a contribution towards fixed costs and profit).

Control. A process that entails a set of organized, adaptive actions directed towards achieving a specified goal in the face of constraints.

Controllable cost. A cost that can be influenced and regulated during a given time span by the actions of a particular individual within an organization.

Conversion cost. The cost incurred in transforming raw materials into finished goods (or in transforming a material from one state to another).

Cost. The amount of sacrifice (or outlay) attributable to a given item, process, etc. This may be actual or notional.

Cost unit/object. An item or quantity of output, a period of time, an area of activity, a process, etc., in relation to which a cost may be ascertained or expressed.

Cost accounting. The techniques and processes of ascertaining the amount of expenditure (actual or notional) incurred in, or attributable to, particular products, processes, or services. This involves collecting, classifying, processing and analysing costing data for either cost control or product costing purposes.

Cost centre. A location, individual, item of equipment, etc., for which costs may be ascertained and used for purposes of cost control or product costing. This is not essentially a personalized concept.

Cost control. The regulation by executive action of the costs of operating an undertaking. The control process essentially involves the setting of cost standards and the study of significant deviations from standard.

Cost reduction. The process of seeking ways to achieve a given result through improved design, better methods, new layouts, incentive schemes, etc. (i.e. the establishing of new standards).

Cost-volume-profit analysis (CVP analysis, break-even analysis). The study of the inter-relationships of cost behaviour patterns, levels of activity, and the profit that results from each alternative combination.

Current assets. Assets that will turn into cash during the next accounting period (e.g. debtors, stocks, etc.).

Current liabilities. Claims that must be met during the next accounting period (e.g. trade creditors, bank overdraft, etc.).

Current ratio (working capital ratio). The ratio of current assets to current liabilities. A measure of the short-term ability of an undertaking to meet its obligations, but a measure that has serious weaknesses.

Depreciation. The diminution in the value of a fixed asset due to use and/or the passage of time.

Differential cost. The difference in aggregate outlays between one course of action and another (= incremental cost).

Direct cost. A cost that can be identified specifically and wholly with a particular cost unit.

Direct costing (variable costing). The process of charging all direct costs to products, processes, or services, leaving all indirect costs to be written off against profits in the period in which they arise.

Discounted cash flow (DCF). A technique of investment appraisal in which an appropriate rate of discount is derived to reduce forecasts of incremental costs and revenues over the life of a project to zero in present value terms.

Discretionary cost. A programmed cost that is subject both to management discretion (i.e. free choice) and management control.

Distribution cost analysis (DCA) (distribution cost accounting). A set of procedures for allocating, apportioning and controlling the costs of distribution (where 'distribution' refers to the set of activities more commonly termed 'marketing').

Effectiveness. The accomplishment of a desired objective or outcome.

Efficiency. The ratio of a system's outputs to inputs; strictly a limiting example of the idea of productivity in that an efficient system is one in which this ratio is optimal. Two categories of efficiency should be noted: *economic efficiency*, which arises when the cost of inputs is minimized for a given level and mix of outputs; and *technical efficiency*, which arises when the output is maximized for a given volume and mix of inputs.

Equity. The claim that the owners of a business have on that business. (This is typically represented by ordinary shares, share premiums, and accumulated reserves.)

Escapable cost. See *Avoidable cost*

Feedback. The flow of information on the outcome of an event that facilitates comparisons of actual with planned outcomes. *Negative feedback* requires corrective measures to counteract deviating outcomes. *Positive feedback* requires corrective measures to amplify deviating outcomes.

Financial accounting. A process and set of procedures for recording, summarizing, classifying, analysing, and reporting financial transactions.

First-in-first-out (FIFO). A method of valuing inventories based on the assumption that the earliest purchases are used first and hence the inventory value is made up of the most recent purchases at the most recent prices.

Fixed (tangible) assets. The long-term physical assets of a business (such as plant, equipment, motor vehicles) by means of which it generates productive activities.

Fixed budget. A budget that is designed to remain unchanged irrespective of the level of activity actually attained.

Fixed cost (period cost). A cost that tends to be unaffected by changes in the level of activity during a given period of time.

Flexible budget. A budget that recognizes the difference in behaviour pattern of fixed and variable costs, and which is designed to change in relation to the level of activity actually attained.

Full cost. See *Absorbed cost*

Functional cost. A cost incurred within a particular section (or function) of an organization (e.g. marketing or manufacturing). Alternatively, this may be defined as the cost of performing a particular function (e.g. typing a letter).

Funds. Funds may be defined as cash, or as working capital, or as liquid assets.

Funds flow. The movement of funds into, out of, and within the organization.

Funds flow statement. A statement, showing the movement (i.e. sources and dispositions) of funds over a given period of time.

Gearing. This refers to the extent to which a company employs debt capital: a highly-geared company has a high ratio of debt to total capital, while a low-geared company will have most of its capital in the form of shareholders' funds (i.e. equity).

Going concern. This describes an organization that is assumed to be continuing its operations on an indefinite basis (i.e. having an infinite life).

Goodwill. The difference between the value of the going concern and the value of the component parts of the organization. Goodwill is an intangible asset that relates to an enterprise's reputation.

Gross profit. The excess of sales revenue in a given period over the cost of goods sold plus the expenses of acquiring those goods (such as carriage).

Historical cost. Actual cost, determined after the event.

Income measurement. The process whereby net profit is determined for a given period of time.

Income statement. See *Profit and loss account*

Incremental cost. The extra cost of taking one course of action rather than another (= differential cost).

Indirect cost. A cost that cannot be allocated but which can be apportioned to cost centres or cost units. Overhead costs are indirect costs.

Inflation. The phenomenon whereby prices in general rise, with the result that the distinction between, say, *real* increases in costs or profits and *monetary* increases becomes confused, and this is compounded by the fact that all prices do not rise at the same rate.

Intangible assets. Assets that do not have a physical presence (such as goodwill and patent rights) but which, nevertheless, facilitate the carrying out of business activities.

Inter-firm comparison. The exchange of comparative information among firms with the aim of helping managements to improve the efficiency of individual firms.

Internal audit. The independent appraisal activity within an organization for reviewing accounting, financial, and other operations as a basis for protective service to management.

Internal rate of return (IRR). The rate of discount at which the present value of future income expected from a project equals that of future outlays. (This is the same as *discounted cash flow*).

Investment appraisal. A means of assessing whether expenditure on a capital project would show a satisfactory rate of return (either absolutely or in relation to alternative uses of funds), and of indicating the optimum time to commit expenditure.

Investment centre. A personalized location for which a named individual is responsible for both the investment base and the rate of return on this investment base. Compare *Cost centre* and *Profit centre*.

Job cost. The cost of a cost unit (= job) consisting of a single order (i.e. a single item or a single batch of like items).

Last-in-first-out (LIFO). A method of valuing inventories based on the assumption that the most recent purchases are used first and hence the inventory value is made up of the earliest purchases at the earliest prices.

Learning curve. A mathematical (graphical) portrayal of the decreasing rate of increase in costs of labour while experience is being gained in a new task.

Liability. A claim by an outsider on the assets of the enterprise. *Current liabilities* are those claims that must be met within the next period. *Long-term liabilities* are claims that need not be met until after the next period. *Contingent liabilities* are those that may not fall to be met at all since their existence will be probabilistic.

Liquid assets. Cash or near-cash resources (such as debtors, stocks, etc.).

Managed cost. A cost that stems from current operations but which must continue to be incurred into the future, at some level determined by management, to ensure the continued existence of the enterprise.

Management accounting. The application of accounting knowledge to the purpose of producing and of interpreting accounting and statistical information designed to assist management in its functions of promoting maximum efficiency and in formulating and co-ordinating future plans and subsequently in measuring their execution.

Management control. The process whereby resources are obtained and used effectively and efficiently in the accomplishment of the organization's objectives.

Marginal cost. The amount at any given volume of output by which aggregate costs are changed if the volume of output is increased or decreased by one unit.

Marginal costing. The process of ascertaining marginal costs and the effects of changes in volume or type of output on profit by differentiating between fixed and variable costs.

Marginal revenue. The amount at any given volume of output by which aggregate revenue is changed if the volume of output is increased or decreased by one unit.

Margin of safety. The excess of budgeted (or actual) sales over the break-even sales volume.

Market value. The value an asset has if offered for sale on the open market in its present condition, less any costs incurred in disposing of that asset.

Master budget. The summary budget that incorporates the key figures and totals of all other budgets.

Mission. A task that is characterized by its end rather than its means, such as 'put a man on the moon by 1970'.

Mixed cost. Typified by semi-fixed and semi-variable costs, mixed costs are those whose behaviour patterns are representative of neither fixed costs nor variable costs, but a combination (stepped) of both.

Model. A simplified representation of reality that may be in the form of a mathematical equation, a chart/flow diagram, a 3-D representation, etc., that can help in defining and solving problems.

Natural expense. An outlay that is classified by its nature (e.g. salary, rent, etc.) rather than by its function (such as marketing, etc.).

Net assets. See *Capital employed*

Net present value. The present value of income arising from a project, less the present value of expenditure on the project, arrived at by discounting at a given rate of interest (usually the cost of capital).

Net worth. See *Capital employed*

Oncost. See *Overhead*

Opportunity cost. The maximum amount that could be obtained at any given point of time if a resource was sold or put to the most valuable alternative use that would be practicable.

Order-filling costs. Costs of distribution (being mainly composed of the costs attributable to warehousing, transport, order-processing, and inventory management).

Order-getting costs. Costs of marketing (being mainly composed of the costs attributable to advertising, sales promotion, personal selling, and product PR).

Out-of-pocket cost. A cost that will necessitate a corresponding outflow of cash.

Over-absorbed cost (over-recovered overhead). The excess of the amount of overhead absorbed (i.e. output × overhead rate) over the amount of overhead cost actually incurred.

Over-capitalized. An excess of capital for the scale of operations being undertaken.

Overhead (burden, oncost). The aggregate of indirect material costs, indirect labour cost, and indirect expenses.

Overhead rate. The expression of overhead in relation to some specific characteristic of a cost centre as a means of providing a basis for its apportionment or absorption.

Over-trading. Carrying on operations with a deficiency of working capital.

Payback period. The length of time it takes an investment to generate sufficient extra net income to repay the additional capital and other outlays involved.

Period cost. See *Fixed cost*

Planning, programming, budgeting system (PPBS) (output budgeting). A system for analysing expenditure by reference to particular (output) objectives instead of under (input) headings such as natural and functional cost classifications.

Present value. The value today of a future payment, receipt, or stream of payments and/or receipts, discounted at an appropriate discount rate.

Primary ratio. This is the apex of the ratio pyramid:

$$\text{the rate of return on investment} = {}^{net\ profit}/_{capital\ invested}$$

Prime cost. The aggregate of direct material cost, direct labour cost, and direct expenses.

Probability. The probability of a particular outcome of an event is simply the proportion of times this outcome would occur if the event were repeated a great number of times.

Process costing. The procedures whereby the costs of operating a manufacturing process are ascertained. This involves dealing with broad averages and large numbers of like units.

Product cost. The aggregate of costs that are associated with a unit of product. Such costs may or may not include an element of overheads depending upon the type of costing system in force—absorption or direct.

Product costing. The process by which product costs are ascertained.

Productivity. The rate of output per unit of input.

Profit centre. A form of responsibility centre in which a manager is held responsible for both revenue and costs, and hence for the resultant level of profit.

Profitgraph. See *Profit-volume chart*

Profit and loss account (income statement, revenue account). A statement in which revenues for a period are summarized along with the costs incurred in securing those revenues. The difference is a profit (if positive) or a loss (if negative). A formalized operating statement.

Profit plan. A fully developed set of budgets that show which activities are to be carried out and how each is to contribute to profit.

Profit-volume ratio. The proportion of each additional unit of sales revenue that consists of contribution (to fixed costs and profit).

Profit-volume chart (profitgraph). A diagram showing the expected relationship between cost and revenue at various volumes with profit being the residual: a break-even chart.

Programmed cost. A cost that is subject both to management discretion and management control but which has little immediate relevance to current operations although it is generally incurred to ensure long term survival.

Ratio analysis. The examination of significant relationships between reported statistics of cost, revenue, profit, assets, liabilities, and capital structure, with a view to better control.

Ratio pyramid. A hierarchy of ratios showing how each ratio is made up and how it relates to other ratios.

Relevant cost. An incremental (or differential) cost (i.e. one that is expected to differ among alternative future courses of action).

Relevant range. The range of activity within which particular cost behaviour patterns are known (or presumed) to exist (e.g. the range within which a fixed cost is actually fixed).

Replacement cost. The cost of replacing an asset at any given point in time, either now or in the future (excluding any element attributable to improvement).

Residual income. The net income from an enterprise (or division) after deducting a figure reflecting the cost of capital.

Residual value. The value of an asset at the end of its useful (economic or technological or physical) life. This will be equivalent to the proceeds of sale net of any disposal costs.

Responsibility accounting. An approach to cost control whereby every item of expenditure is made the responsibility of that individual who can best influence it by his or her own actions.

Responsibility centre. A personalized group of cost centres under the control of a 'responsible' individual.

Retained earnings. The accumulated balance of net profit (after tax) that is undistributed (in the form of dividends) and unappropriated to another use.

Return on investment (ROI). The primary ratio that relates net profit to the capital invested in the enterprise as a whole, or in divisions of the enterprise. Also referred to as return on capital employed (ROCE).

Revenue account. See *Profit and loss account*

Revenue centre. A responsibility centre in which a manager is only held responsible for the level of revenue.

Revenue expenditure. That which is incurred in the normal course of business, the benefit of which is received during the period in which the expenditure is made (i.e. non-capital expense).

Risk. The situation in which a number of outcomes of a decision are possible, but this number can be identified and the probability of each occurring can be estimated.

Secondary ratios. The constituent elements of the primary ratio, namely:

$$\text{Capital turnover} = \frac{\text{Sales}}{\text{Capital invested}}$$

$$\text{Profit margin on sales} = \frac{\text{Net profit}}{\text{Sales}}$$

Segment. A responsibility centre (division, department, etc.) of an organization: or, alternatively, a portion of the market for a given product in which all consumers have important characteristics in common.

Semi-variable cost. See *Mixed cost.*

Semi-fixed cost. See *Stepped cost.*

Sensitivity analysis. A technique that identifies key variables in a system and then assesses the sensitivity of the output of that system to variations in the input variables.

Service costing. A variation on process costing in which the focus of interest is the cost of service outputs (rather than the cost of physical outputs).

Set-up cost. The cost incurred in adjusting machinery, etc., before a production task can be undertaken.

Shutdown costs. The costs incurred in relation to the temporary closing of a department/division/enterprise. Such costs include those of re-opening as well as those of closing.

Standard cost. A predetermined cost that is calculated on the basis of a desired level of operating efficiency.

Standard costing. The process whereby standard costs are developed and used as a comparison for actual costs so that variances can be isolated, investigated if significant, and remedial action taken when deemed necessary.

Start-up costs. The costs incurred in commencing a business.

Stepped cost (semi-fixed cost). A cost the behaviour pattern of which is characterized by steps (i.e. sudden changes) at intervals in accordance with the level of activity, but between these steps the behaviour pattern is typically of a fixed cost nature.

Stewardship. That function of accounting that involves the maintaining of records, etc., on behalf of the (absent) shareholders.

Sunk costs. Those costs that have been invested in a project and which will not be recovered if the project is terminated.

Tertiary ratios. The constituent elements of the secondary ratios:

$$\frac{\text{Gross profit}}{\text{Sales}} \qquad \frac{\text{Sales}}{\text{Overheads}}$$

$$\frac{\text{Sales}}{\text{Working capital}} \qquad \frac{\text{Sales}}{\text{Fixed assets}}$$

Total assets. The sum of fixed assets and current assets.

Trade off. The sacrifice that is involved in choosing one course (or dimension) of action rather than another (e.g. it may be necessary to trade cost for quality).

Trading account. The account in which an enterprise's gross profit is shown by matching sales revenue with the cost of those sales.

Transfer price. The 'price' at which goods are transferred from one division/ department of an enterprise to another division/department of that same enterprise.

Uncertainty. The situation in which the outcomes of a decision cannot be identified in advance, nor probabilities given to the likelihood of any outcome occurring.

Uncontrollable cost. A cost that is beyond the control (i.e. is uninfluenced by the actions) of a given individual during a given period of time.

Under-absorbed cost (under-recovered overhead). The deficit in the amount of overhead absorbed (i.e. output × overhead rate) compared with the amount of overhead cost actually incurred.

Under-capitalized. A deficiency of capital for the scale of operations being undertaken.

Unit cost. The total of a specified cost factor divided by a given volume of units to give an average cost. The unit in question may be of output, of time, etc., depending on the reason for the computation.

Value. This is a measure of preference (e.g. for buying an asset rather than holding cash) which reflects the benefits that one expects to receive from owning the asset.

Value added. The difference between the value of an enterprise's outputs and the value of it inputs.

Variable cost. A cost that tends to vary in accordance with the level of activity (within the relevant range, and within a given period of time).

Variable costing. See *Direct costing.*

Variance. The difference between a planned (i.e. budgeted or standard) outcome and the actual outcome of an event.

Variance analysis. The investigation and explanation of variances with a view to controlling operations.

Venture capital. Funds that are invested in (high-risk) projects in expectation of high rewards.

Wasting asset. A fixed asset that is depleted by use (e.g. a mine or quarry).

Working capital. An enterprise's investment in short term assets net of short term liabilities.

Working capital ratio. See *Current ratio*

Works cost. The sum of direct and indirect manufacturing costs.

Written down value (WDV) (book value). The value, net of depreciation, that an asset has as shown in the enterprise's books of account. Only by chance will this accord with the economic or market value of that asset.

Yield. The rate of return on an investment.

Zero-base budgeting. An approach to budget review and evaluation that requires a manager to justify the resources requested for all activities and projects (including on-going ones) in rank order.

Further Reading

Institute of Cost & Management Accountants (1982), *Management Accounting: Official Terminology*, London: ICMA.
Nobes, C.W. (1985), *Pocket Accountant*, Oxford: Basil Blackwell.
Parker, R.H. (1984), *Macmillan Dictionary of Accounting*, London: Macmillan.

Index